Beyond the Reformation?

Beyond the Reformation?

Authority, Primacy and Unity
in the Conciliar Tradition

Paul Avis

t&t clark

Published by T&T Clark

A Continuum imprint

The Tower Building, 11 York Road, London SE1 7NX

80 Maiden Lane, Suite 704, New York, NY 10038

www.tandtclark.com

All rights reserved. No part of this publication may be reproduced or transmitted in any form or by any means, electronic or mechanical, including photocopying, recording or any information storage or retrieval system, without permission in writing from the publishers.

Paul Avis has asserted his right under the Copyright, Designs and Patents Act, 1988, to be identified as Author of this work.

Copyright © Paul Avis, 2006

British Library Cataloguing-in-Publication Data

A catalogue record for this book is available from the British Library

Typeset by Free Range Book Design & Production Ltd

Printed on acid-free paper in Great Britain by MPG Books Ltd, Bodmin, Cornwall

ISBN 0567083993   (hardback)

BT
88
.A95
2006

CONTENTS

ABBREVIATIONS

BEM   *Baptism, Eucharist and Ministry* (Geneva: World Council of Churches, 1982)

CD   Augustine, *The City of God*

CH   *Church History*

CR   *Corpus Reformatorum*

DP   Marsilius of Padua, *Defensor Pacis*

DS   H. Denzinger and A. Schönmetzer (eds.), *Enchiridion Symbolorum*

ELJ   *Ecclesiastical Law Journal*

EP   Richard Hooker, *Of the Laws of Ecclesiastical Polity*

GS   *Gaudium et Spes*: Pastoral Constitution on the Church in the Modern World, Vatican II

IJSCC   *International Journal for the Study of the Christian Church*

JEH   *Journal of Ecclesiastical History*

JHI   *Journal of the History of Ideas*

JRH   *Journal of Religious History*

JTS   *Journal of Theological Studies*

LACT   Library of Anglo-Catholic Theology

LG   *Lumen Gentium*: the Dogmatic Constitution on the Church, Vatican II

LW   *Luther's Works*, ed. J. Pelikan and H. Lehmann (St Louis and Philadelphia: Concordia and Fortress Press, 1955–)

NIGTC   The New International Greek Testament Commentary

OIC   *One in Christ*

PS   Parker Society Edition of the Works of the English Reformers

ST   Thomas Aquinas, *Summa Theologiae*

UR   *Unitatis Redintegratio*: the Decree on Ecumenism, Vatican II

WA   *D. Martin Luthers Werke* (Weimar: Weimarer Ausgabe, 1883–)

INTRODUCTION

This book is a study of authority in the Christian Church: its principles and theological basis; its structures and organization; and its dynamics, the way it is exercised in practice. The method that I follow is one that comprises historical narrative, theological interpretation and contemporary commentary. But my underlying concern is for beneficial and salutary forms of authority that will promote the unity of the Church in the twenty-first century. The focus is mainly on the past one thousand years, Christianity's second millennium, when the different approaches to authority, broadly monarchical or broadly conciliar, that have come to inform the modern churches, took shape. Unfortunately for the churches and for the people who form their membership, these momentous developments, with their consequences for what Christianity looks like today, are often lost to sight.

Many educated Christian people have only a hazy notion of the massive disruption of the Western Church at the turn of the fourteenth century and of the ensuing conciliar activity that preceded the Reformation by more than a century. Even Reformation specialists do not always give this formative period its due weight in interpreting the period. Some in authority in the Roman Catholic Church would prefer that attention was not drawn to the Conciliar Movement. The long and painful process that resulted in the modern model of the papacy (by the suppression of an alternative tradition) is not given credence. The official line is that the structure that we have now is fundamentally how it has always been and how it was meant to be from the beginning. For their part, the non-Roman Catholic churches are largely unaware of how much they owe in their ecclesiology and structures to pre-Reformation conciliarism. So even to tell the story is important: its significance is clear and does not need to be laboured.

However, the study concludes by drawing out the implications of these historical developments for today's falteringly ecumenical age. The churches desperately need to overcome their inherited divisions in order to present a united witness, a single coherent proclamation (*kerygma*), both to galloping secularism and to resurgent major world faiths. Although up to this point this book is about the Western or Latin part of the Christian Church, in looking 'beyond the Reformation' ecumenically and towards the future of a universal Church whose wounds of division are healed, we bring into play the critique of western developments made over many centuries by the Eastern Churches, the Orthodox tradition.

The title – *Beyond the Reformation?* – has an intentional double reference and points both ways: it looks back and it looks ahead. First, we go back in history behind the Reformation to uncover some of its causes and antecedents (focusing especially on the Conciliar Movement and on both the achievements and the lost opportunities of the General Councils of the early fifteenth century). Second, we look beyond the divisions of the Reformation period – divisions that were provoked equally by the extreme views and violent actions of some on the side of reform and by the Roman Catholic Church's wholesale rejection of the legitimate demands of the Reformers, supported by their appeal to Scripture, the Fathers and conciliar thought. We turn to consider some of the conditions for reconciliation and convergence that are relevant to the current theological debate on the nature of authority and on the structures that best support and embody it. In this respect, we bring forward once again the abiding concerns and insights of the Conciliar Movement as an ecclesiological paradigm and show its relevance to our contemporary situation.

The Reformation is certainly the hinge of the narrative and the pivot of the argument, but it is only one of the several main foci of this study. Our first task is to trace the emergence in history of two paradigms of structures of authority and their ideological supports – broadly labelled 'monarchical' and 'conciliar' – during the centuries preceding the Reformation. The presupposition of this approach is that the Reformation was essentially an unresolved argument about authority in the Latin Church, an argument that was – and remains – internal to western Christendom.

This is the first full-length study, as far as I am aware, that sets the Reformation and the subsequent development of the Protestant and Anglican churches clearly in the context of the legacy of the Conciliar Movement of the late fourteenth and early fifteenth centuries. It explores the extent to which the Reformers invoked the ecclesiological principles and aims of the Conciliar Movement and the degree to which they can be regarded, therefore, as in some sense conciliarists by conviction. My conclusion is that the Continental and Anglican Reformers adhered in slightly different ways to a modified conciliarism and that they should be understood against that background.

This approach obviously places the Reformers in a rather different perspective to the one in which they have often been set in the anti-Protestant polemic of the past. That perspective saw the Reformation as an act of wilful separation from the Western Church with its centre in Rome, an act of rebellion and intransigence with regard to authority, perpetrated by a bunch of renegades from the continuous Christian tradition that stems from the Fathers. It treated the Reformers as though they were of another stripe altogether compared to those other giant figures, such as d'Ailly, Gerson, Zabarella and Cusanus who, firmly and loyally located within the western Catholic tradition, also sought reform of the principles and structures of authority that were dominant in their day and regarded them as corruptions or perversions of the authentic model of the Christian Church.

The method followed here, however, brings out the common ground between the fifteenth-century conciliarists and the sixteenth-century Reformers and underlines the continuity between them. Both groups may, without special pleading, be called 'reformers' and both may, with only moderate qualification, be described as 'conciliarists'. The same arguments were going on; the stakes were equally high and the consequences of failure equally dire. In fact, both movements, that of the fifteenth and that of the sixteenth century, must be judged to have failed, in that both fell well short of their aim of radically reforming the Western Church and permanently modifying its structures of authority. This study implies that the debate, spanning at least two centuries, over the structures and exercise of authority and how it should be reformed in theory and practice, was a debate that was internal to the western household of faith – and that the issues remain worryingly unresolved. The reformers of the Conciliar Movement and the Reformers of the Reformation alike are the discomforting prophetic figures who must both, at all costs, be held within the family of the Western Church.

My motive in undertaking this study, over the past fourteen years (alongside other projects), is then obviously not purely historical, though I believe that the book sheds fresh light on certain aspects of the Reformation, especially on its appropriation of conciliar ideas and its appeal to the cluster of ideas around natural law and the common good. The underlying concern is to assess the validity of the ideas of authority and the structures that embodied those ideas (while being alert to the complex relationship between ideas and institutions and the need for ideological suspicion of all legitimating theories). Both the institutions of the Church and the ideas that sustained them – whether 'monarchical' or 'conciliarist' – were sources of conflict in the centuries on either side of the Reformation. Any examination of their relevance to the Christian churches today is bound to be no less controversial. The major traditions and churches that were involved in the Reformation conflict – Roman Catholic, Protestant and Anglican churches – have been shaped in recent centuries by their response, either positive or negative, to the conflicting monarchical and conciliar paradigms of authority that are discussed in this book.

There is, then, a reforming agenda, drawing inspiration and guidance from a comparatively neglected aspect of Church history, behind this book, an agenda that is motivated by the longing for unity, the healing of the wounds of the Body of Christ, and a passion for authentic expressions of authority in the Church. The approach followed here is born of the conviction that the churches as they exist today, all of whom wrestle with issues of authority and freedom, continuity and innovation, coherence and subsidiarity, need to recognize what has shaped them, to acknowledge that there is unfinished business for them in the pre-Reformation and Reformation periods. The ideas discussed in this book, though very old, are enormously relevant to the churches at this point in their fortunes and carry a challenge to every Christian tradition. The conciliar tradition was an ongoing, unresolved debate about the relation of central church government to the local expressions of the universal Church dispersed among the nations, and in particular about the relation of the authority of the pope to the authority of the episcopate.

The historic conciliar tradition belongs to the Christian Church as a whole, not just to the Roman Catholic Church, which has in fact largely disowned it, at least overtly. Indeed, the Roman Catholic Church has hardly begun to own in practice (to 're-receive') the reforming impulse with regard to authority and the conciliar doctrines that are described here. When Hans Küng recovered aspects of this tradition and promoted conciliar theology, focusing on the Council of Constance, in his *Structures of the Church* during Vatican II, he got into seriously hot water with the Vatican for the first of several times in his life (Küng 1965). Francis Oakley, who has produced a series of books and articles about conciliarism, its history and its political philosophy, over the past forty years, since Vatican II in fact, has gathered and distilled his life's work in *The Conciliarist Tradition* (Oakley 2003). He believes that the Roman Catholic Church needs to rediscover the conciliar tradition – a part of its history that it has suppressed for centuries (he dubs this 'the repression of memory and the pursuit of the politics of oblivion') – in order to reform its practice of authority, in particular by overcoming Vatican centralization under the monarchical papacy of modern times.

The fact that the Protestant churches substantially derive their principles and structures of governance and oversight from the Conciliar Movement is hardly calculated to help the Roman Catholic Church to re-receive that period of its history and that element of its tradition. The polities of non-episcopal Protestant churches, with their hierarchies of interlocking synods or courts, are a one-sided development of conciliar ideas, for the Conciliar Movement pre-supposed episcopacy (as well as papacy). On the other hand, the Anglican polity of the bishop in synod (though this is not generally recognized, even by Anglicans) reflects conciliar ideas in a rather less one-sided way. Almost all of the Lutheran churches, whether episcopally ordered or not, now have synodical government. Lutherans affirm that teaching authority is given to the whole Church, rather than to the episcopate. There is one order of ministry: the distinction between priest and bishop is a matter of human law (*iure humano*), not divinely ordained in some sense. Some Lutheran churches that have bishops, but not (as yet) in the historic succession, do not give their bishops power of jurisdiction but confine jurisdiction to the synod. Episcopal collegiality is, therefore, comparatively weak in Lutheranism and is more aptly predicated of 'the matrix of the Church as a whole' (Aarflot 1988: 372). The Reformed or Presbyterian churches have been distinguished by their hierarchical structures of church courts, from the local presbytery to the national level (cf. Gray and Tucker 1999). The Protestant traditions have inherited the conciliar principles (principles of constitutionality, representation and consent), that inform their synodical systems of Church government, from the pre-Reformation period. But they have not always come to terms with the questions of historical and theological continuity through and beyond the Reformation that this indebtedness implies (for a comprehensive account of synodality in ecumenical perspective see Melloni and Scatena 2005).

What is missing in both the Protestant and the Anglican expressions of conciliarity is, of course, the universal primacy (of some sort – of what sort was precisely the central issue that conciliarism grappled with) of the Bishop of Rome and the role of the papacy considered not simply as a personal office, but as an institution, with a necessary infrastructure. Questions of primacy are considered in the penultimate chapter, where Roman Catholic, Orthodox and Anglican ideas are allowed to interact.

The churches of the Anglican Communion, with all their recent (and current) difficulties over issues of authority, coherence and continuity, have also appropriated conciliar principles and structures and have pioneered a reformed Catholic model of the bishop in synod. Anglicans are thus closer than the historic Protestant churches to the principles of the Conciliar Movement, to which episcopal polity was central. The consecration in the Episcopal Church of the USA (ECUSA) in 2003 of a bishop who, because of the ethical issues relating to his lifestyle, was unacceptable to many Anglicans both in ECUSA and throughout the Communion, was (because its canonical validity has not been effectively challenged) a practically irrevocable sacramental act, one that could not be airbrushed out of the picture, a brutal and unavoidable new fact in the Anglican ecclesiastical landscape. It is because that consecration or ordination was, like all ordinations, a sacramental act, an ecclesial sign with universal intention, of what is true of the Church and of the values that the Church stands for and of the message that it proclaims (for this understanding of ordination see Avis 2005), that at the time of writing it has placed a question mark over the viability of Anglican polity and the cohesion of the Anglican Communion. In that sense, it was parallel to the event that sparked the greatest trauma ever to afflict the Western Church before the Reformation itself: the election in 1378 of two popes (subsequently enlarged to three) who reigned simultaneously, each claiming the allegiance of Christendom and roundly anathematizing the other(s). The sets of responses that have been offered to these two events (so widely separated in time that it seems to be a painful effort for some otherwise educated Christians to discern any connection or analogy between them, an event of the present and an event of the distant past) bear an uncanny resemblance to each other.

There were those in the late fourteenth and early fifteenth centuries who argued that when the two, then three, popes had been elected the rules of the Church had actually been followed and there was therefore nothing much that could be done: only time would tell. The answer given by the leading conciliarists to this defeatist approach was that divine (biblical) law and natural law should override human regulations (positive law) in the interests of the common good of the Church. Divine and natural law mandate action – but action by whom and with whose authority?

Then there were those in the late Middle Ages who argued that the pope in question (whichever of the two or three Bishops of Rome) should be isolated and that canonical obedience should be withdrawn from him if he refused to respond to overtures of concern and should be transferred to the rival candidate (the *via cessionis*). However, this was little more than a gesture and did not solve the structural question of how to remove the offending pope.

Finally, the fully developed conciliar doctrine argued that, because divine and natural law, both inscribed in the Scriptures, took precedence over human, positive laws and moreover because *in extremis* 'necessity knows no law', the whole body of the Church should be consulted, through representative channels, gathered in a General Council, and that the Council was endowed with the power of Christ in his Body the Church to take whatever action was necessary to restore the unity of the Church.

Anglicans surely have much to learn from these events. What the conciliar tradition has to teach us about how best to respond to a situation that threatens the unity of part of the Church is in line with the ideas put forward in the official Windsor Report, but goes well beyond the rather tentative appropriation of these concepts that we find in that report (see Anglican Communion Office 2004).

What of the post-Reformation churches, the Methodists and Baptists, different though they are, in particular? Methodism models a striking form of conciliarity in the Conference, the governing body which is representative of the Methodist community, the Connexion, seen as an organic whole. Does Methodism, that sprang originally from the eighteenth-century Church of England, consciously trace its roots back in visible continuity through the Anglican tradition to the profoundly Catholic reforming impulses of the Conciliar Movement or does it stop at the Reformation, if indeed it tends to get that far? (For discussion of conciliarity and primacy by a Methodist theologian, see Wainwright 1978; 2003.) Can even British Methodism be expected to do so, when its original 'host' church, the Church of England, seems hardly aware these days of its deeper history?

Where do Baptists and other Christians with an 'independent', congregation-centred polity stand with regard to the reforming and conciliar movements that led, through their rejection and suppression, to the Reformation? Do they take the view of some early Anabaptists that corruption set in with Constantine (or even, in the most extreme form of historical suicide, with the death of the last Apostle) and that therefore everything that happened subsequently is actually irrelevant to what the churches should be today and how particular churches should relate to the whole Body? (For a deeply Catholic account of Baptist ecclesiology see Fiddes 2003.)

How does this book proceed? The first chapter, on the Church as mystery and as institution, sets the stage with a discussion of the relationship and tension between the three elements in the Church that were expounded by Baron von Hügel, following some suggestive remarks by Newman: the mystical, the intellectual and the institutional. This triad is picked up again at the end of the book in a brief discussion of continuity and discontinuity through the conciliar and Reformation periods. But to return to the double reference of our title: in the first place we look back 'beyond the Reformation' to the decisive events and ideas of the centuries that preceded the break-up of Western Christendom in the sixteenth century. We trace the emergence of an absolute, centralized ('monarchical') system of authority, located in the mediaeval papacy, especially in the reigns of Gregory VII, Innocent III and Boniface VIII, which developed in the struggle between popes and emperors for supremacy in Christian Europe. We consider the persistent – and persistently unheeded – calls for reform of the top-heavy, hierarchical and economically sapping structures of the Church and we expound the radical political and theological views of Marsilius of Padua, Dante and William of Ockham, before considering the significance of the largely moral reforming fervour of Wyclif and Hus.

We trace the events surrounding the Great Schism of the West in 1378, a trauma unmatched within the Western Church except by the Reformation, when the papacy split, first into two and then into three. The college of cardinals, regretting their recent choice of pope (Urban VI), with his irrational behaviour and violent temper, elected a second pope (Clement VII) – but the first refused to concede. The fact that the same college of cardinals had canonically elected two popes sent a shockwave through Europe. It resulted in a dual system of popes, cardinals, curia and ecclesiastical allegiances, right down to the parochial clergy. Perfectly logically, each side anathematized the other: there could be only one divinely guaranteed structure of salvation and conduit of sacramental grace. But which one was it? The almost metaphysical vertigo induced in many responsible churchmen by this implosion of the pivotal mediaeval principle of unity can scarcely be imagined at this cultural distance. A schism that split the Church from top to bottom was bad enough, but it was exacerbated by the realization that the problem was insoluble within the existing parameters. Because fullness of power (*plenitudo potestatis*) had accrued to the pope, the Roman Church was unable to remedy this catastrophic situation, remaining powerless to reunite itself for forty years.

The schism gave the Conciliar Movement its opportunity. Conciliarism was not an abstract political or theological theory, but arose from this particular historical crisis. Conciliar theory had early mediaeval origins, especially in the debates of canon lawyers on what to do about an heretical or otherwise errant pope. As Tierney (1955 etc.) decisively showed, conciliarism was not in conflict with the canon law tradition, but in fact derived from it. Conciliarism attempted to call in the resources of the whole

Church, dispersed throughout the nations and the universities, in order to redress the failings of the centre.

An impressive roll-call of conciliar thinkers – Conrad of Gelnhausen, Henry of Langenstein, Dietrich of Niem, Pierre d'Ailly, Jean Gerson, Nicholas of Cusa – and their ideas and actions for the healing of the schism and the future governance of the Church, together with the tantalisingly unfulfilled promise of the reforming councils of the first half of the fifteenth century – Pisa, Constance and Basel – forms the substance of the central chapters.

Here we see the crystallization of ideas of constitutional government that had been emerging in ecclesiastical and civil contexts, in canon law and in civic communities, for some centuries. In his study *Constitutionalism*, McIlwain states: 'In all its successive phases, constitutionalism has one essential quality: it is legal limitation on government; it is the antithesis of arbitrary rule; its opposite is despotic government, the government of will instead of law' (McIlwain 1947: 21–22). We consider the late mediaeval ideas of the constitutional exercise of authority, with checks and balances, constraints on power, by means of representative conciliar structures, culminating in a General Council, so that the consent of the governed could be sought.

Linked with these ideas that belong to political philosophy are ideas that belong to the philosophy of law and to moral theology: the validity of natural law, as the highest court of appeal, expounded classically by St Thomas Aquinas; the limitations, therefore, of merely human regulations, of positive law, together with the ancient notion that necessity knows no law; and the overriding claim of the common good of the Church.

A General Council was the most plausible candidate to succeed in uniting the Church and at the same time to implement the age-long desire for reform. A new constitutional instrument that would enable a Council to be convened without the normal authority of the pope was urgently needed. The first full-blooded conciliarists began to invoke the age-old dictum that what affects all should be approved by all (a principle of universal consultation and consent), and to apply it to the resolution of the schism. The premise of the leading conciliar thinkers (Dietrich of Niem, Pierre d'Ailly, Jean Gerson and Nicholas of Cusa) was that the sacred institution itself had failed. The very office (that of the papacy) that was intended to maintain the Church's unity had become the cause of its fragmentation. As d'Ailly put it: 'A community is not sufficiently ordered if it cannot resist its own ruin' (Oakley 1964:64).

The first attempt to unite the papacy, at the Council of Pisa (1409), exacerbated the problem when it simply added a third pope to the two who refused to step down. The papacy was reunited by the Council of Constance in 1417 when it deposed three popes and elected a fourth (Martin V). Constance attempted to perpetuate councils as the normal mode of governance in the Church, of which the pope would be the chief minister. At the Council of Basle (1431–49) the conciliarists over-reached themselves, lost crucial support from leading thinkers such as Nicholas of Cusa, and were tactically out-manoeuvred by the pope (Eugenius IV). Appeals to a General Council against the pope were subsequently outlawed and reform was resisted for a century, until the Council of Trent, when it was too late to prevent the breakup of the Western Church.

The Reformation can be seen as an explosion of pent-up conciliar, reforming energy. It was the execution of John Hus at Constance a century before that caused Luther to question the infallibility of Councils. From that moment of truth for Luther it was a comparatively short step to challenge papal infallibility (then, of course, not a dogma but a practical assumption, though one that was debated within the Church). The minds of the Reformers were seared, with respect to councils, by the betrayal of Hus, but they remained at least critical conciliarists. No one sympathetic to the conciliarist tradition can forget that it was the leading conciliarists Dietrich of Niem, Pierre d'Ailly and Jean Gerson who were the prime movers in the condemnation of Hus on false charges and in the face of an imperial guarantee of safe conduct.

The relationship of the Reformation, not only to proto-reformers such as Wyclif and Hus, and to radical political thinkers such as Marsilius, Dante and Ockham, but to the firmly mainstream thinkers of the Conciliar Movement, is a comparatively neglected aspect of Reformation studies. We consider the views that the Continental and English Reformers took of the fifteenth-century councils and evaluate the persistent appeals to a General Council that were made by some Reformers (e.g. Luther and Cranmer). As far as the Church of England is concerned, we look at Richard Hooker and other exponents of a conciliar type of ecclesiology among the Anglican divines of the seventeenth century and later and carry the account forward to the establishment of conciliar structures in the Anglican Communion.

The penultimate chapter looks at ideas of conciliarity, universal primacy and Church unity in the Western and Eastern Churches – Roman Catholic, Anglican and Orthodox – during the past century and a half. The historical fierce hostility of the East to papal claims is matched by irenic proposals from ecumenical theology. The remarkable congruity of Orthodox and Anglican ecclesiologies stands out here.

As we have already noted, an appeal to natural law, whether explicit or implicit, informed conciliar thought, enabling the conciliarists to appeal to a higher principle than positive law (laws that were of merely human institution and seemed to prevent the reform of Church structures), and ultimately to override it in order to secure the common good of the Church over party or personal advantage. The place and significance of natural law in the theology of the Reformers is a neglected – and to the extent that it has been addressed, controversial – area. A treatment of the role of natural law in Luther, Zwingli, Calvin, Bucer and the English Reformation as far as Hooker, brings out the strong continuity of Reformation theology with the mediaeval natural law tradition and marks one more strand in the ties that link the Reformers to the schoolmen and the conciliarists. The final chapter offers some reflections on the use of these ideas in recent discussion: the common good of the Church and the relation between natural law and the law of the Church. The chapter includes some reflections on issues of continuity and discontinuity in the history of church traditions from the Conciliar Movement, through the Reformation to the present. The way in which the imperative of reform, the *leitmotif* of the Reformation, has been articulated in modern Roman Catholic theology, by Congar, Rahner and Vatican II, and the need for realism, not utopianism, in ecclesiology, combined with a vision of true authority, are the concluding topics of this book.

Finally, I need to say that any theological value judgements expressed in this book have not been discussed by the Council for Christian Unity of the Church of England, for which I work as its General Secretary. This study is offered, in my personal capacity, as a contribution to ecumenical study and discussion, in the cause of the mission and unity of the one Church of Jesus Christ. I am grateful to Louise Walton for compiling the index.

Chapter 1

The Church as Mystery and Institution

This book is about some of the struggles and conflicts of the Christian Church during a thousand years of its history. The focus is on the tension and conflict between the Church as an institution and the Church as a mystery 'hidden in Christ with God'. The life of the Church is grounded in a mystical vision of participation in God and sustained by beliefs and teachings that are derived from revelation. But its historical existence is inescapably the life of an institution, with all that that implies about structure, organization and authority.

In order to hold together in time and space, any great community needs to organize itself and to provide itself with structures. It is precisely that organizational framework that enables it to promote its distinctive values and to carry forward its corporate purposes. Any living community is sustained by intrinsic collective values and is thus constituted as a moral community. A moral community is marked by a strong sense of living from an authoritative tradition and a commitment to perpetuating that tradition. Its sustaining values are enshrined in the tradition, and loyalty to the tradition gives authenticity to its life. The values so enshrined are both moral and social, so the moral community is at the same time a society. *Communitas* and *societas* belong together. Where the community is structured in such a way as to make it self-sufficient and a law unto itself we may say that it is a *societas perfecta* – which means not (as is sometimes supposed) a morally perfect, flawless and immaculate society, but one that is complete in itself and not accountable to any external authority. Most of the leading protagonists that figure in this book – not only the papal publicists, but the conciliarists too, and even such Reformers as Calvin – believed that the Church was a *societas perfecta*. The term is not in itself a value judgement, but it does suggest a self-contained and self-confident institution, robust in its defence of its sustaining ideology.

Institutions and their Ideology

In today's culture – the cultural epoch of late modernity – we say that we believe in community (though actually we believe much more in individualism), but we are certainly suspicious of institutions. 'Institutional' is often thrown around as a pejorative term, especially when applied to the Church. The expression 'the institutional church' carries overtones of distaste for something that is monolithic, rigid and probably fossilized. The phrase implies a preference for an alternative form of church that is more credible and socially acceptable. We are allergic to most historic institutions because we have learned to treat the traditions that they embody and the structures that give them hard edges with a hermeneutic of suspicion. We have learned from certain strands of social science (notably the Marxist and Critical Theory schools) that all institutions instantiate unequal power relations, privileging some and not privileging others in terms of the power that they hold. More sharply, from a liberationist perspective, the distribution of power is perceived as always unjust, oppressing those who do not have it and placing them at the disposal of those who do. In all institutions some people (comparatively few) have the right to rule, or shall we say to manage or to lead; others (the majority) have the duty to obey, or shall we say to co-operate or to follow. The rulers enjoy a disproportionate share of the desirable goods that belong to the community (whether these are mainly wealth or mainly esteem, but certainly always authority). The Christian Church in virtually any of its Promethean manifestations, but glaringly so in its hierarchical and clerical forms, evinces the dichotomy of ruler and ruled, those who decide and those who obey, those who lead and those who follow. Again, this analysis cuts right across the controversies presented in this book: high papalism, conciliarism, the Reformation: all alike involve unequal power relations.

So far all this is mere description and is obvious, so to speak, to the naked eye: you don't need to be a sociologist to see it. But the really insidious element resides in the area of legitimation. Legitimation purports to tell us why the present structures are the correct ones and should on no account be changed. The conceptual constructs that give rulers the right to rule and to impose the duty of obedience on all the rest comprise the ideology of the institution. Ideology provides the rationale for unjust power relations. But ideology is irrefutable from within the institution because it tells the rulers the welcome news that their position is a responsibility thrust upon them by higher authority for the good of the disenfranchised majority. Ideology tells the masses that to serve and to obey are their proper station, their due place in the great scheme of things. The conceptual frameworks that informed the words and actions of the papal monarchists, the conciliar thinkers, and the Reformers and their successors were all ideologies. In that sense they are all tarred with the same brush. The high papalist argues that the pope can be judged by no one (*papa a nemine judicantur*). The conciliarist claims that by persisting in schism the rival popes have committed what amounts to heresy and so qualify for deposition under canon law. Wyclif asserts that, because the property of the Church had been given originally by the laity, when its true purpose has been lost the laity should confiscate it back again. Luther makes a persuasive case for the German nobility to set up conciliar machinery for the reform of the Church in their lands. Hooker defends without the slightest concession every aspect, however accidental, of the Elizabethan settlement of religion in England. As MacCulloch says, if Parliament had commanded clergy to preach standing on their heads, Hooker would have found persuasive reasons to justify this (MacCulloch 2003: 507). All are defenders of ideology according to their lights – and its prisoners.

This book shows how the mediaeval papacy and its advocates, the papal publicists, heaped up claims for papal sovereignty that would not be defended by the most ardent Ultramontane Roman Catholic today. It describes the alternative vision for the institutional Church that the conciliarists worked out when the papal hierarchy became dysfunctional. It includes accounts of the attacks of Wyclif and Hus on the abuses of the institution and their radical remedy of calling in the state to reform the Church. It shows how the sixteenth-century Reformers rejected aspects of the late mediaeval institution and appealed to the Church of Christ as they saw it in the New Testament and in the early Fathers, the period of primitive purity. In every case, not only were ideological factors at work, but the integrity of the institution (a sacred, God-validated institution) was believed to be at stake. There was no proposal on the table in these debates (except perhaps in the radical programmes of Wyclif and Hus) that did not involve the redemption of the Church as a visible divine society. The conciliarists (notably Gerson) held to an equally hierarchical view of the Church as that of the papal publicists, but it was one where the balance between the papacy and the episcopate was redressed. The discussion of the conciliar elements in the theology of the Reformers gives no succour to the idea that any of them defended the notion that the Church was essentially or primarily invisible.

The Mystical and the Institutional

In his great work *The Mystical Element of Religion* (1908, 2nd edn 1923) Baron Friedrich von Hügel, the lay Roman Catholic theologian and polymath, has a famous chapter on 'The Three Elements in Religion' (von Hügel 1923: I, ch. 2). The three elements are the institutional, the intellectual and the mystical. We have begun with the institutional dimension and must now turn to the mystical and the intellectual as they apply to our thesis. Not only the sixteenth-century Reformers, but also the pre-Reformation conciliarists (for they were reformers of a sort, too) invoked the mystical against the institutional. Both conciliarists and Reformers wanted the Church to return to its true meaning, its authentic existence, in conformity to Scripture and the early tradition. The conciliarists were high-minded moralists and were appalled at the corruptions of Rome (Dietrich of Niem, who had seen it all at first hand, is filled with disgust). They aimed to rectify the structures so that the institution would function more effectively in the cure of souls. The Reformers attacked the structures of the late mediaeval Church in the name of its true essence, its christological centre. The institution had lost touch with its *raison d'être*. The gospel must renew and transform the Church. The papal and episcopal hierarchy was persecuting the preachers of the gospel. Like the conciliarists, the Reformers also appealed to the mystical against the institutional. We might say that for Luther the centre of gravity lay with the mystical, and structures were things that made no difference to salvation (*adiaphora*). For Calvin, however, the centre of gravity lay with the institutional: the structures of pastoral oversight were ordained by God; but the structures enshrined the mystical core of union with Christ through the Holy Spirit and the sacraments and he seldom lost sight of it.

The conciliarists and the Reformers also invoked the intellectual (in the form of the theological) against the institutional. They critiqued the dominant structures with theological arguments drawn from Scripture, the Fathers, and Roman and canon law. The Conciliar Movement saw a flourishing of ecclesiology; indeed, it is arguable that the crisis of the late mediaeval papacy and the reformist or conciliarist response gave birth to ecclesiology as a theological discipline. Out of a burning passion for the reform of abuses, Wyclif and Hus both wrote treatises entitled *De Ecclesia*. The Conciliar Movement generated major works of ecclesiology, not least Gerson's conciliar writings, particularly his *De Potestate Ecclesiae* (1416–18), and Cusanus' great work on Catholic concord. The later crisis, that of the Reformation, spawned innumerable minor and major writings on the Church, from Luther's *Babylonian Captivity* (1520) to the definitive edition of Calvin's *Institutes* (1559). Luther was a one-man printing industry and Calvin and Bucer were not far behind. Of course, the Reformers were answered from the Roman Catholic side by equally heavy theological artillery. In England, Jewel's *Apology* (1562) and Hooker's *Ecclesiastical Polity* stand out among the major Anglican contributions to ecclesiology of this period. Erasmus is, however, an example of a reforming spirit who shrank from direct political or popular action and who did not identify with the conciliar strand, entertaining no great hopes of a council. For Erasmus, the crisis, the theological polarization, should be resolved by the community of scholars (the *studium*) calmly considering the best course of action and advising the powers that be. A learned consensus would prevail. The pen, whether pious, polemical or satirical, would prove mightier than political action. Thus, through intellectual renewal, all the protagonists of this period that spans more than two centuries sought institutional renewal and reform.

Three Essential Elements and Three Phases of Development

In *The Mystical Element of Religion,* von Hügel shows that the three elements – the institutional, the intellectual and the mystical – correspond to three stages of spiritual development in the individual: childhood, adolescence and adulthood. In the first stage, that of spiritual infancy, we are guided by authority; in the second stage, that of spiritual adolescence, by reason; and in the third stage, that of spiritual maturity, by our own inner experience or intuition. Von Hügel's basic scheme has become known to a wider audience in Gerard Hughes' widely read book about spiritual growth, *God of Surprises* (1996).

The first stage of development in the Christian life, according to von Hügel, is spiritual infancy and corresponds to the institutional element of religion. Children need security and protection. They do not question what their parents provide for them. They learn through the senses and the memory, using their imagination. Children are comparatively passive recipients of a world that is largely given. So too with the institutional element in religion: it is the given fact of the Church, its beliefs and its worship, that is significant. We learn prayers, creeds and rules by heart. We are nurtured by the unchanging action of the Church in its liturgy, especially the sacramental cycle of baptism, confirmation and Holy Communion. The formation that the Church provides is appropriated through the senses, the imagination and the memory. The source of religious formation is external and is received on authority. Von Hügel calls this religion as fact and thing. We could sum up this stage of faith and its corresponding component of religion as 'growth through trust'. This accepting kind of faith will continue to form the bedrock of the spiritual life.

The second stage is spiritual adolescence or youth and corresponds to the intellectual element in religion. Young people no longer take everything on trust. They are compelled to question and argue and they need to be convinced. This is the stage of rebellion against accepted beliefs and standards and of working out meaning for oneself. So too with the critical element in religion: it is the critical evaluation of beliefs that is significant. Now it is the intellectual aspect of the faith that comes to the fore: Christianity as thought, system and philosophy of life. We begin to reflect critically on the inherited beliefs of the Church and try to square them with other truths that we have come to believe. We try to work out a meaning and framework for life using the resources of the Church's tradition. We could not do this unless we had already passed through stage one and so had appropriated, once and for all, the institutional element of religion. However, a purely critical and intellectual faith would prove arid and impossible to sustain. In isolation it would lead to a destructive rationalism. Hence the need to pass on to the third stage.

The third stage is spiritual maturity or adulthood and corresponds to the mystical element of religion. Adulthood is the time of responsibility, of taking decisions, of facing the future, and of engaging in constructive activity. The middle period of life is the time when we become more aware of our own psyche, especially the unconscious, and have to take matters to do with inner experience more seriously. So too with the mystical element in religion: the emotional, the volitional, the ethical and the practical are welded together as we live out our faith in the midst of the practicalities of life, but live it out, we trust, from ever stronger inner depths. This third stage/component is concerned with our becoming more in harmony with spiritual reality. Von Hügel writes: 'Here religion is rather felt than seen or reasoned about, is loved and lived rather than analysed, is action and power, rather than either external fact or internal verification' (von Hügel 1923, I: 53).

Each stage is carried forward to the next, while being surpassed by it. Each element contains traces of the other two. They have to be passed through in order: difficulties and resistance arise when individuals or groups are hustled from stage one (infancy – institutional) to stage three (maturity – mystical) without being allowed to pass at their own pace through stage two (adolescence – critical). They must first begin to question spontaneously what they have been taught on authority and to feel dissatisfaction with what they have been brought up on.

A Protestant Parallel

There is something of a parallel to von Hügel's scheme in a Protestant theologian, Paul Tillich. Tillich spoke of the tension between 'Catholic substance' and 'Protestant principle' (Tillich 1948). Catholic substance is the inherited content of Christian faith and practice and belongs to the whole Church. Protestant principle is the prophetic critique of all human institutions, which have an inveterate tendency to claim the absolute and final authority that belongs to God alone. It maintains the boundary between the conditioned and the unconditioned. The Protestant principle is seen most clearly in the witness of the sixteenth-century Reformers, but it also really belongs, like the Catholic substance, to the whole Church and is integral to the wholeness and health of Christianity. Jaroslav Pelikan used Tillich's formula in an apologetic for Luther's Reformation (Pelikan 1964): while it reverenced tradition and the inherited structures of the mediaeval Church, it brought them to the touchstone of the gospel with radical consequences. It preserved what is truly Catholic and could pass the test of Protestant principle. Luther and colleagues undoubtedly professed this intention: the Augsburg Confession (1530) is premised on this approach. Abuses were to be corrected; the gospel must be freely available; beyond that nothing would be affected. However, the question remains whether this approach was consistent with Luther's theology, that was actually highly subversive of all institutions, and therefore to what extent the strategy was implemented. We shall pick up that issue in relation to structures of authority in due course.

Catholic substance and Protestant principle correspond very broadly to von Hügel's institutional and intellectual elements in religion. But does Tillich have anything corresponding to von Hügel's third element, the mystical? Not explicitly as part of any threefold scheme. But Tillich's work is of course infused with a powerful existential dimension, which we see most clearly in *The Courage to Be* (Tillich 1962), and in his notion of 'ultimate concern'. However, in order to echo von Hügel's interpretation, Tillich would have to show how his existential component presupposes both Catholic substance and Protestant principle and I am not confident that he intends to do this.

According to von Hügel, the richest faith is found where all three stages or aspects are operative in relative harmony and creative tension. 'I believe because I am told, because it is true, because it answers to my deepest interior experiences and needs' (von Hügel 1923: I, 54). Von Hügel suggests Newman as someone who succeeded in combining all three. But each of these elements is imperialistic and will attempt to dominate the others. There is a need to be alert to those factors that tend to suppress one or other element in the life of the individual or in the corporate life of the Church.

Three Criteria of Ecclesial Integrity

I now propose to adapt von Hügel's three elements – the institutional, the intellectual and the mystical – into three *criteria of ecclesial integrity*: let us call them the principles of conservatism, criticism and contemplation. Because the Church is indefectible and cannot finally fail in its stewardship of the gospel, whatever its deficiencies may be (as the Reformers as well as the high papalists and conciliarists held), it will always have an integrity given to it by God. It is not for us, needless to say, to presume to offer the Church of Christ integrity! But the integrity of the Church is both gift and task: it belongs to grace and it belongs to human responsibility. In all the areas covered in this study – authority and unity, reform and liberty – there is an obligation on all Christians, and especially on those entrusted with oversight, to work for the integrity of the visible Church, in other words for the common good of the Church.

The institutional dimension equates broadly to the principle of *conservatism*: this means preserving all that is sound and fruitful and that has proved its worth in the life of the Church in the past. It means garnering the well-winnowed harvest of our heritage and not dismissing it simply because it has been around for a long time. Christianity, like other historical religions, draws its strength from the resources of the past and adapts them to enable it to face the challenges of the present. Though it must be

constantly changing (and has, as a matter of historical fact, done so continuously), it will be most true to its own nature by changing not by revolution but by evolution, in critical continuity with its previous history.
MacIntyre's idea of tradition-constituted and tradition-constituting enquiry
resonates here: there is no intellectual progress in detachment from the
givens of tradition within the moral community that embodies it
(MacIntyre 1985). The principle of conservatism resists passing fashions,
takes a long-term view, and is mindful of all that we owe to those who have
gone before. In biblical language, it looks to the rock from which we were
hewn. The principle of conservatism has a marked affinity with the
Catholic substance of Christianity as Tillich defines it. It is secured by the
institutional continuity of the Church, even though what is conserved (the
mystical vision and the cognitive tradition) may prove subversive of the
institution at times. One thread that runs through this study is the conservatism of the magisterial Reformation; and one strand within that thread
is the tradition of conciliar thought.

The intellectual dimension equates broadly to the principle of *criticism*:
this means that all human traditions and institutions should be scrutinized
for their tendency to become an end in themselves, and so to quench the
Spirit. Only God is the ultimate good; created, finite things, however
precious, must never be absolutized. To give to God's creatures the
reverence that is due only to God is idolatry. The principle of criticism
means that we must never forget that the Church's perfection is eschatological and will not be realized in this world. The principle of criticism is
subversive of ecclesiastical complacency and stagnation. It relativizes ecclesiastical structures and resists the imperialistic claims of one over against
another. This principle clearly has an affinity with Tillich's Protestant
principle. The criterion of criticism impelled the reforming movements of
the mediaeval period. They were fired with a vision of what the Church
was for and what it should be.

The mystical dimension equates broadly to the principle of *contemplation*: it means that we must always ask of any institution or programme
how it enhances our spiritual vision and our relationship to God. The
principle of contemplation constantly relativizes both the institutional and
the intellectual aspects of Christianity. They are simply means to the *visio
dei*. It insists that administrative efficiency and academic soundness are
never enough (just supposing that we ever reached the point of achieving
them!). The contemplative principle cries out for reality, for vitality, for the
experience of God. Mere conservatism can be stifling. Mere criticism can
be arid. It is the mystical and contemplative dimension that is the ultimate
test of a church's integrity, of its standing before the face of God (as Luther
typically puts it: *coram Deo*). If conservatism binds us to our historic institutions and criticism holds us to our studies of Scripture and theology, contemplation drives us to our knees.

Newman's Seminal Schema

Immediately behind von Hügel and his three elements stands John Henry Newman and his seminal remarks about the three functions of the Church. Newman made these comments in the preface that he wrote in 1877 to the reissue of his Anglican work *The Prophetical Office of the Church*, under the title *The Via Media of the Anglican Church* (Newman 1990; all references in his section are to pp. 24–26). Just as Christ is Prophet, King and Priest, so the Church has a triple office: teaching (prophetic), ruling (regal) and worshipping (priestly), or as we might say, theological, governing and liturgical. These three functions correspond to three dimensions of Chistianity. 'It is at once a philosophy, a political power and a religious rite.'

Each dimension and function, according to Newman, has its 'guiding principle': the guiding principle of theology is truth; that of worship is devotion and edification; that of government is expediency.

Each dimension or function also has its special faculty or 'instrument': theology employs reason; worship relates to our emotional nature; governance uses command and coercion.

Each has its own besetting temptation or weakness: theological reasoning can become mere rationalism; devotion can degenerate into superstition and 'enthusiasm'; authority can be debased into proud ambition or tyranny.

Newman, like von Hügel, sees an order of development in the stages – they are not random or interchangeable – but Newman applies this socially rather than individually. His theory is, as we might think today, unashamedly hierarchical. In the beginning, says Newman, Christianity appealed particularly to 'the lower ranks of society', the illiterate, ignorant and dependent, and here its devotional potential was first realized. As Christianity developed (presumably in the early Patristic age) it began to attract intellectuals and sophisticated people, the 'cultivated class', and at this stage its theology began to be elaborated. Later still the faith was adopted by rulers and princes (beginning with the Emperor Constantine, presumably), who began to tap its potential for power and authority. It emerged at this stage as 'an ecclesiastical polity', and 'chose Rome for its centre'.

Newman was drawing here on his reading of Anglican divines, especially early Evangelical influences on his theology, on the Anglican Calvinist tradition, in fact (cf. Weidner's introduction to Newman 1990: xlix–lxxv). Anglican writers had taught the doctrine of the person and work of Christ under the threefold rubric of prophet, priest and king, the three Old Testament types of Christ, the Messiah or Anointed One, who were anointed with oil, with the Spirit of God, or both. Though this tradition had been mediated to Newman by Thomas Scott, the Evangelical biblical commentator who made an indelible impression on him, there was nothing exclusively Evangelical or even Calvinist about this scheme.

Calvin and Anglicans on Christ's Triple Office

Christ's triple office as prophet, priest and king was indeed classically expounded in Calvin's *Institutes* (Calvin 1962: Bk II, ch. xv). He alleged that, under the papacy, the doctrine of Christ's triple office, though known, was 'frigid', 'of no great benefit' and not fully understood (Calvin 1962: I, 426). Christ's anointing with the Spirit was primarily with a view to his kingly office: this 'pertains to the whole body of the Church' as well as to each individual member. It secures and safeguards the continuity and perpetuity of the Church (its indefectibility, as we might say). The prophetic unction was given to Jesus Christ as preacher and teacher of the good news of the kingdom, not only for himself, but for his whole body, so that a corresponding efficacy of the Spirit might always accompany the preaching of the gospel. He also takes us into his priestly ministry, so that we, 'though in ourselves polluted, in him being priests (Revelation 1.6) offer ourselves and our all to God, and freely enter the heavenly sanctuary, so that the sacrifices of prayer and praise which we present' are pleasing to God (I, 425–32; cf. Jansen 1956).

While it is clear that in Calvin the triple office applies to the Church as well as to Christ himself, he expounds it under the heading of Christology and does not return to it in his fourth book, on the Church. Moreover, the treatment is not as systematic or comprehensive as one might expect. The kingly office is related to the divine preservation or indefectibility of the Church, rather than to its governing ministry. The priestly office is expounded in purely individual terms, and not in relation to the ministry of the sacraments. The prophetic office is related to the Church's mission and is not given an individual application: teaching and preaching were strictly controlled in Calvin's Geneva.

Within Anglican theology the theme is extensively expounded in John Pearson's *Exposition of the Creed* (first edn 1659; Pearson 1864: 165–86, 385–88) and even crops up in Joseph Butler's *Analogy of Religion* where it is said to be a standard approach (first edn 1736; Butler 1889: 251–52). Newman would have been familiar with it not only in these and other Anglican divines, but in Fathers such as St John Chrysostom and Eusebius of Caesarea. It is indeed found in most Christian traditions and in all ages. It was not unknown to Aquinas and the mediaeval schoolmen. But it has not been taken up to the same extent by Lutherans (for a slightly pedantic critique from a Lutheran theologian see Pannenberg 1964: 212–25; on the tradition see Wainwright 1997: Pt 2; for a brief exposition of the biblical material see Avis 2005: 65–69).

The Triple Office of the Church

The significance of Newman's use of this venerable hermeneutic of Christology lay in his application of it to the Church in a more thoroughgoing way than Calvin. This was what some Protestant, especially Anglican Evangelical, writers were reluctant to do, since it seemed to divinize the Church as a human institution. For Newman the Church is Christ's 'representative ... his mystical Body and Bride', and is, therefore, not so much a human as 'a divine institution'. It is the shrine and organ of 'the Paraclete', the Holy Spirit, 'who speaks through her till the end comes'. Pearson had said that, just as the oil of anointing flowed down Aaron's head and beard to the robes that covered his whole body (Psalm 133), so Christ's anointing with the Spirit as Messiah flows down to all his people. Newman says that 'after his pattern, and in human measure, Holy Church has a triple office too' (for what 'in human measure' represents for Newman in allowing for imperfection and worse in the Church, see Weidner 2001).

No doubt it was partly Newman's influence that explains the prominence of the theme of the three offices or tasks (*munera*) of the Church and its ministry in the teaching of the Second Vatican Council. In Vatican II, the whole people of God (*laos*) is prophetic, priestly and royal. Not only bishops and clergy, but laypeople too, are entrusted with the responsibility of teaching and sanctifying – though where we might expect the regal office of governing to be applied to the people of God as whole it is conspicuous by its absence, though recognized elsewhere (LG 10–12, 34: Abbott 1966: 26–30, 61). The approach is not the slightly static one of von Hügel's three elements, nor the apparently functional one of Newman's three functions, but is the dynamic one of three tasks comprising the Church's mission.

Interestingly, Newman seems to give special prominence to the teaching and ruling functions. (Evangelical and Tractarian he had been and at heart remained: the sacerdotal dimension of Church and ministry was not major for Newman; it was the theological and the authoritarian that fired him.) The prophetic, teaching function has primacy because of its intimate relation to theological truth. 'Theology is the fundamental and regulative principle of the whole Church system.' Theology is the exposition of divine revelation and, since revelation is 'the initial and essential idea of Christianity', theology could hardly be more central. It is theology that gives substance to the prophetic office (as its subject matter, formal cause and expression, as Newman puts it) and as such virtually creates the priestly and kingly offices of the Church. Moreover, it has a certain 'jurisdiction' over them and can judge whether they are being exercised properly.

Having said that about the prophetic office of the Church, Newman goes on to elevate particularly the pastoral or governing office (just as Calvin did). He has already shown that it represents the pinnacle of the process of historical development in which the priestly (devotional) emerged first and the prophetic (intellectual) second. He has also assured his Roman Catholic readers (and no doubt the Roman censors) that 'the Pope, as the Vicar of Christ, inherits these offices and acts for the Church in them'. Now he elaborates: 'the Papacy and its Curia' constitutes 'the special centre of action'

of the Church's governing or ruling office. The exercise of this office is by
means of command and coercion. Since the beginning, Newman claims, the
Church has had 'a hierarchy and a head, with a strict unity of polity, the
claim of an exclusive divine authority and blessing, the trusteeship of the
gospel gifts, and the exercise over her members of an absolute and almost
despotic rule'. Altogether, the Catholic Church comprises 'a sovereign
State'. Newman explicitly identifies this aspect with the catholicity of the
Church: it is her authority structures that make the Church Catholic; universality means hierarchy and centralization.

In the 1877 Preface to the *Via Media*, Newman is arguing for an uncompromising version of the Church as a *societas perfecta*, a unitary, uniform,
complete, self-sufficient and self-regulating body. Although he had
deplored the formal definition of the dogma of papal infallibility at the First
Vatican Council (1869–71) several years earlier, he is now endorsing what
had been achieved at the Council in terms of magisterial authority and
universal ordinary jurisdiction of the papacy. The pope, he says, inherits
Christ's prophetic, priestly and pastoral offices and exercises them on
behalf of the Church. If Christ teaches infallibly, as he surely does, then the
pope can teach infallibly (Newman had never, as a Roman Catholic, ques-
tioned the principle of papal infallibility, only the expediency of promul-
gating it as dogma). If Christ's kingly rule is universal, as it surely is, then
the pope's jurisdiction is world-wide (obviously Newman had accepted this
when he became a Roman Catholic in 1845).

An Anglican Alternative

Newman is finally and decisively repudiating the Anglican alternative
(basically the 'branch' model of the Church, where the Roman and
Anglican churches, together with the Eastern churches, are streams of the
one apostolic tradition) that he had expounded in *The Prophetical Office
of the Church* and very soon found wanting, dismissing it as a mere paper
theory that had never had a real, concrete existence. What Newman meant
by this incredibly arrogant judgement on Anglicanism, that its ecclesiology
only existed on paper, in the writings of its divines, is – though one hesitates
to say it – that it had not been able to accommodate him. Newman's
attempt, particularly in Tract 90, to take Anglican ecclesiology in a sharply
new direction – Romewards – had been turned down firmly by the
University of Oxford and (more gently) by the Bishop of the diocese. This
rebuff, to Newman's sensitive spirit, had the effect of discrediting the whole
tradition, of which he had been so eminent and eloquent an advocate and
apologist, not least in *The Prophetical Office of the Church* (cf. Turner
2002).

The Anglican divines, from the Reformers, through the Jacobaean and
Caroline divines, to the eighteenth-century High Churchmen and those

Tractarians who did not follow Newman to Rome, understood catholicity differently. They worked with a dispersed or distributed concept of catholicity, one that did not entail a single hierarchical authority and that was resistant to global centralization. For classical Anglicanism, the Catholic Church was not a unitary, uniform, self-sufficient and autonomous body, where decisions are made hierarchically and centrally (a *societas perfecta*). It was a complex, diverse, interdependent communion made up of particular (mostly national) churches, sharing a common faith and common principles of order, but with differences of liturgies, ceremonies and traditions, and where responsibility for decision-making was dispersed and operated at various levels of conciliarity – and it worked in partnership with the state, which had obligations to the Church.

The practice of the Roman Catholic Church, more than a century after Newman's death, is much as he described and defended it in the terse remarks of his 1877 Preface – only more so. The Second Vatican Council, which is sometimes called Newman's Council because it reflected certain aspects of his ecclesiology that are in some degree of tension with the remarks of 1877, provided a theoretical corrective to the First. Its theology of communion, grounded in baptism; its concept of the local church or diocese and of episcopal collegiality; and its recognition of elements of ecclesial reality beyond the Roman Catholic Church are all moves in the direction of the model of a reformed Catholicism (of which Anglicanism happens to be an – obviously very imperfect – instantiation). But Roman Catholic theologians constantly question whether Vatican II has been 'received' (e.g. Tillard 1985). To put it mildly, its vision has not been fully implemented. It is arguable that what the late Basil Cardinal Hume called the 'pyramid' model of hierarchical communion and the centralization of all authority and jurisdiction have become intensified since Newman wrote, notwithstanding Vatican II.

Anglican ecclesiology, both practice and theory, though it has of course developed since Newman rejected it in 1845 and again in 1877, is essentially what he rejected. The Anglican Communion of Churches existed only in embryo in 1845: it consisted of the Scottish Episcopal Church and the Church of Ireland, together with the Church of England (although since 1800 the Irish and English Churches were constitutionally one church, in practice they were regarded as two). The term 'Anglican Communion' occurs before 1845 (Podmore 2004) and may possibly have been known to Newman. The first Lambeth Conference took place in 1867 as an expression of non-hierarchical and non-coercive conciliarity. The Anglican Quadrilateral (basically Scriptures, Creeds, sacraments, historic episcopate) was proposed first at Chicago in 1886 and then at Lambeth in 1888 (being further refined in 1920). The nature of the Anglican Communion as a fellowship of particular or national churches was classically defined by the Lambeth Conference of 1930 and the essentially dispersed character of authority in Anglicanism was set out by Lambeth 1948. The coherence of the Communion has been tested by the issue of women priests and bishops and by that of homosexual clergy and bishops. These challenges and the way that they are met bring out concretely the meaning of Anglican conciliarity. They test to breaking point what is at stake for a communion that is distributed, an authority that is dispersed, a conciliarity that is not centralized and a collegiality that is not hierarchical.

The Conciliar Tradition, the Reformation and the 'Three Elements'

This book explores the historical sources of the issues that were so sharply posed by Newman in his Preface to *The Via Media of the Anglican Church*. Within the context of the three offices and functions of the Church, this study focuses on the regal office and on the governing or ruling function (the one that arguably came to dominate Newman's thinking after he rejected Anglicanism and the one that most interested Calvin). This book concentrates on the political or institutional dimension of the Church and on the distribution of power and the exercise of authority within it. This approach inevitably raises the issue of the relation of the political or pastoral office/function to the other two: the devotional/sacramental and the magisterial/theological. Was it merely wishful thinking that led Newman to assert the priority of theology over the other two? Had he not in fact already conceded the issue in favour of the political office – game, set and match – by professing his loyalty, in 1845 and at numerous subsequent moments, to the centralized structure – a structure that, through censorship and policing of the academy, would dominate the theological function and, through centralization of the liturgy and resistance to inculturation, would hold the devotional one in an iron grip for the next century and a half at least?

To put it in von Hügel's terms: what is the *modus vivendi* between the three elements of religion – the institutional, the intellectual and the mystical – in a model of authority that is both Catholic and reformed? It is arguable that, in the history of the Western Church up to the eve of the Reformation, the institutional element progressively dominated and eventually absorbed the intellectual and the mystical elements, thwarting the development that von Hügel believed to be vital. The events of the sixteenth century can plausibly be seen as the intellectual and the mystical elements reasserting their claims over against the institutional element.

It is well known and not controversial that the early Lutheran Reformation sat lightly to the structural and institutional aspects of the Church. The essential requirement, the one thing needful, the pearl of great price, was the free course of Evangelical theology and the uninhibited expression of Evangelical piety. Structures of authority and oversight – particularly legal structures – were not the concern of the gospel. What mattered was the actual event of word and sacrament. The political, juridical element was external to the gospel and should be administered by Christian princes, and so on. This phase did not last long and there was soon a flourishing of Lutheran legal studies and an energetic programme of creating ordinances and institutions to reflect these (Witte 2002). However, until the end of the First World War, church affairs in Lutheran Germany were administered by the civil authorities and it remains the case that in much of Lutheranism the 'magisterium', the teacher and judge of true doctrine, rests with the academics, the professors of theology.

It was the fact of the Reformation, and the consequent separation of the Church of England from papal jurisdiction and thus inevitably from the Roman Catholic communion also, that created Newman's dilemma in the early 1840s: could he be a catholic and apostolic Christian within the Church of England? In this study, I delve back beyond the watershed of the Reformation to the mediaeval period, and particularly to the Conciliar Movement, to recover the sources of a catholic and reformed approach to structures of authority. It was in this period, the half century from the Great Schism of 1378 to the failure of the Council of Basel in the early 1430s, that the issues of authority structures in the modern Church emerged and crystallized. Of course, they had been fermenting for centuries before the crisis of 1378 and would continue to develop from the Reformation to the present day. But the questions were framed, the agendas were set and the alternatives were posed at this time.

Newman and Historical Perspective

I am not aware that Newman had any interest in the late mediaeval Conciliar Movement or much knowledge of it, or that he had come to grips with conciliar theory. Newman's heart was in the patristic period: he needed to feel at one with the Fathers and martyrs of the early Church. Although he was consummately versed in the early councils of the Church, his theological centre was located prior to the developments and crises that called forth conciliarism. He was not at home in any other period of Church history: the Reformation was alien in its ethos to him (Avis 2002: 237, 242–44) and as for the Enlightenment, it represented the apostasy of western civilization. Newman viewed the rise of the historical and physical sciences in the nineteenth century with a disdain bordering on aversion. He was not comfortable with the modern, Ultramontane Roman Church and reconciled himself to it by intellectual dexterity and emotional economy. Newman was an arch-reactionary, an atavist, a throwback, who hankered for the society of the western Fathers as he imagined them. Again and again he called them in aid of his positions. However, a Cyprian, an Ambrose, even an Athanasius, with their penetrating vision of what really mattered in truth and error, in life and death, would have made short work of the fastidious, casuistical, logic-chopping and self-obsessed Newman. Much of

Newman's theological development was influenced by the illusion that he would feel at home in the rough-house of the early Church. But Newman was something of a homeless theologian, alienated from ecclesiastical domesticity: the successive institutions to which he belonged, from Oriel College onwards, always caused him grief and he them. His ideal was a select group of celibate male disciples, in retreat from the rough and tumble of the world, with himself as their teacher and guide, such as he fleetingly achieved at Littlemore while still an Anglican. Newman was held by a spiritual vision, of God, Christian truth and the Church – in that order. For Newman the mystical won out against the intellectual and decisively trumped the institutional (cf. Turner 2002).

Chapter 2

MODELS OF AUTHORITY IN THE CHURCH

The Monarchical and Conciliar Paradigms

Two rival models of authority and governance in the Church have dominated western Christianity for the past thousand years and continue to exist in tension today (we will say something about authority in Eastern Christianity later). It is convenient to call these western models 'monarchical' and 'conciliar', provided we remember that the first thing to say about the monarchical and the conciliar models of church authority is that they are stereotypes. They are not invariably found in their pure forms: elements of each are found in most churches and there are grey areas where they merge into each other. Neither do they imply straightforward value judgements, so that the monarchical is always bad and the conciliar is always good (or perhaps, for some, the other way round): both types are capable of being debased and corrupted. Monarchical Catholicism embodies a principle of primacy, a personal ministry of oversight, that is realized at every level of the Church's life, whether it is explicitly acknowledged or not. On the other hand, conciliarity has sometimes become debased and extreme, as we shall see, and in any case becomes feeble and paralysed where there is a lack of leadership, of primacy. Both models can be perverted to ideological ends where they serve the vested interests of those who have the power to place their dominant conceptual construction on the effects of human action.

Although I am drawing a contrast between the monarchical and the conciliar paradigms and perhaps, therefore, unintentionally accentuating the differences, it is important to bear in mind that they have much in common. In fact they share a set of very basic presuppositions about the nature of the Church. Both are forms of Catholicism; that is to say, they each express in different ways a Catholic understanding of the Church. They presuppose that the Church is a universal, divinely instituted, structured, visible society – a community that is given stewardship of the means of grace: principally the saving doctrine of the faith and the sacraments that are also normally necessary for salvation. So both models are stating an ecclesiology and both say a good deal about how the Church is envisaged and understood.

Furthermore, those who magnified papal authority and those who sought to check it were not as far apart as is sometimes assumed (cf.

McCready 1975). Though the papal monarchists (the 'publicists') tend to make absolute statements about the untrammelled power of the papacy – statements that have been taken at face value by interpreters such as Ullmann and Wilks – they often go on to qualify the application of those outright declarations in practice. Both the publicists and their opponents (including the conciliarists) accept the spiritual basis of society and deny ultimate autonomy to the civil order. The anti-papal-monarchists admit that the spiritual power is superior to the temporal, while denying that the temporal is derived from the spiritual; and the publicists accept the independent integrity of temporal authority. For both sides any papal intervention in temporal affairs must be justified, not by pretensions to temporal jurisdiction as such on the part of the pope, but by spiritual considerations because the pope is responsible for the spiritual welfare of Christendom. In all that follows we should think of these passionate and sometimes violent debates as an ongoing argument within the family.

The Monarchical Model

The historical exemplar of monarchical Catholicism is the Roman Church of the later Middle Ages, in which full authority (*plenitudo potestatis*), both spiritual and temporal, was held to be concentrated in the papacy. Accelerating claims for papal authority were challenged by the Conciliar Movement at the turn of the fourteenth century and for several decades afterwards, but were reasserted with a vengeance when that movement was effectively defeated. The Ultramontanism that marked the Roman Catholic Church's reaction to the Enlightenment, the French Revolution and the rise of nationalism was an resurgence of monarchical Catholicism. The Vatican I decrees on the universal jurisdiction and infallible teaching authority of the Petrine office were the theoretical high watermark of the Ultramontane tide. But the concrete practical implementation continued and in the twentieth-century, the papacy was more centralized and authoritarian than it had ever been. These claims were not retracted by Vatican II (1962–65) which continued to assert the supreme, full, ordinary and immediate jurisdiction of the pope over all local churches and all Christians. Even the authority of bishops, which the Council affirms as a counterbalancing factor, is held to be nugatory apart from their relation of 'hierarchical communion' to the pope.

However, it is important to say that the monarchical model of authority is not confined to Roman Catholicism. Wherever ecclesiastical power is concentrated disproportionately and unrepresentatively in the hierarchy, whenever lay people and the majority of clergy are excluded from responsibility for the affairs of the Church, we find the monarchical principle at work. The history of the Church of England provides abundant examples of monarchical government in the form of high-handed kings such as

Elizabeth I, James I and Charles I, autocratic archbishops like Bancroft and Laud, not to mention the innumerable company of pompous prelates and self-important parsons through the centuries. But Rome remains the classic case of monarchical Catholicism because its model of ecclesiastical governance received elaborate ideological underpinning over many centuries, much of which is still upheld theologically and implemented effectively today. 'While the ideology of papal monarchy was forged in mediaeval times, its implementation has occurred only in modern times' (T. Nichols 1997: 316).

Monarchical Catholicism entails a descending, centralized, hierocratic ecclesiology with a pyramid structure. Authority is concentrated in the hierarchy which flows down from the papacy. In the period before the Great Schism of 1378 – when the cardinals elected a replacement pope, so giving rise to rival structures of jurisdiction running parallel throughout Europe, even down to parish level – canon lawyers and theologians competed with each other to supply the popes with ever more inflated claims in order to bolster their power over against the emperor and other civil rulers. The pope was invested with God's power on earth and there were few curbs, theoretically at least, on his authority. There was no higher court of appeal than the pope, not even the emperor, for spiritual power included and exceeded temporal power. We shall pick up the historical thread again shortly, but meanwhile it may be helpful to enlarge on what is actually at stake.

In the Roman Catholic tradition this supreme authority is expressed in teaching, jurisdiction and sacramental power. In teaching, the Church's magisterium (teaching office, essentially the pope) has an authority at least equal to, and in practice greater than, that of a General Council. In jurisdiction, an immediate universal jurisdiction, superior both to provincial synods and to the authority of the local bishop, is claimed for the papacy. In sacramental power, the grace of the sacraments flows down from its God-given matrix in the pope as the successor of Peter and the vicar of Christ to the bishops and thence to the priests and the faithful – so that in the last analysis there can be no true priestly orders or efficacious sacraments apart from communion with the pope, even if, as in the case of the Eastern Churches and the Old Catholic Churches, that communion has subsequently become broken without Roman recognition of the validity of their orders and sacraments being lost.

The Emergence of the Papal Monarchy and the Longing for Reform

In the development of monarchical Catholicism practical, political developments went hand in hand with the elaboration of ideology. Beginning in the second half of the eleventh century and continuing throughout the twelfth, the papacy was centralized and its administration was made more rigorous, so that the pope and the curia took direct administrative control of the Western Church and sought to impose uniformity of practice, according to the Roman model, throughout the Church. By the thirteenth century papal power was at its height: it had successfully encroached on the secular sphere in England and elsewhere against the opposition of both the bishops and the kings (Brooke 1931: 29, 41, 227).

Running parallel with the escalation of ideological claims for papal authority was the progressive centralization of church administration across Europe in the papacy, particularly during the Avignon period, 1305–1403. Nomination to various ecclesiastical offices and benefices accrued to the papacy and so did a proportion of their revenues. Clement IV's Bull *Licet Ecclesiarum*, 1265, claimed for the papacy the disposal of all benefices and cures of souls. Ecclesiastical benefices were material items and treated as articles of private property with a commercial value. The pre-schism period saw a massive expansion of the papal civil service and its conversion in many respects into 'a great fiscal machine' (Oakley 2003: 30). Jedin, the historian of the Council of Trent and no friend of conciliar theory, pointed out that 'a rigid centralisation of authority characterised the papal government of the Church' and that 'it was above all the centralization of authority in the Curia, the procedure adopted in granting benefices, and the system of taxation connected therewith, that cried out for reform' (Jedin 1957: 5, 7).

Ideas of reform and renewal, both personal and communal, are inseparable from the Christian religion and are bound up with the grace of Christian liberty through redemption. The properly ordered, adequately reformed Christian life is one in which God's service is experienced as perfect liberty. As Ladner showed in his major work *The Idea of Reform: Its Impact on Christian Thought and Action in the Age of the Fathers* (Ladner 1959), the idea of reform is arguably unique to Christianity and belongs to its very essence, being enshrined in its original trust deeds, as it were. The cluster of interrelated ideas, found in the New Testament and the early Church, of penitence, conversion, baptismal regeneration and the life of discipleship, shaped the concept of reform. The notion, so central to St Paul's epistles, of the renewal of the image and likeness of God in humankind, inspired the reform movements of early and mediaeval Christianity. St Augustine of Hippo was a seminal influence on concepts of renewal and reform, but Augustine's vision was limited: he was interested only in individual sanctity and in small communities of kindred spirits in the midst of a decadent and crumbling earthly city. It was not until the late eleventh century, the age of Gregory VII (Hildebrand), that the reform agenda embraced the whole Church; and it took a further century, until the age of Innocent III and St Thomas Aquinas, before the vision of reform became extended to Christendom itself. The idea of reform, Ladner concludes, 'was to remain the self-perpetuating core, the inner life spring of Christian tradition' (Ladner 1959: 423).

Attacks on the Roman Church, inspired by the hunger for a Church that would be pure, simple and chaste, were already prevalent before the Great Schism; they were intensified, but not inaugurated, by this catastrophic failure of the hierarchy, the cardinals and popes. Leff describes the 'widespread attitude of distaste and criticism', 'a sense of betrayal', not only with regard to the moral and 'professional' deficiencies of the clergy, but with regard to 'the malfunctioning of the church as an institution'. Its very constitution as an hierarchical system was being widely challenged long before the sixteenth century (Leff 1967a: I, 25, 29). What was at stake was the nature of the Catholic Church as a political community, as an ordered society, and particularly its structures of authority.

By the beginning of the fifteenth century intense frustration over the continuing schism – a combination of disillusionment with the behaviour of the rival popes and growing suspicion about their intentions – effected a fusion of the rhetoric of reform and the political theory of the conciliarists. Though some (such as Gerson) still agonized about the appropriate theological way forward, the synthesis of the reform crusade and constitutional ideas created a practical platform for remedial action.

Recent scholarship has tended to emphasize the underlying unity between the late mediaeval and the Reformation periods. Both were characterized by fervent piety, the consecrated energy of lay Christians and the consequent eliding of the received boundaries between the sacred and the secular. The search for a state of holiness in the midst of everyday life is the common thread that binds the pre-Reformation and the Reformation epochs together (Trinkaus and Oberman 1974: xii; cf. Leff 1967b). Holiness brought peace of mind to the individual – tranquility of conscience – and harmony to society. The passion for reform and the longing for peace are intimately linked. Obermann notes that the two most prominent themes in the reform literature of the later Middle Ages are *pax* and *concordia*. Marsilius of Padua's *Defensor Pacis* and Nicholas of Cusa's *De Pace Fidei* between them span this period. The longing for change, for reform, that would bring peace and harmony to Christendom remained undiminished by the beginning of the sixteenth century. Martin Luther, echoing the words of Jeremiah against the false prophets, echoed it in the 92nd of his Ninety-five Theses in 1517: '"*Pax, pax*", *et non est pax*' (Obermann in Trinkaus and Oberman 1974: 15–16).

Owen Chadwick points out that in the early sixteenth century the impulse for change at a local level often came from a group of people 'who suddenly felt nausea towards what was happening in their church' and wanted 'to rid themselves of a pollution felt to be a stain upon the community' (Chadwick 2001: 39). The urge for reform was powered not only by the longing for a pure, abstract ideal, but also by revulsion against the corruptions of the system. As Cameron observes, ecclesiastical literature was 'saturated' with the language of reformation long before the Reformation itself (Cameron 1991: 38).

In this climate, late mediaeval scholars, particularly Roman law jurists, began to discount the mystification surrounding papal claims. It became increasingly apparent that the sphere of papal sovereignty was itself a 'state' whose origins and constitution were essentially temporal. The papal *regnum* began to seem no different in principle to that of 'secular' monarchs. The papacy was evaluated as a merely human institution and its claims as inventions of human legitimation (Canning in Wood 1991: 245). This radical, subversive vision formed the premise for ever louder rumblings of discontent and opposition to ecclesiastical privilege and papal interference in Germany, England, Scandinavia and elsewhere in Europe, and the legal and constitutional ideas that accompanied them (for a useful survey see Skinner 1978: II, 50–64). But it took the fusion of the imperative of reunion after the schism with the campaign for reform in head and members to make constitutional ideas a force to be reckoned with. Pierre d'Ailly and Dietrich of Niem brought together programmes of reform and proposals for reunification: both were to be achieved through the calling of a General Council.

The Conciliar Model

The Conciliar Movement in the Western Church developed as a challenge to monarchical Catholicism and as a response to the disasters that the latter had produced: above all the Great Schism of the West, but also the chronic failure to address urgent issues of reform. The conciliar tradition accepted unquestioningly the premise of catholicity: the Church as a divinely ordained visible society with appointed structures of authority and sacramentality. Conciliarists, as much as papalists, regarded the Church as a *societas perfecta*, a self-sufficient body having all the power it needed to rule itself and rectify its deficiencies. Conciliarism is definitely a form of Catholicism: hence I want to insist that the expression 'conciliar Catholicism', which might be considered by Ultramontane papalists to be a contradiction in terms, an oxymoron, is entirely appropriate – unless Catholicism is to be rigidly identified with the sky-high papalism of the late Middle Ages and of the First Vatican Council.

Conciliar thought advocated a form of distributed authority in which fullness of authority was located in the whole body of the Church and came to focus and expression in councils – local, provincial and general – of which the papacy was the moderator. Apologists for the conciliar ideal were able to claim that the conciliar model of Church governance long predated the monarchical model, since councils went back to the beginnings of the Christian Church, to the Council of Jerusalem described in Acts 15. Several General Councils took place before the emergence of papal hegemony in the Western Church. The first, at Nicaea in AD 325, was called by the Emperor Constantine and he it was who presided over it.

The Western Church had a full conciliar life for many centuries. Regional and national councils were a regular feature of mediaeval Christendom. In the Frankish church, the practice of consulting in council went back to early mediaeval times (Wallace-Hadrill 1983: ch. 6). In the English Church, Archbishop Lanfranc did much to restore the conciliar life that had fallen into decay. The councils over which he presided, both diocesan and national, were grounded in worship and were significant liturgical, not merely administrative or judicial, events. They contributed to the renewal of the Church on the basis of Scripture and the teachings of the Fathers and early councils (Cowdrey 2003: ch. 9).

Conciliar theory originated in the fairly routine work of canon lawyers, but underwent accelerated development at the hands of theologians and political philosophers in the spate of writing on ecclesiology that occurred from the early fourteenth century onwards. Not the least of the predisposing factors was the resentment of the episcopate at direct papal intervention in the form of the new international mendicant orders that traversed dioceses and on whom the popes heaped privileges at the expense of the bishops. While the bishops did not question the universal writ of the pope's authority, they maintained (against certain papal publicists such as Augustinus Triumphus), that their own authority was not derived from that of the pope (Tierney 1982: 60–61). Roman Catholic theory, from Trent to the two Vatican Councils, has supported the bishops, but often theory has been belied by practice.

These ideological developments were compounded by the increasing weight given to national interests and, at the end of this period, by the rise of the nation-state. The long-standing mediaeval contest between *Sacerdotium* and *Imperium* was transposed from the context of a unified sacral realm in which pope and emperor were the greater and lesser lights, the sun and the moon in the one firmament, to the new context in which nation-states, supported by their episcopates, began to seek sovereignty and to claim imperial status for themselves.

Conciliar ecclesiology stands, therefore, for an alternative form of Catholicism and a different model of authority. Conciliar thought was articulated in the late mediaeval period, building on well-winnowed principles of canon law. The council of Pisa (1409) and the General Councils of Constance (1414) and Basel (1431) attempted to implement conciliar principles and in fact developed them further. Conciliar theory located plenary authority in the whole Church within which the papacy had a constitutional role which was variously interpreted: interpretations ranging from maximalist to minimalist views. Councils – local, provincial and general – were seen as the executive expression of this authority. Conciliar authority recognized national identities and aspirations, endorsed a kind of subsidiarity, invited academic contributions and gave a role (albeit a limited one) to the laity. The Conciliar Movement re-united the Western Church, but it failed to effect the reforms which were crying out for redress.

The conciliar model drew on sources considerably more ancient and more 'official' than used to be supposed and came to a head rapidly in the face of the Great Schism of the West. The partial success of the Councils of Pisa, Constance and Basel in the first half of the fifteenth century temporarily damped down extravagant papal claims, but when the papacy emerged, actually strengthened by the contest with conciliarism, these claims were revived – with interest.

Brian Tierney, who pioneered research into the Conciliar Movement, comments that in the study of ecclesiology, 'the beginning of wisdom is an awareness that the medieval church was the mother of all the western churches' (Tierney 1982: 104). This is as true of conciliar ideas as of other things. The Reformation, in its ecclesiological aspect at least, was a violent outburst of dammed-up conciliar aspirations. Continental and Anglican Reformers alike appealed to conciliar principles and urged a free General Council which would be called and presided over by the civil magistrate rather than by the pope. The Anglican Reformers and the seventeenth-century divines have a great deal to say about the authority of councils. They uphold the classical conciliar ideal of a free and fully representative council to arbitrate on the points of dispute between the churches. In more modern times, that is to say around the end of the nineteenth and the beginning of the twentieth centuries, when these things were more thought of than they are today, some of the most distinguished interpreters of Anglicanism from an historical point of view, such as R.W. Dixon, Mandell Creighton and J.N. Figgis, lamented the failure of the Conciliar Movement and attributed the tragic divisions and excesses of the Reformation to that failure (as Lord Acton also did: 1952: 246). These Anglican historians were agreed in seeing Anglicanism as an expression and continuation of the conciliar ideal, that is to say, of a reformed Catholicism in the area of authority.

Matthew Spinka, the doyen of Hus studies, underlines the pivotal importance of conciliarism: 'The conciliar period is one of the most significant eras in the history of Christianity. Had its principles prevailed, the Roman Church would have become a constitutional, instead of an absolute monarchy. The Council of Constance was the culmination of a daring effort to change the direction of papal development' (Spinka 1965: 3). But the fact is that the trajectory that runs from Pisa, through Constance and then to Basel ended in failure. That failure led unswervingly to the breakup of Western Christendom in the sixteenth century.

Chapter 3

The Emergence of Monarchical Authority

The monarchical, centralized character of modern Roman Catholicism was the product of gradual historical development over more than a millennium. In the present chapter we shall trace in outline some milestones in this unfolding process before considering, in the next chapter, the conciliar alternative, that of a more distributed pattern of authority that could become focused in a General Council when that was required. For what follows in this chapter see generally: Ullmann 1949, 1961, 1962; Wilks 1963; Morris 1989; Morrison 1969; Kelly 1986; Robinson 1988; Watt 1988; H. Chadwick 2003. For text and commentary see O'Donovan and O'Donovan 1999; Nederman and Forhan 1993; an older but valuable resource, with texts, is Tierney 1964.

There are several issues in play in the developments that concern us in this chapter. First, there is the relationship between spiritual and temporal, ecclesiastical and civil (rather than 'secular') authority, which was focused respectively in the pope (and other prelates) on the one hand and the emperor (and other kings and princes) on the other. Second, there is the relationship between the spiritual and the temporal aspects within papal authority or jurisdiction itself: what were the proper scope and limits of papal authority? And third, there is the relationship between temporal and spiritual goods and property in this earthly life and the issue of to what extent, if any, the Church should be implicated in the ownership or management of temporal possessions.

What we do not find, of course, is a dialectic between Church and State in the modern sense, for these were not yet fully or clearly differentiated. The spiritual and the temporal were twin aspects of a single, unified Christian commonwealth in which the spiritual dimension embraced civil life and the temporal dimension was Christian. That does not mean, however, that there was harmony between them. On the contrary, the tensions and struggles between kings and popes during the period 1050–1300 were so continuous and merged into each other in such a way that they appear to constitute 'one long, continuing crisis' (Tierney 1964: 1).

Spiritual and Temporal

Political theory in the Middle Ages and well beyond can be construed as a series of attempted legitimations of the rival claims of the temporal and the ecclesiastical powers, emperor and pope, king and bishop. An unresolved duality of structured authority stemmed from the first great power struggle between empire and papacy, the Investiture contest of c.1100 over the respective rights of pope and king in making ecclesiastical appointments, in which 'neither side was able to make good its more extreme theocratic pretensions' (Tierney 1982: 10). The struggle was a see-saw in which first one claim and then the other predominated. The most extreme claims on behalf of the papacy were matched, by the time we reach the fourteenth century, by equally extravagant pretensions on behalf of king and emperor. In both cases only the integrated hierarchical, sacral and sacramental vision of the universe can provide an intelligible framework for language that to modern ears sounds sacrilegious. Pope emulated emperor and then emperor pope. Kings and bishops were both anointed. The ascriptions of Christlikeness and Godlikeness were snatched from one to the other and back again. Mediaeval rulers were hailed as 'the image of Christ' and 'the vicar of Christ'. The emperor was styled by civilian lawyers, relying on Roman imperial precedents, *deus in terris*, *deus terrens* and *deus praesens*. The king was subject to divine (revealed) law, but above positive (human) law and was the living embodiment of law on earth (*lex animata in terris*). The cross-fertilization of attributes took sartorial form: 'the pope adorned his tiara with a golden crown, donned the imperial purple, and was preceded by imperial banners... The emperor wore his crown like a mitre, donned the pontifical shoes and other clerical raiments, and received, like a bishop, a ring at his coronation' (Kantorowitz 1957: 193). To put it crudely, first the king aspired to be pope and then the pope to be king (for the dynamic of ideas see Tellenbach 1940).

A genuine philosopical and political dilemma was being played out. Which was preferable: one body with two heads or two bodies with one head? Either option seemed to produce an ugly monster and fuelled the competition to achieve a single body with a single head, on the presupposition that only monarchical government, civil or ecclesiastical, could hold Christendom together and maintain the vital principle of unity that directed Christian society towards its God-given end. But which would it be: Christian community as empire, ruled by the Christian Emperor, or Christian community as Church, ruled by the pope? Was the Church to be seen as an integral part of the empire, or the empire to be included as part of the Church?

Both monism and dualism had to receive their due; first one and then the other see-sawed to dominance. After Ambrose had insisted that the Emperor was within the Church, not above it, a *modus vivendi*, a fairly balanced duality of the two powers, pertained during the patristic period in the West. Gelasius I (pope 492–96) set the tone at the end of the fifth century. 'Two there are, august Emperor,' he wrote, 'by which this world is ruled: the consecrated authority of priests and the royal power.' However, of the two, it is the clergy who have the greater responsibility in that they will have to give account at the Judgement for those who have exercised kingship under their guidance (O'Donovan and O'Donovan 1999: 179). The papacy pursued a consistent policy of hierocratic dominance, with minor variations of emphasis, throughout the Middle Ages. However, 'the flaw in the papal theory of the relations of *papatus* and *imperium* was that no pope could ever find an emperor who would accept the subordinate role devised for him' (Watt 1988: 396; Ullmann 1962: x–xi, 1).

Under Charlemagne the bishops did their best to advocate a dualism that would preserve their rights over against the king, while Charlemagne himself rehearsed a royal monism of the Christ-like monarch, seeking parity with the emperors of the Eastern Roman Empire who saw themselves as Christ-like priest-kings (*Rex-Sacerdos, basileus kai hierus, isochristos*). Charlemagne exercised ecclesiastical jurisdiction and legislated for the church on liturgy, catechesis, baptism, the discipline of clergy and religious, various sacraments, and feast days (Ullmann 1962: 6–17 and ch. 3; Morrison 1964).

Whatever the tensions, rivalries and power struggles, in high mediaeval thought the spiritual and the temporal were not separate realms but twin aspects of a unified reality. 'Sacred and secular' is as anachronistic when applied to the Middle Ages as is 'Church and State'. As Wilks put it, in his massive account of theories of sovereignty in the late Middle Ages: 'In the great papal-imperial struggles which convulsed most of the Middle Ages the nature of society was not in dispute, but only the proper distribution of authority within it' (Wilks 1963: 84). Unity was the ultimate principle of mediaeval thought and the *argumentum unitatis* was the presupposition of its political theory (Gierke 1958a). Humanity was one community, whether considered in its spiritual aspect as the universal Church (*ecclesia universalis*) or in its temporal aspect as the human commonwealth (*respublica generis humani*). There were not two classes of person, 'sacred' people and 'secular' people: each individual was subject to dual jurisdiction, spiritual and temporal. Until this idea was decisively challenged by Marsilius of Padua and Dante, the Church was seen as the one divinely ordained true 'state', possessing the fullness of all spiritual and temporal power and embracing under its jurisdiction civil authority. To postulate any autonomous authority outside the authority of the Church was heresy (*Duo principia ponere, haereticum est*) (Figgis 1916: 113).

Thomas Aquinas articulates the *argumentum unitatis* when he states in *On Kingship* that 'every multitude is derived from unity' and that peace consists in 'the unity of a multitude' (Aquinas in Nederman and Forhan 1993: 103, 115). While the Church's Head is Christ, its earthly ruler is the pope who is a spiritual and temporal monarch, possessed of an empire (*principatus*). As the publicist for papal supremacy Augustinus Triumphus put it: *tota multitudo et tota respublica vel spiritualis vel corporalis* (Wilks 1963: 65). As Gierke wrote: 'Throughout the whole Middle Age there reigned, almost without condition or qualification, the notion that the oneness and universality of the Church must manifest itself in a unity of law, constitution and supreme government' (Gierke 1958: 18). The argument that took place within this framework was about whether the pope's jurisdiction in temporal matters was direct or indirect, proximate or ultimate. The papal publicists deployed the *reductio ad unum* ruthlessly in favour of sole papal sovereignty, temporal as well as spiritual. For them unity and monarchy were interchangeable terms (Wilks 1963: 32, 45).

However, according to this world-view the distinction between spiritual and temporal modes (*Sacerdotium* and *Regnum* or *Imperium*) had also been willed by God, and proceeded from the same divine source – the one to minister to the divine part of man, the other to the human part – so that it belonged to the divine economy that the pope should delegate his temporal authority. Though, as the successor of Peter, he possesses the two swords (*utrumque gladium*) that Peter had in the Garden of Gethsemane, the pope has entrusted the day-to-day exercise of the temporal sword to the emperor. As Bernard of Clairvaux put it in his letter to Pope Eugenius III urging him to launch a new crusade in 1150: 'Peter has them both to draw when necessary; one by his command, the other by his hand' (Bernard in Nederman and Forhan 1993: 22; cf. Watt 1988: 300–302). The pope has *plenitudo potestatis* as the Vicar of Christ who is both priest and king. The pope therefore has jurisdiction over the *saeculum*, as well as over the *sacerdotium*, but he hands the civil sword to the prince to exercise while remaining accountable to the pope for how he discharges his delegated responsibility.

As Ambrose had argued, the emperor was within the Church, not above it (*intra ecclesiam non supra ecclesiam*). The emperor, therefore, should never forget that he owes his authority to the pope, for just as the soul is superior to the body (argued the canonists), the pope is superior to the emperor, and 'as the body is to the mind, so is the emperor to the pope'. Moreover, the spiritual power embraces and transcends (as it were) the temporal, so that the Church includes the Empire (*Ecclesia continet imperium*). The administrative and executive actions of the temporal power were of too mean a character to be carried out by the spiritual power. John of Salisbury (c. 1120–80) develops the ancient metaphor of the body politic in the cause of a harmonious community with a division of labour. Like a healthy body, it will be guided by the soul (the spiritually minded clergy) and ruled by the head (the wise king). The temporal sword is accepted by the ruler from the hand of the Church, which makes the ruler a sort of minister of the clergy, carrying out those more earthy but necessary tasks (such as executions) that would demean the priesthood. The ruler's duty to the Church is to advance its standing in the commonwealth and to promote the practice of religion (John of Salisbury in Nederman and Forhan 1993: 33, 52; O'Donovan and O'Donovan 1999: 277–96, esp. 289–90).

It was heresy to postulate an equality between pope and emperor, for that would mean two co-vicars on earth (*duos vicarios equales in terris*). The emperor was therefore the most inferior servant of 'the servant of the servants of God' (*ultimus servus papae et ecclesiae*). It was on these premises that the canonists claimed for the pope the power to depose emperors and kings and to release subjects from their allegiance, invoking as precedent the deposition of Childeric III in favour of Pepin by Pope Zacharias in 751, 'the first concrete political action of the papacy in the secular field' (Ullmann 1949: 178).

For the high papal theorists, temporal and spiritual power is that jurisdiction usually granted by the pope to laypeople and clerics respectively. All lay officials in the commonwealth were for them simply papal nominees. The papal publicists did not need the 'Donation of Constantine', in order to ascribe imperial power to the pope: as the embodiment of the Christ who reigns at the right hand of God and to whom all authority in heaven and earth is given, the pope is king as well as priest. *Papa est verus imperator.* The pope merely awards executive power (*potestas executionis*) to emperors and kings to carry out a mandate received from the pope; his temporal responsibilities are exercised through the laity (Wilks 1963: 65, 176, 254–56, 268).

The centripetal force of the political ideal of unity was combined with Platonic metaphysical realism to produce a concentration of identity in the persona of the pope. The pope not only represented St Peter, Christ and God, but also the clergy, the body of the faithful and the whole Christian commonwealth. He is *in persona ecclesiae* par excellence. Conversely when the Church is spoken of it may be the whole body, the clergy or the pope that is meant. As Augustinus Triumphus said, echoing (or, as it seems to us, parodying) St Paul in The Acts of the Apostles, in him (the pope) we live and move and have our being (Acts 17.28). Christ is as truly manifested in the pope as he is in the Eucharist (Wilks 1963: 31, 33, 37, 41).

If the Church was a body, so was the 'state'. If the Church was a mystical body, no less could be claimed for the 'state'. When Thomas Aquinas used the expression *corpus Ecclesiae mysticum* he seemed to be raising the jurisdictional structures of the Roman Church to a transcendent level: it became a mystical corporation. But advocates of the temporal power could match this, as Vincent of Beauvais did in the thirteenth century when he spoke of the mystical body of the commonwealth, *corpus reipublicae mysticum*, which was a step beyond *corpus morale et politicum* (Kantorowitz 1957: 201–11). In such ways, these apologists for the spiritual and the temporal powers respectively attempted to outbid each other. What would the end be?

Early Foundations of Plenitude of Power

The first western writer to assert that Peter was superior to the other Apostles and alone received the keys of the kingdom, which he then shared with the other Apostles, was Optatus, c. 370 (H. Chadwick 2003: 31). Nearly a century later, Pope Leo I ('The Great', 440–461) made explicit what had long been implicit, the identification of the Bishop of Rome with St Peter, in both his office and his actions (see Ullmann 1975: ch. 4). Leo claimed to function as Peter's vicar (*vice Petri fungimur*). According to Leo, while Christ gave the power of order (sacramental power) to all the Apostles equally, he gave the power of the keys and the power to bind and loose to Peter alone in his person and not as the representative of the college (so to speak) of the Apostles. Just as Peter had then imparted the power of jurisdiction to the other Apostles, so the pope (not the emperor) grants jurisdiction to the bishops. The pope is prince of the bishops just as Peter was the prince of the Apostles. Peter was given juridical powers to bind and loose (*Ligare, solvere*): the Old Testament prophetic resonances of this in the Greek New Testament were transposed into familiar Roman legal idiom in the Vulgate. Christ imparts to Peter his own divine sovereignty. The popes inherit (in a legal sense) Peter's authority, even though they lack his personal grace.

In the mid-ninth century Nicholas I (858–897) claimed that Rome had received from God all that God willed to give to the universal Church and that St Peter lived and presided in that see. Rome was *magistra, mater et caput* of all churches – mistress, mother and head – and its bishop was Peter's *vicarius*. Nicholas employed the 'False Decretals' that undermined the earlier doctrine that papal authority was derived from conciliar decisions and was not inherent in the 'Petrine' office. In the period from the mid-eleventh century to the Great Schism of 1378, when (as we shall see shortly) the papacy became fragmented (though not for the first time), papal claims became intensified. Canon lawyers and other ecclesiological theorists readily supplied the popes with ever more inflated claims.

Gregory VII

The concentration of power in the hands of the papacy owed much to the dynamic reforming pontificate of Gregory VII (Hildebrand) which began in 1073 (definitive study Cowdrey 1998; discussion of ideas Tellenbach 1940 and Ullmann 1962: ch. 9). Gregory intensified the identification of the pope with Peter, claiming: 'Blessed Peter answers by me.' Gregory consistently styled himself 'Vicar of St Peter', not Vicar of Christ (though the latter title was both ancient and current). He identified completely with Peter, believing that Peter lived in him and ruled the Church through him. What was said and done to Gregory was said and done to Peter. Because

Christ appointed Peter as 'Prince of the Apostles', 'this principate and authority have passed through St Peter to all who have succeeded to his throne, or who will succeed to it until the end of the world, by divine privilege and by hereditary right (*iure hereditario*)' (Cowdrey 1998: 525, 528, 520). Appealing to the spurious 'Donation of Constantine' (*Constitutum Constantini*) and the Forged Decretals, Gregory and his supporters magnified the claims of the Roman see. A few Gregorian texts contain the germ of every later papal claim, the foundational elements of the fully developed Roman Catholic system (MacDonald 1932: 242; cf. O'Donovan and O'Donovan 1999: 240–49).

The curious document known as the *Dictatus Papae* (text in O'Donovan and O'Donovan 1999: 242; Tierney 1964: 49–50), which appears to consist of headings for draft canons and was almost certainly drafted by Gregory, pushes out the boundaries of papal authority. It asserts that the pope has power, without a synod, to depose and restore bishops; he may translate bishops, unite bishoprics and ordain clergy of any church; he should be asked to adjudicate in all major disputes; his legates take precedence over bishops, and so on. The Bishop of Rome was the only universal bishop. He could be judged by no one. Rome enjoyed the primacy over all other churches; it had never erred and never would err. To be Catholic it was necessary to agree with the Roman Church. The pope has the power to depose not only bishops but kings and emperors (the first explicit claim to be able to depose the emperor). His 'feet are to be kissed by all princes'. Unsurprisingly, no concerted attempt was made to implement or execute these claims. To make that attempt was not at all beyond Gregory's ambition, but he may have been deterred by close advisers and responded to the call to exercise circumspection and to temper absolute claims to particular situations (Cowdrey 1998: 502–505).

According to Ullmann, Gregory's pontificate saw the hierocratic theory become embodied in an ecclesiastical system, 'the essence of which is the conception of the universal Church as a body corporate and politic, comprising all Christians,' the *societas Christiana*. While it is primarily spiritual, this society is also earthly and has all the apparatus to constitute a civil society, legislative, consultative, administrative and executive offices and these are exercised by the clergy, who become the instruments of ecclesiastical government, the implementers of Church law. The clergy can stand for the whole Church and be called the *ecclesia*. The Church is becoming consciously a *societas perfecta*, a complete, fully organized and self-sufficient society. The body of Christ was the *fidelium congregatio*: 'This body has all the concreteness and tangibility of an organically integrated and earthly society' (Ullmann 1962: 271, 276).

What Gregory was doing was arrogating to the papacy the universal jurisdiction of the Roman Empire. The steps he initiated at the beginning of his papacy brought him into direct conflict with Henry IV of Germany. The clash was a continuation of the long-running lay investiture contest (the claim of 'secular' rulers to appoint to ecclesiastical office), but it fore-shadowed the struggle between hierocratic centralization and 'secular', national aspirations that would become more pronounced during the conciliar period. Henry could not renounce his claim to appoint bishops without abandoning all hope of uniting Germany under a single monarchy. As far as Gregory was concerned, any king who was unwilling to accept papal direction was guilty of the sin of *superbia*, pride or arrogance, and was on that account unworthy to reign. In a series of decrees Gregory threatened with excommunication any cleric who accepted investiture with a bishopric, abbey or church from a layperson and any layperson who purported to offer it. The prohibition of lay investiture was a demand that no king of the time either could or did accept (Tierney 1964: 47). For his part, Gregory could not acquiesce in the imperial claims, which included the claim to appoint the popes themselves, without jeopardizing the reform of the Church (of simony and clerical marriage). When Henry turned to the bishops for support against the pope, and Gregory appealed to the German princes to help him depose the king, it became clear that 'the whole leadership of Christian society was at stake in the dispute' (Tierney 1964: 45).

Henry invoked the older 'dualistic' model of pope and emperor each wielding his proper sword, spiritual and temporal respectively, received direct from God. 'He usurped for himself,' protested Henry indignantly, 'the kingdom and the priesthood, without God's sanction, despising God's holy ordinance which willed essentially that they ... should remain not in the hands of one, but as two, in the hands of two.' Two swords, the spiritual and the 'carnal', are to be wielded, says Henry significantly, 'in the Church' (Ullmann 1962: 346).

Gregory excommunicated and 'deposed' Henry, claiming to release his subjects from their obedience, just as Pius V was to do with regard to Elizabeth I in 1570. Gregory, who initiated the claim to suzerainty over the kings of the West, was the first and Pius was the last to do this. Gregory laid territorial claim to those parts of Europe, especially Spain, that were being reconquered from the Saracens for the true faith, since all pagan Europe was nominally under papal jurisdiction and certain territories were held in fief to the pope by princes. He also writes to rebuke Solomon, King of Hungary, for having accepted the fiefdom of his kingdom from the king of Germany, not from 'St Peter', for long ago the kingdom of Hungary had been 'devotedly surrendered to St Peter by King Stephen as the full property of the Holy Roman Church under its complete jurisdiction and control' (text in Tierney 1964: 50). Although Gregory did not go so far as to claim, as later popes or their champions would, that temporal power was delegated by the spiritual power and was invalid without its blessing, his radical agenda began to undermine the accepted principles of obedience to traditional authority, temporal and spiritual (Morris 1989: 129). The papal dignity was degraded: to Henry, before he did penance barefoot at Canossa, Gregory was 'not Pope, but false monk'. The king's temporal authority was undermined as he was excommunicated, re-instated and then excommunicated again by the pope. Such behaviour on both sides was bound to upset the balance and undermine the cohesion of Christendom.

In his last encyclical, in 1084, Gregory insisted that his greatest concern as pope had been that the Church, the Bride of Christ, 'should return to her former glory and stand free, chaste and catholic'. The freedom he had in mind was the freedom to obey the successor of St Peter rather than the emperor, to submit to the authority of the clergy without interference from the laity. Gregory paved the way for the mediaeval papal monarchy, but construed the aggrandizement of the papacy in terms of monastic obedience to a superior, rather than in legal or canonistic terms (cf. Cowdrey 1998: 583, 696–97).

Innocent III

At the Second Lateran Council (1139), held to consolidate his victory over the antipope Anacletus II, Innocent II asserted: 'Rome is the head of the world.' Nearly a century later, his namesake Innocent III (pope 1198–1216; see principally Tillmann 1980: ch. 2 and Appendix 1) claimed for the pope both priestly and kingly power, as the vicar of the one prefigured by Melchizedek who was both priest and king. He asserted in principle an omnicompetence of jurisdiction: there was no dispute or case of a spiritual nature that was not potentially within his authority and there were circumstances in which temporal matters also came under his jurisdiction. All churches and church matters fell within his power (*omnes ecclesiae et res ecclesiarum sunt in potestate Pape*: Jacob 1963: 19). Innocent explicitly adumbrated the doctrine of *plenitudo potestatis*, proclaiming in a sermon: 'Others are called to the role of caring, but only Peter is raised to fullness of power.' As he put it in his consecration sermon:

> Now therefore you see who is the servant who is set over the household, – truly the vicar of Jesus Christ, the successor of Peter, the Christ of the Lord, the God of Pharoah; established in the middle between God and man, lower than God but higher than man; less than God but greater than man; who judges all, and is judged by none (Morris 1989: 431; cf. Tierney 1964: 132).

The pope was the sun, the greater light, to preside over human souls, while the emperor was the moon, the lesser light, presiding over human bodies. 'Just as the moon derives its light from the sun and is indeed lower than it in quantity and quality, in position and in power, so too the royal power derives the splendour of its dignity from the pontifical authority' (Tierney 1964: 132). Christ left to Peter not only the universal Church but the whole world to govern, and the pope was not only Peter's successor, but *vicarius Christi*.

At the Fourth Lateran Council, 1215, Innocent defined the position of the Roman Church as a *principatus ordinariae potestatis*, a primacy of ordinary power over all the churches by virtue of divine institution. 'Innocent, therefore, deems himself entitled to exercise concurrently in every respect the rights of the bishops, archbishops, primates and patri-archs' (Tillmann 1980: 34). He is the universal bishop with an unrestricted right of intervention in the affairs of any diocese or province.

However, Innocent III was careful to define the limits of his jurisdiction: his was the *plenitudo ecclesiasticae potestatis*, while in the temporal sphere the emperor was similarly invested with *plenitudo potestatis*. Innocent respected the Gelasian doctrine of the separation and independence of the Two Swords, citing the text, 'Render unto Caesar...'. He affirmed the limits set by divine law in the Church and confined his discretion to matters of human institution – though in the sphere of human law there were no further legal or constitutional limits.

There were also circumstances when the pope had the right to exercise a conditional temporal authority: *ratione peccati*, where sins were concerned, and on the whole Innocent resisted the temptation to abuse the potential that this loophole offered. He chastised rulers for their public mortal sins in the same way that he subjected other laypeople to the disci-pline of the Church and he branded political actions, such as breach of an oath and waging unjust war, as examples of such mortal sins. The pope also claimed ordinary temporal authority in papal fiefdoms, notably England.

Citing the claim of Innocent III that popes were invested with God's power on earth (*vices Dei gerit in terris*), Ullmann comments, 'In the con-ception of the canonists, the pope was truly God on earth' (Ullmann 1949: 79). Tillmann's verdict, however, is more balanced: Innocent neither asserted papal world domination in the sense of a papal universal monarchy ..., nor claimed it for himself in the sense of a fundamental sub-ordination of the temporal to the spiritual power' (Tillmann 1980: 26). He should not be assimilated to Gregory VII and Innocent IV who not only released subjects from their oaths of allegiance (as Innocent III had done on occasion), but claimed the power to depose emperors and kings from their thrones. Nevertheless, Innocent III wielded his fullness of spiritual jurisdic-tion so rigorously and consistently that he permanently affected the con-sciousness of the Western Church.

'Fullness of Power'

The canonistic writings, commentaries on the canons, were ransacked on behalf of papal claims. The papal publicists deployed canonistic material in support of the enlargement of papal authority. The less chance the popes had of implementing the totality of jurisdiction that theorists devised for them, the wilder the claims could become, released from the constraints of practice (Wilks 1963: 151).

Panormitanus, who was active in the conciliar period, asserted that the pope could do and say whatever he pleased, being answerable to no one. In fact, the pope could do whatever God could do (*Papa potest facere, quicquid Deus potest*). The canonists proclaimed that the pope was above the law, divine or human, and that whatever the pope approved thereby had the force of law (Ullmann 1949: 50–51). For Augustinus Triumphus (d. 1328) the pope's will is the criterion of what is right: what pleases the pope has the force of law. 'Thus there is only one act absolutely bad in itself – the rejection of the pope's authority, and the only absolute ethical norm is the obligation to obey him' (Wilks 1963: 154).

The conception of papal fullness of power (*plenitudo potestatis*) goes back to Leo I (Robinson 1988: 282), but it was Bernard of Clairvaux who explicitly applied it to a reigning pope in the case of Eugenius III in the first half of the twelfth century. 'According to your canons,' Bernard wrote, 'some are called to a share of the responsibilities, but you are called to the fullness of power. The power of others is confined within definite limits, but your power extends even over those who have received power over others' (Robinson 1988: 282; Morris 1989: 206; O'Donovan and O'Donovan 1999: 269–76). That is to say, the pope's authority was both spiritual and temporal. The canonists developed this rhetoric into a claim of universal jurisdiction, both spiritual and temporal. In the spiritual sphere the pope's jurisdiction penetrated every episcopal see: bishops had no rights in their own sees but held them at the pope's pleasure (Wilks 1963: 384). Everyone was subject by divine right to papal jurisdiction (*Omnes subsunt ei jure divino*), and the pope had no equal in power on earth. Ullmann points out that both parts of this statement, which recurs over and over again in canonistic writings, have to be taken literally: 'the idea of hyperbole was foreign to the canonists' (Ullmann 1949: 77). Some publicists accorded to the pope *plenitudo deitatis* as the ground of *plenitudo potestatis*. The latter then becomes 'sovereignty pure and simple, the power to do all things: *Papa omnia potest*' (Wilks 1963: 169).

The claim to temporal sovereignty reached its term in the concept of papal world monarchy (Tierney 1955: 88–89). Innocent III had insisted that Christ left to Peter the government not only of the Church but of the whole world. The only legitimate government, anywhere in the world, was government that acknowledged the pope. The canonists came to argue that, strictly speaking, there had been no regal power before Christ and that, similarly, those infidel states that refused the supremacy of the pope could not be classed as lawful governments. Without lawful government there could be no rightful possession of goods and property. Therefore (argued Petrus Bertrandi) the pope was the rightful owner of the whole world. In the fourteenth century both John of Paris and William of Ockham contested the claim that the temporal goods of rulers belonged ultimately to the Pope. As Johannes Teutonicus put it, *Extra ecclesiam non est imperium*. The pope was the vicar of God on earth, not just in the Church (*Summus pontifex Dei locum tenet in terris*). Some canonists went as far as to claim that all power in heaven and on earth (Matthew 28.18) was given to the pope. The idea of papal world sovereignty was bound up with the Crusades, which were considered to be a stepping stone towards the eventual establishment of a world monarchy – though this could not come about by force. Innocent IV, from whom these ideas mainly derived, proposed that wherever Roman emperors – pagan or Christian – had exercised their power, it was the prerogative of the pope to reclaim these countries for himself.

Boniface VIII

In July 1294 Peter the Hermit, a naïve, unworldly and illiterate saint, was elected pope as Celestine V, amid acclamation that the 'angel pope', foretold in prophetic oracles of the thirteenth century, had at last appeared. Peter, the leader of a poor brotherhood of friars, brought Franciscan ideas of a reformed and more spiritual Church to the throne of Peter. He proved utterly incompetent to rule; the administration of the papacy lapsed into confusion; in policy Celestine was the puppet of Charles II, King of Naples and Sicily, who compelled him to reside at Naples. By the end of the year, in an unprecedented act, Celstine had renounced his see. His successor was the canonist Cardinal Benedetto Caetani who had misled Peter into believing that there were precedents for papal abdication. As Pope Boniface VIII, Caetani presided simultaneously over the most extreme claims and the lowest fortunes of the mediaeval papacy.

Boniface's reign (1294–1303) represents the high water mark in the assertion of the supremacy of the papacy in the temporal as well as the spiritual sphere. Boniface sometimes dressed in imperial insignia, boasting that he was emperor, no less than pope.

> Boniface VIII personally, his curia collectively and his loyal theologians and canonists, produced a hierocratic dossier of unprecedented proportions and ingenuity, whose general trend was to assail or abandon every moderating or qualifying tenet about papal omnipotence suggested by past theory and experience (Watt 1988: 400).

Boniface's incursions into temporal jurisdiction (not least his interventions in Florentine politics) earned him the utter opprobrium of Dante: he was 'the prince of the new Pharisees' who waged war on Christians (*Inferno*, XXVII, 85–88), 'Christ made captive in his vicar' (*Purgatorio*, XX, 87). His spectre haunts the *Divine Comedy* (Dante 1981; Ferrante 1984: ch. 2).

Ironically, while popes such as Boniface tightened their grip on the Church, they ceded power in the empire. They intensified divided loyalties among the bishops and alienated Christian rulers. Ecclesiastical centralization and royal consolidation of power, playing into the rise of national sentiment, were on a collision course. The struggle for supremacy between Boniface and Philip the Fair of France was the first conflict that can properly be described as a dispute over national sovereignty. The idea of the state was emerging in France and the relevant administrative machinery was being developed. If the Roman doctrine of universal lordship had been realized in practice it 'would have rendered the rise of national states impossible' (Tierney 1964: 172).

In a direct attack on the principle of national sovereignty, Boniface asserted in the bull *Clericis Laicos* (text in Tierney 1964: 175–76) that kings had no power to tax the clergy without papal consent and incited the clergy to disobey their king in such an event. He was forced to climb down in humiliating circumstances.

His defiant bull *Unam Sanctam* of 1302 was promulgated in the face of impending disaster and humiliation in his battle with Philip IV 'The Fair' of France. As Philip's henchmen advanced, intending to drag Boniface before a General Council where he could be deposed for 'heresy', Boniface insisted that 'it is absolutely necessary for the salvation of all human creatures that they submit to the Roman Pontiff' (Neuner and Dupuis 1983: 218 [no. 804 = DS 875]; Tierney 1964: 188–89). It has been said that 'the bull's greatest novelty is its absence of involved proof. Amid the controversial literature of the period it sounds a note of solemn and eloquent certainty' (Boase 1933: 318; on the circumstances of the bull see 315–37). The decree was no aberration; it recapitulated, albeit in a provocative way, the papal claims as they had been inflated over centuries and was entirely consistent with what had been said by Boniface's predecessors (Ullmann 1978: 73). But it was called forth by the challenge of contemporary secularizing intellectual trends and constitutes a brave riposte to them. Neither did it mark a dying fall: *Unam Sanctam* was re-promulgated (with minor changes) on the very eve of the Reformation by the Fifth Lateran Council (1512–17), as a riposte to Gallican conciliarism, in the bull *Pastor Aeternus Gregem* (text in Alberigo *et al.* 1962: 616). Nevertheless, as Tierney puts it, 'Boniface VIII's defeat marks the end of the road that Innocent III had marked out for the papacy a century earlier' (Tierney 1964: 185). Renouard highlights the momentous significance of Philip the Fair sending Guillame de Nogaret with an army to arrest Boniface at Anagni and drag him before a General Council; it marked the end of an era (Renouard 1970: 13). The claims to temporal jurisdiction obviously rang hollow in these circumstances, but the aggrandizement of the papal office from a position of political weakness also invited sceptical doubts. 'It called the bluff of the high mediaeval doctrine of the papacy, for it measured the distance between inflated religious rhetoric and cold reality' (Duffy 1997: 122).

The contest between Philip IV and Boniface generated some of the most energetic political theorizing of the later Middle Ages. Giles of Rome's *De Ecclesiastica Potestate* was probably written early in 1302 and influenced

Boniface as he drew up *Unam Sanctam*. It expounds 'at unprecedented length and with a degree of elaboration never previously attempted' the hierocratic ideology of the mediaeval papacy (Dyson 1986: xiii). It is more extreme than the bull itself in that it deduces from the principle that papal power is supreme, that it is total and all-encompassing, and that all other power derives its force and legitimacy from it. There is in Giles no meaningful conceptual distinction between the power of the Church and the power of the pope, no distribution of authority throughout the Church, no constitutional checks and balances – even the material goods of the faithful revert to the pope if required. As the O'Donovans put it: 'Giles portrays the *corpus Christianum* as a seamless spiritual and temporal garment: at once a universal, indivisible, mystical communion and an earthly hierarchy of law and power' (O'Donovan and O'Donovan 1999: 362; extract 365–78; translation in full Dyson 1986).

James of Viterbo (d. 1308) produced *De Regimine Christiano* in support of Boniface in 1302. He modifies the extreme position of Giles of Rome. He does not accept Giles's claim that temporal power is illegitimate unless it is validated by the spiritual power. It is natural to man and therefore willed by the Creator. However, it needs to be completed and perfected by the spiritual power. The Church is 'a glorious kingdom', universal, self-sufficient and hierarchically structured (a *societas perfecta*, one might say). The pope holds imperial power by concession of the Emperor Constantine (the Donation of Constantine).

James defines the Church of Christ as a *regnum ecclesiasticum*, a term (in which the emphasis falls of the substantive) translated by E.F. Jacob as 'a divinely commissioned monarchical government' (Jacob 1963: 7). James has the rudiments of the notion of Christ's triple office, as prophet, priest and king, in the form of priest, king and worker of miracles (prophets were expected to perform miracles to validate their message) and shows that these have been communicated to the Church (O'Donovan and O'Donovan 1999: 379–87, at 382). The hierarchy of the Church is not only priestly but royal, possessing regal authority over spiritual and temporal affairs.

> By making jurisdiction the defining criterion of royal power, James was able to bestow the status of king on both pope and bishops. By distinguishing between earthly royal power and spiritual royal power, he was able to apply all the ideology of kingship to the exercise of authority within the Church (Kempshall 1999: 281).

Both Giles of Rome and James of Viterbo invoke the hallowed idea of the common good to support the doctrine of papal *plenitudo potestatis*. The common good of Christendom may require the pope to depose an errant king. John of Paris (whom we shall meet shortly) turned this idea on its head. Kings may act, in the interests of the common good, to depose an errant pope. Here the notion of the common good is being used to validate 'a secularized plenitude of power' (Kempshall 1999: 287).

Chapter 4

Precursors of Conciliarism

The Ideological Background

Tendencies towards absolute authority and indications of a more constitutional approach went on in parallel in the later Middle Ages and the early modern period. Both received succour from the reception of Roman law (Skinner 1978: II, 124–34). The influence of Roman legal concepts not only strengthened the doctrine of papal headship through the idea of sovereignty, but also brought to the forefront the concept of *universitas*, corporation or collectivity. This carried with it ideas concerning the rights of the whole body in relation to its head, representative or rector, as the case may be, together with doctrines delimiting the respective powers of each. The Roman law maxim, derived from Justinian, that what affects all alike must be approved by all (*ut quod omnes similiter tangit, ab omnibus comprobetur*) was pivotal in conciliar thought. Although it was originally concerned with property rights, this principle came to be applied to the obligation laid on the head of the body to seek the consent of its members where their interests were affected. The emphasis on consent, approval or reception was strengthened by Gratian's statements that 'laws are confirmed when they are approved by the custom of those using them'. Furthermore, nearly all the mediaeval canonists defined the Church as the congregation of the faithful (*congregatio fidelium*), a definition which supervened on and transcended the distinction between clergy and laity. As Tierney in particular has emphasized, the Conciliar Movement was not something alien to the Western Church and forced upon it by design, as its papalist antagonists have tended to claim, but on the contrary represented the culmination of ideas that were embedded in the law and doctrine of the Church itself, the culmination of the theories that the canonists themselves had evolved (Tierney 1955: passim, esp. 237; see also Pelikan 1983).

The Decretists, in stressing the sovereignty of the pope, at the same time laid down limits to papal authority, invoking the counter-balancing idea of the general well-being of the Church (*generalis status ecclesiae*). This type of appeal was generic: both Roman and canon lawyers, and not only popes but kings used it. In the civil context, it was concerned with the public welfare, the state of the realm (*status regni*); in the ecclesiastical context, it referred to the *status ecclesiae*, the well-being or flourishing of the Church

(Post 1964: 12). In the hands of the Decretists, the touchstone of the *status ecclesiae* meant, for example, that the pope could not give a dispensation against a decree of a General Council in any matter affecting the general well-being of the Church. The Decretists considered the circumstances in which a pope could be brought to trial and subsequently deposed for a notorious crime that caused grave scandal to the Church. While they did not elucidate the relationship of a General Council to the pope, their thought contains the seeds of the idea that a Council might assume authority over a pope in certain circumstances (Tierney 1955: 50–51, 56, 47–48).

Before the idea of the superiority of a Council to a pope in defined circumstances could be practically entertained, however, corporation ideas needed to develop. Within a corporation, as it was understood in Roman civil law, authority could be exercised by the members as well as by the head. Corporation was inimical to hierarchy. Corporate institutions within the Church (orders of friars; universities) became stronger. By about 1200 corporation theory began to be extended from particular groups within the Church to the whole Church as such. The thirteenth century saw the gradual extension and systematization of the powers of members over against the head, until by the end of the century corporate representation by delegates who were given full powers to act was flourishing throughout western Europe (Tierney 1955: 96–103, 130; Post 1964: 62).

Thomas Aquinas: Natural Law and the Common Good

'It was no accident,' wrote Michael Wilks, 'that conciliar theories of government received a sudden access of energy following the penetrating investigation of the idea of natural law by Aquinas and his successors' (Wilks 1963: 153). To play up the authority of natural law is to put positive law in its proper place, and so to relativize and make contingent particular human rules and structures. The orbit of natural law contains ideas of natural justice, giving to each their due, equity and moderation in the conduct of authority. It orientates to the common good both the making of law and its execution and so curbs excesses of power. It has in view the proper liberty of the individual and of every constituent community of the commonwealth. Aquinas insisted that those who have entered into the glorious liberty of the sons of God (cf. Romans 8.21) through the indwelling Holy Spirit may submit only to a regime that is directed to the well-being (*utilitas*) of its subjects and does not take away that liberty (Black 1992: 30).

When the concept of the common good is unpacked it is seen to elevate the claims of the whole above the claims of its parts; and then it is only a few short steps to the idea of the community being the best judge of its own good. But how can the community come to a mind and make this judgement without some form of representative government? Notions of constitutionality and consent require structures of representation to give effect to them. Although natural law is not necessarily opposed to hierarchy (hardly in the case of St Thomas), it is subversive of absolutism and counteracts abuses of authority. And its implications are ultimately even more radical: our response to an emergency cannot be hidebound by positive law, for 'necessity knows no law' – an idea that goes back to classical Greece and was handed on to the mediaevals by Justinian (Post 1964: 18–21).

The application of natural law arguments to questions of authority in the Church was closely pursued by a number of major conciliar thinkers: John of Paris, Pierre d'Ailly, Jean Gerson, Nicholas Cusanus and later Jacques Almain, John Mair (Major), Edmond Richer and their successors in the University of Paris who kept conciliar ideas alive in a hostile atmosphere (see Oakley 2003: 74, 124–29; 1981). Behind them and informing their thought lay the work of Thomas Aquinas on natural law and the common good. Though Aquinas did not devote a separate treatise to the idea of the common good and did not tackle the common life of the body of Christ as a specific sphere of reflection, his comments on the idea of the common good are extensive (see Eschmann 1943 for copious citations). Though he invokes Aristotle, Aquinas' deepest sources are Roman and patristic, especially Augustine's teaching on the peace that can be esteemed and enjoyed in this world (Augustine 1972: 599–600 [CD XV.4]; O'Donovan and O'Donovan 2004: 48–72).

The effect of the Thomistic affirmation of natural law within the sphere of the Church was to subject positive laws, such as those made by papal decree, to a higher authority and to bring them to the bar of reason that was a universal human possession. For Aquinas law is the reasonable ordinance or prescription which is formally promulgated, is intended to promote the common good, and comes from the one who has charge of the community (Aquinas, n.d. 28: 16–17 [ST I–II q. 90 a. 4]). On this understanding, law has several determining characteristics: it is reasonable, not arbitrary; it is for the common good and not for personal or party advantage; it is promulgated by the authority that is responsible for the community. Laws that are made for private or party advantage are not true law and unjust because of wrong purpose (for exposition see Lisska 1996; briefly Sigmund 1993).

The form of reason with which law is imbued is not speculative or theoretical reason, but Aristotle's practical reason (*phronesis*). This reasoning faculty is orientated to the good or to the common good. It works things out in the light of circumstances, guided by prudence and with the flexibility (*epieikeia*) that takes unusual circumstances and anomalies into account (ST I–II q. 96 a. 6; q. 120 a. 1; for detailed analysis see Westburg 1994). Law is an expression of reason (the practical, rather than the theoretical reason), not of mere will. The reason directs the will, not vice versa. This means that commands that claim divine authority (decrees of the Church) must be in accordance with the divine law as revealed in Scripture which discloses the mind of God towards us. The ability to exercise practical reason in this way is given through the acquisition of moral virtue and is an expression of responsible moral agency. 'Moral actions and human actions are the same.' To take due responsibility, rather than to give blind obedience and deference, is the mark of moral agency. This is true in both the political and the ecclesiastical spheres and thus suggests that they are brought within a common framework of philosophy of law. Arguments from political thought (such as the principles of representation or consent) have – and this claim has obvious subversive consequences – equal relevance to Church as to State. Political life has God's blessing and political activity fulfils our divine calling, just as contemplative activity does. Every part of the community has a stake in the making of law: there are the seeds of constitutionalism in Aquinas.

Law is given for the common good, the well-being of the whole community. The common good reflects the social, collective nature of humankind. That nature or essence has certain inherent inclinations or dispositions: in the first place to survive; then to flourish; ultimately to know God and to enjoy the *visio dei*. 'Everything according to its own nature tends to preserve its own being' (Aquinas n.d. 28: 81 [ST I–II, q. 94, a. 2]). Human nature has a right to have these needs met, rather than denied. To survive, to flourish and to serve the ultimate end applies to communities and institutions as much as to individuals. The common good of the community is 'greater', 'better' or 'more divine' than the individual good, though not necessarily 'more perfect' of its kind (Kempshall 1999: 86–87). To seek the common good leads to greater human well-being, the harmonious realization of what is natural to humankind: happiness in this life (*eudaemonia*) and ultimately blessedness in the next (*beatitudo*). The more perfect in virtue a society is, the closer it is to God (see also on the common good in late mediaeval thought, Black 1992: 24–28).

The very existence of a common good requires that society be governed. Order and hierarchy are needed for the common good to be realized, but a particular agent of that order, a particular stage in the hierarchy, is not as important as the whole body. Aquinas assumes that temporal laws are promulgated by the civil rulers and ecclesiastical laws by the pope (though he is not completely clear or consistent about the relation of spiritual and temporal authority). But the crisis of the Great Schism, more than a century after Aquinas' death in 1274, began to make it an open question as to where this responsibility lay and who was ultimately responsible for deciding what was best for the community – the pope or a council? Aquinas and the Thomist school did not subscribe to the monistic realism that led to the identification of the Church and the pope. For them the *ecclesia* comprised the universal Church together with the pope: the body and its earthly head as distinguishable elements, the whole being greater than the parts. Even to see it like this was to begin to prise apart the practical identification of head and members that was characteristic of the high papal theory.

Pre-conciliar Thought

We turn now to look at some of the mediaeval thinkers who, though by no means full conciliarists themselves, nevertheless contributed to the development of conciliar theory. They do this in three ways. First they challenge the doctrine of papal *plenitudo potestatis*, particularly the claim of temporal jurisdiction over the bodies, goods and powers of Christians living in this world, and seek to recall the papacy to its proper spiritual and pastoral role. In other words, they reform and refocus the concept of ecclesiastical authority. Second, they vindicate the sole-legitimacy and God-given vocation of the civil ruler in the purposes of God and look to the magistrate to reform the Church. In other words, they hand back temporal authority where it belongs and restore a rival or (more euphemistically, a complementary) centre of authority to that of the papacy. Third, they begin to replace the pyramid model of a vertical, sacral hierarchy with the rounder model of the whole body legislating for its common good. In other words, the touchstone and criterion for the exercise of authority in the Church becomes the well-being, the benefit and the flourishing of the whole body – which is no longer to be identified *tout court* with the good of its earthly head, or of the hierarchy or even of the clergy.

John of Paris

John of Paris, sometimes known as John Quidort (c. 1250–1306), wrote his *On Royal and Papal Power* (*Tractatus de potestate regia et papale*) at the time of *Unam Sanctam* (1302–3). Texts in translation: John of Paris 1971 (ed. Watt); John of Paris 1974 (ed. Monahan). Selections: Nederman and Forhan 1993: 158–67; O'Donovan and O'Donovan, 1999: 400–412). Although he enters the lists in support of Philip IV and his right to tax and direct the French Church, John remains his own man, an independent, balanced and judicious thinker. He subjects both ecclesiastical and temporal power to the same set of basic constitutional criteria. He does not merely transfer totalitarian authority from the papacy to the king. While John does not challenge the divine institution of the papacy, he sees the Church as a corporation made up of many lesser corporations and has a sense of the community of the whole Church that is not merely the co-efficient of an all-absorbing papacy.

John thinks constitutionally about authority, defending the rights of subjects, emphasizing consent and election, the rule of law and political office as stewardship, the integrity of property and the need to defer to the common good. His political theory is informed by a modified Aristotelianism in which appeal to the common good, guided by natural law, is central. Temporal authority is rule over a community by one person for the sake of the common good. Kingship is justified by natural law and the law of nations, for humankind is by nature a political or civil animal, as Aristotle taught in the *Politics*, and in both material and cultural goods man is not self-sufficient. The common good of a political society is not merely a material but a moral good: as rational and moral beings men are orientated to the moral good of virtue and that must find communal expression.

The argument of *On Royal and Papal Power* rests, as Watt puts it, on the double foundations of the Bible read in the light of standard exegesis and the canon law read in the light of canonistic commentary. 'The one provided the underlying principles of perennial validity, the other the evidence of their implementation in the life of the Church through the ages' (Watt, introduction to John of Paris 1971: 37; see also 36–46). Among John's sources the Scriptures are supreme. He cited directly 150 biblical texts, some more than once, twice as many from the New Testament than from the Old. He accessed the Scriptures both directly, from the biblical text, and indirectly, from standard mediaeval compendia of patristic and biblical texts. He uses the Fathers as exegetes of Scripture in order to rescue key texts (such as the appeal to the 'two swords', Luke 22.38) from the armoury of papalists and locate them back in their proper context. In this respect, John of Paris is a champion of hermeneutical integrity. Second to the Bible, John cites canon law, fifty texts from Gratian's *Decretum* and seventeen from the Gregorian decretals, many of them cited more than once. John also depends massively on two other types of source: the legacy of the ancient world, particularly the writings of Cicero and Aristotle, which is implicit, and the contribution of contemporary and near contemporary political and theological writers who are (with one exception) not mentioned by name.

In the *Tractatus* John charts what he calls a middle way between two extreme views of the Church's competence in the temporal sphere. Radical sects, such as the Waldensians, deny the Church (and therefore the pope) any temporal goods and property. On the other hand, those who claim that the pope has received temporal authority directly from God fall into the error of King Herod who, on hearing of the birth of the Messiah, believed him to be an earthly king. Against the first opinion, typified by the Waldensians, John asserts that it is not wrong for prelates to have lordship and jurisdiction in temporalities, provided it is understood that they do not have this *ex officio* as vicars of Christ and successors of the Apostles. They can only receive such power by delegation from those to whom it properly belongs, the temporal rulers. Against the second view, that of the extreme papalists, he defends the integrity of temporal authority over against papal encroachment.

First, John establishes the relative independence of the temporal realm on the basis of chronological priority. Biblical history shows that, since the Aaronic priesthood was a foreshadowing and type of the priesthood of Christ and was defective in itself as priesthood, there were true kings before there were true priests. Second, he shows that, although the dignity of the priesthood is superior to that of kingship, it does not follow that the latter derives from the former. Neither is derived from the other, but both stem from a common source, being awarded by a power greater than either. The temporal power is greater than the spiritual in temporal things and the spiritual exceeds the temporal in spiritual things. Temporal power is not contained within spiritual power, but is established by God in its own right. John was, according to Watt, 'the first to provide a systematic demonstration that the political traditions and practices of a national kingdom had their fundamental justification in divine, natural and ecclesiastical law' (Watt, introduction to John of Paris 1971: 63).

John believes that temporal political society is embodied in a plurality of forms, corresponding to the various circumstances of peoples in the world, differentiated by climate, language and condition. The Church, in contrast, is a unitary society. 'One man alone is not enough to rule the entire world in temporal matters, although one man is adequate to rule in spiritual matters. For spiritual power can easily exercise its censure, which is verbal, on all persons near and far; but the secular power cannot so easily apply its sword, which is manual, to persons who are distant. It is easier to extend a word than a hand' (John of Paris 1974: 14, ch. 3). John here sets up the interesting scenario of a unified Church relating to a plurality of political societies. He thus escapes the remorseless logic of the mediaeval power struggle between emperor and pope that was premised on the unitary character of temporal as well as of spiritual authority and on the question that inevitably followed as to which one of them should be subordinate to the other. In place of the hierarchical struggle, John of Paris works out a doctrine of reciprocal indirect power (*potestas indirecta*) that avoids a mere polarity or dualism of spiritual and temporal authority. Spiritual and temporal authorities alike, exercising legitimate power in their own spheres also relate to the other sphere in the form of indirect power, that is to say power that is conditional (constrained) and accidental (contingent).

Having secured the integrity of temporal authority against the papacy, John proceeds to perform the same office for the episcopate. Just as temporal rulers receive their authority directly from God (not via the pope) and from the people who elect them or consent to their election, so bishops receive their authority directly from God (not via the pope) and from the people who elect them or consent to their election. It was not Peter who sent forth the Twelve and the Seventy-two, but Christ. And it was not Peter who breathed the Holy Spirit on the Apostles, giving them authority to forgive sins, but Christ. This power of the keys is entirely spiritual (though John struggles a bit at this point and we can see that there is a grey area here) and impinges only incidentally on the temporal (for example, through temporal penances). The Church's sanctions are its control of admission to the sacraments; temporal authority, on the other hand, is concerned purely with physical or material punishments. The pope is subject to both civil and ecclesiastical law and may be called to account by the college of cardinals or by the emperor. Radical changes in the constitution of the Church can only be effected by a General Council.

John's doctrine of the power of the Church (or pope) over temporal goods is shaped by a robust notion of private property, one that is, however, moderated by an almost equally strong notion of communal ownership. In so far as the Church is involved in temporal possessions, these belong to the whole community of the Church and not to the pope as the principal member. What the pope has is stewardship, not proprietorship, of ecclesiastical property for the common good. It falls within his jurisdiction to determine what is just or unjust regarding temporal goods over which he does not have dominion. The pope has no rights over the temporal goods of the laity (except perhaps in an emergency, such as a major threat to Christendom), for these are not held in trust by the community, as are ecclesiastical goods, but have been acquired by the efforts of individuals and now remain in their possession ('...they are acquired by individual persons through their art, labour or their own industry; and individual persons as individuals exercise right, power and true dominion over such goods. As lord over such goods, a person can order, dispose, keep or transfer what is his as he sees fit, without injury to anyone else': John of Paris 1974: 28, ch. 7). The pope is not even the steward of lay goods.

The issue at stake is not simply whether kings can tax the clergy, but whether the pope, the universal steward but not the owner of ecclesiastical wealth, has the right to appropriate church property for reasons other than the sake of the common good (Coleman in Wood 1991: 219). The pope does not have this because Christ himself did not have it, and if he did not have it, he could not have bestowed it on Peter. John treats the 'Donation of Constantine', which supposedly conveyed temporal possessions to Pope Sylvester, in a generally sceptical manner, with a marked lack of deference, and insists that in any case it conferred no imperial power over the realm of France, because the Franks were not included in the original compact (John of Paris 1974: 112, ch. 21).

There is a neat even-handedness about John's view of the possible impeachment of emperor or pope (ch. 22). If either were to betray their office, the one could take remedial action against the other. The two swords are bound to assist each other in the common bond of charity. If the emperor became an incorrigible heretic and flouted the sanctions that the Church brought against him, the pope would be right to withdraw support from him and to encourage his deposition from office. If, on the other hand, the pope were to commit criminal acts in the temporal sphere (for example, by expropriating lay property), it would be right for the emperor to take action against him. Should the pope go off the rails spiritually (for example, by embracing heresy or, says John menacingly, by depriving churchmen and chapters of their rights or by disposing of ecclesiastical property for reasons other than that of the common good), he should first be warned by the cardinals who represent the whole body of clergy. If the cardinals fail, Christian men can turn to the emperor as a member of the Church. In a crisis, any Christian may reprove the pope for his faults out of mere charity. It is within the authority of the college of cardinals to accept a papal resignation and even to act to depose a pope, since the college represents the clergy and the people, but it is more appropriate for deposition to be handled by a General Council. An errant pope's position has become untenable when he has lost the consent of the faithful for his tenure of office (John of Paris 1974: 129, ch. 25). In the conciliar period John's views on conciliar authority were referred to explicitly by Pierre d'Ailly and Jacques Almain and used without acknowledgement by Jean Gerson.

Dante

Dante (1265–1321), whom we tend to think of as the consummate exponent of a hierarchical sacral universe, with its detailed geography of a world beyond and its divinely decreed rewards and punishments, is actually one of the great 'secularizers' (in the literal sense of *saeculum*, the present age) of the later Middle Ages. Auerbach has called him 'the poet of the secular world'. Dante's *Monarchy* has been hailed as 'the first act of rebellion against scholastic transcendence'. The *Divine Comedy* reveals an incandescent passion to uphold moral responsibility in this world and to follow through the consequences of immoral actions (Ferrante 1984: 3). With Aquinas, Dante holds that natural reason is capable of guiding action to bring about the good life in this world, a life of moral, social and political well-being (Gilson 1963).

Dante is both the representative of the municipal spirit of the independent Italian city-states and the harbinger of the civic humanism of the early Renaissance. He bridges those two tributaries that feed into conciliar theory. But his secularity in this respect was radically qualified by a patrician abhorrence of the commercial, acquisitive spirit of the cities and the pragmatic, amoral policies that went with it (later codified by Machiavelli). This aesthetic, hedonistic paganism was repugnant to him (Auerbach 1961). The selfish, cruel and amoral cockpit of Florentine politics made the city and its corrupt society a type of Hell to Dante (Ferrante 1984: ch. 3).

Dante subscribed at first to the view that the state was founded merely on force – a notion that harked back to the Augustinian doctrine that the state was ordained as a remedy against sin and pointed forward to the unsparing political realism of Machiavelli and Hobbes. But Dante moved to the belief that the state was the highest expression of human aspiration, the sphere of human fulfilment in this life. Force was merely the instrumental, not the moving, cause of the state: its true origin is in divine reason (Dante 1903: *Convivio* IV, iv; Dante 1954: *Monarchia* II, i). Dante's fundamental humanism is revealed in the way that he goes a step beyond Aquinas in seeing life in this world not only as a means to a higher end in the next world, but as a sufficient end in itself. He recognizes happiness in this life, not just blessedness in the next, as the appointed goal for humanity. Dante postulates two final goals for humanity (*duo ultima*), corresponding to our dual nature, physical and spiritual, generated and created, corruptible and incorruptible: one to be attained in this life before death, the other in the next life after death (Dante 1903: *Convivio* IV, xvii; Dante 1954: *Monarchia*, III, xv, 3–8; cf. Gilson 1963: 104–105, 191–92; d'Entrèves 1952; Reeves 1965; Boyde 1981: 293–95; Ferrante 1984: ch. 2).

Corresponding to these two ends of human life is a division of orders in the world and of authorities to rule them. For life in this world, reason is an adequate guide: Aristotle is the supreme, indeed the perfect exponent of reason and the emperor is reason's executive. But, for humanity to attain its eternal destiny, revelation is required. The pope presides in the sphere of revelation (but not of reason), of grace (but not of nature). There is therefore no part of *natural* life in the human community over which the pope can rightly claim jurisdiction. Dante thus drastically curtails the authority of the papacy, denying it *plenitudo potestatis*, and thereby negating the early mediaeval and Thomistic hierarchical conception of the universe with the pope at the apex of the pyramid. Dante's quasi-biblical revelation (for that is what he claimed for the *Divina commedia*: see Hawkins 1999) is postulated as the antithesis of the totalitarian sacral/papal nexus. That was not the way to the common good nor was it the path of truth.

However, Dante goes even further (and this highlights his contribution to the conciliar mentality), for there is a sense in which the emperor has the pre-eminence so far as this world is concerned. Though we have reason, which is interpreted by the philosophers, and supernatural truth bestowed by the Holy Spirit, to guide us in the twin aspects of human aspiration, human nature is such that men would turn their backs on both reason and revelation and run wild like untamed horses if they were not curbed by the bit and bridle of the emperor's authority (Dante 1954: *Monarchia*, III, xvi). As far as human life in history is concerned, Dante's longing gaze is directed decisively to the emperor rather than to the pope. Dante's imperial ideology, though reinforced by the rise of national feeling, itself stimulated by the strong corporate identity that activated the city states, was informed by secular sources. These were principally Roman law which had little room for the pope and continually emphasized the role of the emperor; the myth of an eternal Rome ordained by divine providence; and the Latin classics, especially Virgil (Lenkeith 1952; Davis 1957).

Significantly Dante effects a transposition of attributes from the Church to the empire and from the pope to the emperor. In *Monarchia* he envisages a universal community of the human race (*universalis civilitas humani generis*), unified by the emperor who is presented as a saviour figure, appearing in the fullness of time as the fulfilment of prophetic hopes. Dante 'envisaged the descent of an emperor from the Alps as both a temporal and a holy event, long prophecied in the context of apocalyptic time' (Pocock 1975: 50). Dante's *humana civilitas*, though it derives from the two-cities scheme of Augustine and Orosius, has come a long way from the earthly city of earlier dualistic theology. It has acquired some of the attributes of the City of God.

Dante invested the city of Rome with the attributes of the biblical and Augustinian City of God. For Davis the central theme of history for Dante is 'the unfolding of God's providence through the instrumentality of Rome' (Davis 1957: 235). The city that had been the seat of both Augustus and St Peter had been brought low by imperial weakness and by ecclesiastical corruption. St Peter tells Dante in Paradise that the papal see is vacant, meaning that it is occupied by an unworthy incumbent and perverted to evil ends (*Paradiso* XXVII, 22–24; Dante 1981). Dante's attack on the ecclesiastical hierarchy is endorsed by Beatrice, Virgil and St Peter himself. What had led to the debasement of the Church, the degradation of the empire and the destruction of the civilized world was the 'Donation of Constantine', which included the city of Rome (not of course the *conversion* of Constantine, as later Anabaptists and modern opponents of 'establishment' would hold: Dante is emphatic about that). In Paradise, Constantine repents of his 'donation' (*Inferno* XIX, 115–117; *Paradiso* XX, 58–60; Davis 1957: 195–96). Temporal power has turned the Church into a monstrosity.

Rome, on the other hand, takes on a twofold eschatological aura: spiritual and temporal. The former pointing to a reform of the papacy after Boniface VIII had sullied its spiritual mission with claims to total temporal jurisdiction; the latter pointing to the promised emperor who would reign for the common good. As Dante argued in *Monarchia* (III, iv), the temporal and spiritual powers are equal in standing. In *Purgatorio* he calls them 'two suns (*due soli*) by which could be seen both the road of the world and the road to God'. But now they have eclipsed each other as the temporal sword is combined with the shepherd's crook, leaving the world to stagger like a blind man into the ditch (XVI, 107–108, 66, 109; cf. Mazotta 1979: 313).

Dante has given European civilization a push in the direction of secularization by removing the emperor from the shadow of the papacy. This is not the separation of Church and State advocated by radical groups at the Reformation and inscribed in some post-Enlightenment political constitutions. The language of 'separation of Church and State', used by Ferrante

(1984: 126) is utterly inept. The empire is not completely secularized nor is the state completely absolutized. Imperial authority knows that it owes its existence directly to God, while the pope provides not legitimation but merely a blessing, like the light of the sun shining upon the moon (Dante 1954: *Monarchia* III, iv) – though to appreciate the exact force of this simile we have to translate it back into Ptolemaic cosmology where sun and moon are both planets circling in their spheres around the earth, not a star at the centre of the solar system and the satellite of a minor planet of that system, respectively: a greater equality is entailed for Dante than for us.

Dante's secularizing philosophy of history takes the form of an inter-weaving of the events of imperial history with those of the biblical narrative. The birth of King David coincides with the coming of Aeneas who was, according to Virgil, the founder of the city of Rome. The Incarnation synchronizes with the perfection of the Roman Empire under Augustus (Dante 1903: *Convivio* IV, v). Here, Dante is doing more than the adroit harmonizing of classical and biblical chronologies that we find in the work of the chroniclers and apologists from the early Middle Ages up to Ussher and Bossuet, which tied together, for example, the Trojan War with the exploits of Sampson in an age of heroes that transcended the division between sacred and secular. Dante is in fact incorporating the empire into the scheme of salvation history. The disposition of classical figures in the *Divine Comedy* confirms this: Trajan and Justinian are placed not far from Christ in Paradise, while in the deepest abyss of the Inferno, Lucifer grinds up the worst traitors: Judas Iscariot the betrayer of Christ and Brutus and Cassius the assassins of Caesar (Dante 1981; Lenkeith 1952: 82–83).

What has Dante actually done here? Has he sacralized the empire or has he secularized the Church? He has actually done both of these things: with one hand he has relativized the papacy and deprived it of *plenitudo potes-tatis* by denying it all except spiritual authority; with the other he has elevated secular history, personified by the emperor, to a plane where it acquires new significance as the appointed sphere in which humanity fulfils itself in this life. At the same time, with his conception of the total human (Christian) community, he has given a boost to that notion of *universitas* – the whole body, the corporate sense of humanity – that became an indis-pensible part of the conciliarists' platform.

Marsilius of Padua

Marsilius (or Marsiglio) of Padua (c. 1275–1342) is designated by his translator and exponent Alan Gewirth as 'the founder of conciliarism' because he turned the mediaeval hierarchy on its head by making the pope dependent on a council and the council dependent on the laity (Gewirth 1951: 286). To put it like that, however, is to adopt a partial perspective on conciliarism. What Marsilius did was to radicalize the pre-conciliar concept of 'the whole Church', but in a way that played off council against pope, laity against clergy, and State against Church (the terms 'Church' and 'State' cease to be crassly anachronistic with him). He did not resolve the mediaeval conflict between emperor and pope: the teams simply changed ends.

When Marsilius' authorship of *The Defender of the Peace* (*Defensor Pacis*) became known, a couple of years after its publication in 1324, he was condemned as a heretic by Pope John XXII in the Bull *Licet Iuxta Doctrinam* (1327) and forced to flee from the University of Paris, of which he was Rector. Marsilius took refuge with the emperor Ludwig (Louis, Lewis) of Bavaria and accompanied Ludwig to Rome in 1328 where the latter was crowned by a Roman nobleman and proceeded to depose John XXII with Marsilius assisting. When the popular tide turned in favour of the Pope, they were forced to vacate Rome and Marsilius remained at Ludwig's court, together with William of Ockham and other dissident thinkers, for the rest of his life (Gewirth 1951; Watt 1988: 416–18; for the text of *Defensor Pacis* see Marsilius of Padua 1956, hereinafter cited as DP by section).

Drawing particularly on Aristotle's *Politics*, Augustine's *City of God* and the secular rationality of Averroism, Marsilius launched a broad attack on papal absolutism and the claim to *plenitudo potestatis* which mandated papal intervention in temporal affairs. Human happiness, in the form of the stable, self-sufficient civil community that Aristotle had evoked, was threatened by papal interference. 'Civil happiness' (*civilis felicitas*) constitutes 'the best of the objects of desire possible to men in this world and the ultimate aim of human acts' (DP I, i, 7). To say that civil happiness is 'the ultimate aim' is to take a further step in the trajectory marked out by Aquinas and Dante and is a frankly secular agenda. Like them, Marsilius echoes Aristotle: 'Those who live a civil life not only live, which beasts or slaves do, but they live well, having leisure for the liberal functions that derive from the virtues of both the theoretic and the practical soul' (DP I, iv, 2). Where Augustine had prescribed that humans should *use* (*uti*) temporal goods only in order to *enjoy* (*frui*) the spiritual goods that belong to eternal life, Marsilius boldly states that humans should 'enjoy' (*frui*) civil happiness. He sets temporal happiness and eternal bliss side by side, as two forms of the 'sufficient life', as though they were of equal value (Gewirth 1951: 78).

The defender of the peace of Marsilius' title was not an individual ruler, but the state which was founded on the sovereignty of the people and governed with their consent. That consent was not understood at that time, of course, as elicited by means of democratic machinery and calculated by weight of votes, but was a participative, reflective investment in the deliberative process, effected representatively by those with the social, moral and educational competence to do so.

Marsilius pushes the dualistic motif in mediaeval political thought a step further, widening the gap between State and Church within the Christian commonwealth, but he is far from seeking to divorce them. Aristotle had memorably said that the city (*polis*), the self-sufficient community, exists not just for the sake of living but for the sake of living well; it is ordered to the good life (Aristotle 1995: 10: *Politics*, I, 2). There is therefore for Marsilius a division of labour, a distinction of function within the one body corresponding to the twofold nature of the good life, of moral virtue: temporal and spiritual. The State delegates spiritual functions to the Church, which lacks all inherent jurisdiction, whether spiritual or temporal.

All power is invested in the people and elected rulers are answerable to them. The legislator, the primary and proper efficient cause of the law, is 'the whole body of the citizens, or the weightier multitude (*pars valentior*) thereof' (DP, I, xiii, 3). Aristotle had concluded in the *Politics* (III, 15) that the community, acting collectively, would tend to come to sounder decisions, those in the interests of the common good or common advantage, than a single individual, even though the individuals concerned, taken separately, might be morally and intellectually inferior to that individual (the king) (Aristotle 1995: 124). Leff describes the *Defensor Pacis* as 'a re-assertion of the common good over private interest ... of law duly enacted over arbitrary rule' (Leff 1967b: 65). Marsilius also echoes the venerable Justinian maxim: 'What affects the benefit or harm of all ought to be known and heard by all.' Marsilius frequently invokes the axiom: 'the whole is greater than any of its parts' (e.g. DP I, xv, 4). The *pars valentior* (or *pars principans*) can represent the whole; it is almost synonymous with *universitas* (Gewirth 1951: 182–85).

The Church consists, for Marsilius, not of the hierarchy and its obedient subjects, but of 'the whole body of the faithful, who believe in and invoke the name of Christ, and all the parts of this whole body in every community, even the household... And therefore all the Christian faithful, both priests and non-priests, are and should be called churchmen' (DP, II, ii, 3). The Church exists for the faithful and is governed by them. The principal means whereby the body of the faithful governs the Church is through a General Council. What Marsilius says about General Councils deserves to be quoted at length as a formative early expression of the conciliar ideal:

> The principal authority, direct or indirect, for such determination of doubtful questions belongs only to a general council composed of all Christians or of the weightier part of them, or to those persons who have been granted such authority by the whole body of Christian believers... The procedure is as follows: Let all the notable provinces or communities of the world, in accordance with the determination of their human legislators whether one or many, and according to their proportion in quantity and quality of persons, elect faithful men, first priests and then non-priests, suitable persons of the most blameless lives and the greatest experience in divine law. These men ... are to assemble at

a place which is most convenient according to the decision of the majority of them, where they are to settle those matters pertaining to divine law which have appeared doubtful, and which it seems useful, expedient, and necessary to define. There too they are to make such other decrees with regard to church ritual or divine worship as will be conducive to the quiet and tranquillity of the believers (DP, II, xx, 2).

Just as the authority to legislate and govern in a state belongs to the whole body of citizens, so the whole body of the faithful (which is coterminous with the citizenry) must elect the Council, define articles of faith, elect the priesthood and the pope ('head bishop') and control excommunication. 'The lawful sovereign, the whole body of the citizens (*universitas civium*) reappears as the whole body of the faithful (*universitas fidelium*) or, more pertinently, as the general council of believers (*generale concilium creden-tium*)' (Watt 1988: 420). The hierarchy, including the pope, is a human arrangement, just like any other office in the community, and is subject to the General Council (DP, II, xxi, 5; xxii, 9). The Church is without power to enforce its rules and must leave all coercion to the State. Naturally, Marsilius deprives the pope of *plenitudo potestatis*, defined as plenitude of coercive jurisdiction, unlimited by any human law – a 'perverted opinion ... pernicious to the human race'.

This account of authority leads Gewirth to decribe the Marsilian Church as 'a purely spiritual congregation of believers, connected by ... their common faith and participation in the sacraments' (Gewirth 1951: 277). However, Marsilius does not in fact challenge the mediaeval understanding of the fundamental unity of Church and State as distinguishable elements within the one Christian commonwealth. The *universitas civium* and the *universitas fidelium* are coterminous. The numerical identity of the two communities means that the spiritual congregation should be seen in functional, not sociological, terms (cf. Kempshall 2001: 327). Marsilius is not a prophet of modern pluralism or of the separation of Church and State. Neither does he intend to secularize the Church, assimilating it to the civil community: a priesthood and the liturgical life of the Church signify and represent the whole integrated community's final cause or purpose (DP I, 4, 4–5). 'Here, at once, near the beginning of the *Defensor Pacis*, the limits of naturalism have been exposed' (Leff 1967b: 67).

Marsilius reverses the accepted relation between the pope and a General Council. The state, not the pope, convokes the council. The council elects and may depose the pope. The Council confirms and makes binding its decisions, not the pope. The council, not the pope, is infallible and belief in its doctrines is necessary for salvation. The council is elected by nations, proportionately to the quantity and quality of persons, and includes laypeople and clergy as well as bishops. There is a principle of incipient democracy and egalitarianism in Marsilius: he believes that the more exten-sively competent people are consulted, the more reliable the decision will be. Quantitative enlargement brings qualitative enhancement in the pursuit of truth (Gewirth 1951: 289–90).

Marsilius was too radical in his subordination of the Church to the State to be an acknowledged influence on the conciliarists. His influence on conciliarism took place behind the scenes and was selective. Dietrich of Niem and Nicholas of Cusa use him without acknowledgement. Like Ockham (who did not accept Marsilius' doctrine of the infallibility of General Councils), Marsilius is important for the role that he gives to laypeople and the lower clergy in councils which generally had been confined to bishops.

Even more subversive of a papal monarchy exercising temporal jurisdiction than Marsilius' specific proposals was his underlying method. This was informed not by a political pragmatism or opportunism that merely reversed the roles of Church and State, but by an inspiring vision of apostolic purity and simplicity instantiated in the primitive Church. The New Testament became a reformer's manifesto. Christ and the Apostles had lived lives marked by poverty and simplicity, without temporal possessions. Jesus repudiated temporal authority for himself, declaring that his kingdom was not of this world. The primitive Church was not hierarchical and was ministered to only by deacons and priests. There is no papacy to be seen in the New Testament. Marsilius' polemical deployment of the biblical pattern of the Church as a realizable alternative was, suggests Leff, 'the most devastating weapon of political criticism in late mediaeval ecclesiology' (Leff 1967b: 67). Marsilius advocated a return to the ideal of the primitive Church, not only for particular religious communities, monastic or medicant (which had been a recurring theme throughout the Middle Ages), but for the whole structured institution of the Church, from top to bottom. This vision of apostolic purity and simplicity also motivated such diverse figures of the late mediaeval period as Dante and Ockham, Wyclif and Hus, several of the classical conciliarists and the sixteenth-century Reformers.

William of Ockham

William of Ockham (c. 1285–1347), while not himself to be numbered among the conciliarists, provided intellectual underpinning for the Conciliar Movement and his insights reach out, as it were, towards the Reformers. Texts in O'Donovan and O'Donovan 1999: 457–75; Nederman and Forhan 1993: 208–20; Ockham 1995, 1927, [*Dialogus*] www. britac.ac.uk/pubs.dialogus. Studies: McGrade 1974; Ryan 1979. What drives Ockham's ecclesiology is the realization that the nightmare scenario entertained by the canonists hypothetically – a pope becoming a heretic – had become real in the person of John XXII when he condemned the doctrine of evangelical poverty, grounded on the absolute poverty of Christ, that was espoused by the Franciscan Spirituals. Ockham, outraged to the depths of his being, launched a violent attack on this pope. But if the truth of the gospel could not be found in the pope, where could it be found:

in a General Council, in the whole body of the faithful, in the heart of a simple believer? And if the pope could become heretical, what assurances attach to his office after all?

Ockham's political writings grapple with the question of the rights and limits of papal power, of *plenitudo potestatis*. He treats the papacy, which he had seen at close hand at Avignon (Kelley 1987), more in terms of its limits than its privileges and it has been said that he qualifies the *plenitudo potestatis* out of existence (Ryan 1979: 9). Ockham does not underestimate the force of the arguments in favour of the temporal jurisdiction of the pope, but his judgement is ultimately against it. A significant move is his assertion that the empire is in no way derived from the pope but is received 'solely from God'. The emperor's jurisdiction in temporal matters is supreme by divine right and even the pope is subject to him in this respect.

Ockham acknowledges that the papacy is *de jure divino*; there is a papal monarchy, but it is, so to speak, a constitutional one. As Jacob says of Ockham's *De Imperatorum et Pontificium Potestate*: 'it is the view of a constitutional liberal, not of an anti-papal zealot' (Jacob 1963: 103; Latin text in Ockham 1927). The papacy is the soul of the Christian body, animating the whole. Unlike Marsilius of Padua, Ockham defends papal independence against secular jurisdiction. But like Dante and Bernard of Clairvaux, Ockham attributes *ministerium*, not *dominium*, to the pope. The papacy remains the final court of appeal and the final arbiter of disputed questions:

> Though not all the faithful are immediately subject in all things to the pope, nor is the pope in many matters their judge, yet, because in the necessary definition of every question by a judge, whether in the ordinary course or on special occasion, by divine law there should be some one deciding authority, therefore we must concede that the pope below Christ is head and judge of all the faithful [*papa sub Christo est caput et iudex summus omnium fidelium*] (Jacob 1963: 104; Latin text in Ockham 1927: 26).

Jacob comments: 'In the last resort Ockham cannot escape from a unitary theory of papal sovereignty; it was Marsilius who knew how to do that. The liberal tries to curtail the operation of papal power; the revolutionary does not argue about the *plenitudo*. He denies it altogether' (Jacob 1963: 104–105). Ockham simply urges the papacy to turn away from legalism and to embrace evangelical liberty. The pope should seek the voluntary co-operation of his subjects and avoid harsh measures of government. Ockham regards popular consent as the normal original basis for legitimate secular authority (the power to make laws and give rights resided originally in the people who, however, subsequently transferred it to the emperor), though he refrains from applying this theory directly to the Church as Marsilius and the later conciliarists do. However, the principle constantly invoked by the conciliarists, 'What affects everyone ought to be approved by everyone', is central to his thinking (Ockham in Nederman and Forham 1993: 211). McGrade believes that 'Ockham's appeal to the gospel as a law of liberty was his most significant argument against curialist views of *plenitudo potestatis*' (McGrade 1974: 219).

In *A Short Discourse on the Tyrannical Ascendancy of the Pope* and more extensively in the *Dialogus*, Ockham attacks the thesis that by virtue of his *plenitudo potestatis* the pope can command by right anything that does not violate divine (biblical) or natural law. Ockham is aghast at the idea. Following the canonists, who had argued that the pope was without authority to legislate or otherwise act against the *generalis status ecclesiae*, Ockham claims that since the pope had received spiritual power from God purely for the good of the whole Church, he did not have the authority to act in ways detrimental to the common good (*bonum commune*) of the Church. Implied in his riposte is the fact that revealed, divine law is positive and specific, leaving many areas untouched, while natural law is general and often permissive. The thesis that he rejects would give appalling scope to the abuse of papal power. It would mean that Christ's law, the gospel law, the law of liberty, would be turned into 'a most horrendous servitude', a greater bondage than that of the Old Testament law. Christians would become the pope's slaves. Augustine and Aquinas had made the same point, but they had limited it to an exhortation to those in authority to be moderate; Ockham concludes that this sort of power is illegitimate: the pope simply does not possess *plenitudo potestatis* (Kelley 1987: 13–14). The pope does not have the sort of power that would permit him to act against the common good – and that must take into account the natural moral frailty and physical infirmity of many folk. Responsibility for the common good belongs to all the faithful; it transcends the sacredness of ecclesiastical office, levelling all Christians (Ryan 1979: 19–20; Tierney 1954: 46, n. 23; Ockham *Dialogus*, Pt III, Tract 1, ch. 5).

The same points are made more concisely in *Eight Questions on the Power of the Pope*. The best regime should exist for the sake of the common good of the subjects; church government does not exist for the personal good of the pope. Peter received power from Christ purely to serve the common good in a way that leads the faithful to salvation. He had no authority to impose commandments that did not conduce to salvation and were not in accord with divine and natural law. Even if the pope had the power to legislate freely in any area not contrary to divine and natural law, the faithful would effectively be slaves of the pope 'for no lord can by right have a power over his slaves greater than this power' (Ockham 1995: 312–13, 318–19).

Ockham's aim is not simply to curtail the exercise of papal authority, nor is it merely to widen the distance between the spiritual and the temporal powers (cf. Kempshall 2001: 328–30): it is to curb absolute power, whether spiritual or temporal, in the interests of a radical evangelical grasp of the truth which is to be apprehended in freedom by the whole body of the Church. It is the truth of the gospel that is sovereign and the truth shall make you free (John 8.32). Liberty is a central value of human existence and the God-given right of every person. For Ockham the intellectual, truth element in authority is crucial: he distinguishes cognitive authority from political authority. 'Legitimate correction' on the part of the institution demands that errors be clearly refuted by arguments grounded in Scripture and for this purpose scholars are better equipped than ecclesiastics (J.L. O'Donovan, 1991: 15). However, for him there is no guarantee that an individual or a body will master the truth or possess it in its entirety. We must give weight to what is human as well as to what is divine in the Church. The papacy is divine in that it was instituted by Christ, but human in that human beings decide who should be appointed pope, who should take part in the election and who should be responsible for correcting the pope if necessary.

Ockham denies infallibility to the Church: popes, cardinals, councils and all Christians are capable of falling into heresy (*Dialogus*, Pt I, bk 5). If the reigning pope had turned out to be a heretic, what hope was there for lesser mortals? The true faith might be preserved only in the soul of one baptized infant. 'The whole faith of the Church can stand in one alone.' Indefectibility with regard to the truth of the gospel was promised by Christ to the whole Church, but since no part of the Church can be identified with the whole, no part can claim unfailing truth. As McGrade comments: 'Hence, there can be no "fail-safe" ecclesiastical constitution, no purely constitutional solution to so radical a crisis as papal heresy' (McGrade 1974: 73).

Councils come into their own in tackling this and similar emergencies. Laymen and women may take the initiative in convening a council; kings will be intimately involved and their consent to decisions will be required. A General Council is called 'by human convocation'; it cannot perfectly represent the whole *universitas fidelium* and so exercise its inherent powers. Therefore – and here Ockham parts company both with the canonists who preceded him and the conciliarists who followed him – General Councils are not infallible, as the Scriptures are; they are not in receipt of divine revelation. Prophets and Apostles who received revelation waited on God in prayer, but General Councils rely on study and debate to attain truth. Divine illumination is granted to those who are holy, not to those who are more learned or wise. But Councils proceed by using the intelligence of those assembled and by relying on general divine guidance. Error is present in all things that rely on human wisdom and virtue, General Councils not excepted. We can be assured that a particular Council was convened in a Catholic way if its teaching is true to Scripture. The fact that the pope approved the Council's decrees is sufficient authentication. However, like so many in these centuries who wrestled with the question where truth was to be found, Ockham's position is circular, for it is the role of a Council to correct and convert the errors of the pope in matters of faith (Ryan 1979: 14).

While Ockham is less hostile to the developed corporate structures of authority than are some of the later full-blooded conciliarists, he massively relativizes the papacy. Fundamentally, as the case of John XXII showed, the pope is not needed to maintain the Church in truth. There does not always have to be a pope; there could be an interregnum for a century or two. There could be a plurality of popes ('many popes'). Ecclesiastical offices and structures are contingent and provisional in relation to the mystical nature of the Church. It is the latter, the union of true believers in the truth, that endures (Ryan 1979: 20–21, 29). At the same time, Ockham is more sceptical than are the conciliarists of the ability of councils to solve problems.

The element of contingency and relativism in Ockham's polity is pronounced: there is no gleaming blueprint, no panacea. No one part holds the key to perfection: only the whole endures with full integrity. As Black comments, for him 'every clause of the church's constitution was riddled with exceptions' (Black 1992: 172). Ockham's greatness as a pre-conciliarist is found not only in his principled constitutionalism and his vision of liberty in the Church, but in his theological daring: he thinks the unthinkable – the possibility that the whole institutional structure of the Church could fall into error – and in the last resort he looks to its ordinary lay members (the *congregatio fidelium*) to lead it back to truth.

Chapter 5

WYCLIF AND HUS: SUBVERSIVE NON-CONCILIARISTS

Wyclif and Hus: Similarities and Differences

We cannot look back beyond the Reformation to the major formative influences that shaped authority in the Church in the late mediaeval period without referring to John Wyclif and Jan Hus. Their destinies are forever linked together through the condemnations that led to Hus' martyrdom. There can be no question that Hus was massively indebted to Wyclif for his theology. Loserth (1884) documented the impressive direct textual dependence, though without bringing out the remarkable freedom that Hus evinced in simply leaving out the elements in Wyclif's theology that were of doubtful orthodoxy. Although Hus was in fact scrupulously selective and discriminating in what he borrowed from Wyclif, he did not trouble to distance himself from Wyclif's reputation or from aspects of Wyclif's teaching that he rejected. To distance himself from such a warrior for truth would have been repugnant to him. As a result, Hus was condemned to execution as though he had propagated Wyclif's worst errors. Wyclif was for Hus a symbol of fearless, reforming zeal. Both of them belong securely to the pre-Reformation ferment in the sphere of authority. We need to register their attacks on the late mediaeval Church–State authority matrix and their call for radical scriptural renewal and reform. However, we cannot smuggle them in to the story as crypto-conciliarists. Conciliarists they certainly were not. For a doctrinal comparison between Wyclif and Hus see Leff in Kenny 1986: 105–25; also Wilks 2000: ch. 4; for Wyclif's influence see Keen in Kenny 1986: 127–45; for his notoriety among Roman Catholics, see Kenny in Kenny 1986: 147–68; and for his reputation among Protestants see Aston 1965.

Wyclif lived most of his life before the Great Schism of the West and his appeal for reform was not to a General Council but to what a later generation would call 'the godly prince'. The conciliar model of the Church as the *congregatio fidelium*, a visible, ordered community with power to govern itself independently of the state, a *societas perfecta*, left him cold. The Church was simply not a visible body in any important sense. And Wyclif was more anti-papal than any conciliarist could ever be. However, he resonates with conciliar ideas when he urges that the 'whole church', nobility and clergy alike, must join forces to reform corruption and when he appeals, in tune with contemporary notions, to the general welfare or common good (*utilitas*) of the realm (Farr 1974: 89, 139–41, 146). Hus too, who embraced Wyclif's notion of the Church as the body of the predestinate, but on practical and ethical, rather than on philosophical grounds, often invokes the universal Church against the restrictive interpretation of the papalists that the Church comprised the pope and the cardinals.

Hus, who did hope for vindication from a council (though he professed not to expect it), was destroyed by conciliarists, principally Dietrich of Niem, Pierre d'Ailly, Jean Gerson and Cardinal Zabarella, who all saw him as an enemy of the fabric of authority (including a 'constitutional' papacy) in the Catholic Church and perceived that his concept of the Church was incompatible with the juridical, hierarchical ecclesiology that they promoted (Spinka 1966: 393–95). These eminent churchmen all had feet of clay. Their witness to essential truths of the Church is tainted by lack of integrity in their treatment of Hus, by blind zeal. This fact has troubled many who have appealed to conciliar principles, from Martin Luther to Hans Küng. It continues to inhibit any unhistorical romanticizing about conciliarism and takes much of the gloss off the Council of Constance. No one who is sympathetic to conciliarist ideas can ever forget that it was the cream of conciliarists who implacably condemned Hus on false charges, refused to hear his protestations that he had never taught the views attributed to him and secured his execution in spite of a safe-conduct.

Although neither their views nor their characters should be treated as identical, Wyclif and Hus remain profoundly subversive twin witnesses, harbingers of the trauma of the sixteenth-century Reformation, whose passionate denunciations helped to destabilize the hierocratic, centralized structures of authority focused on the papacy. While some of Wyclif's theories were so extreme that they could not catalyse any coherent movement, Hus's more attainable and practical agenda galvanized the reform movement in Bohemia that had been smouldering for decades. Wyclif and Hus were hailed by some Protestant Reformers as forerunners of the Reform. For English Protestants Wyclif became (as John Bale first put it) 'the morning star' of the Reformation, even though the image of clear, cool steady light is seriously awry as a metaphor of Wyclif's teaching. While the influence of Lollardy on the progress of the English Reformation is still debated (see recently Rex 2002, who holds that it was negligible), Wyclif himself was both the symbol and the stimulator of reform. Hus was seen as the Reformation's proto-martyr, a century before the event. Luther hailed them from afar as kindred spirits. He endorsed Wyclif's Bible-based agenda for reform of a corrupt hierarchy and priesthood and his call for a return to primitive simplicity and purity. The same tide of revulsion against the wealth, power and privileges of the Church swept Wyclif, Hus, Luther, Zwingli and many others forward into irrevocable action against authority. It was the condemnation and execution of Hus at the Council of Constance that convinced Luther that General Councils were not infallible, but could err in their judgements.

Both Wyclif and Hus anticipated major areas of the Reformation programme: not only the scathing denunciations of endemic abuses such as simony and the clarion call to return to the simplicity and purity of the Apostles, but the invoking of the magistrate (king, prince, duke) to initiate reform, the harnessing of national aspirations and resentments against an imperial papacy, the paramount authority of Holy Scripture and the witness of the Fathers over against accumulated human traditions. It has often been pointed out that Wyclif's agenda anticipated with uncanny accuracy the developments of the 1530s in England under Henry VIII every step of the way. Hus, however, cannot plausibly be claimed as a Protestant *avant la lettre*: he remained an orthodox mediaeval catholic in his beliefs and he instinctively held fast to the received devotional forms. Hus was a Catholic reformer, more genuinely Catholic than those who silenced him. But to say this is not to imply that the magisterial Reformers of the next century, though more radical in their rejection of certain inherited structures, were not equally catholic. However, even to raise the issue is to beg the whole question of the authenticity of the Reformation impulse within Western Christendom.

John Wyclif

John Wyclif (1330–1384) left an ambiguous legacy to the reforming movements of the fifteenth century. His ideological extremism and doctrinal aberrations tainted the cause of reform and created a stereotype of destructive reformation for opponents of reform to throw at later reformers. On the other hand, his fearless radicalism shouted from the housetops what was whispered within and so give impetus to the cause of reform generally.

Workman 1926 is a not very theological but immensely thorough biography. McFarlane 1972 is a rather unsympathetic account of Wyclif's role and influence. Farr 1974 defends the coherence of Wyclif's appeal to English law. Kenny 1985 provides a superb general introduction to his thought. See also O'Donovan 1991: 29–42 and especially Leff 1967a: II (a substantial account of his reforming ideas and their impact) and 1987. Hudson 1992 offers an excellent brief introduction. For unusual twists see Wilks 2000. Most recently Rex 2002 sets Wyclif in his context. It remains doubtful whether any of the English works that have been attributed to Wyclif, such as the treatises on the pope and on the Church, are actually from his hand. Several relevant treatises are available in English in Spinka 1953 and the *De Ecclesia* of Wyclif 1886 has marginal summaries in English.

Wyclif's *Tractatus de Ecclesia* (Wyclif 1886) is the first major treatise on ecclesiology since patristic times. It was called forth by a burning indignation against the corruptions, abuses and failings of the Western Church (possibly combined with some personal grievance). However, it is not the first blast of the Reformation trumpet: it still speaks the mediaeval language of 'holy mother church' (*sancta mater ecclesia catholica*: 85); it works with the shorthand designation 'the Roman Church' for the *una sancta*; it assumes that deceased believers are in purgatory and that the saints intercede in heaven for the church militant. The three parts into which the host is broken at the mass signify the three parts of the Church: triumphant, dormant and militant (*partem in celo triumphantem, partem in purgatorio dormientem et partem in terris militantem*: Wyclif 1886: 8). Outside the Church there is no salvation (*extra sanctam ecclesiam non est salus vel remissio peccatorum*: 11). The Church is like Noah's ark: no animal was saved that was not in the ark (12). The reprobate, the foreknown, are not part of this body, but are like limbs cut off it (12). The Church is the whole body of the predestined (*una universitas fidelium pre-destinatorum*: 37). To be in the Church is not necessarily to be of the Church (89).

Wyclif re-interprets Boniface VIII's Bull *Unam Sanctam* (1303 – relatively recent to him), that every creature must submit to the Roman pontiff in order to be saved (Wyclif 1886: 14–15, 26). He professes not to be able to believe that the pope intended the obvious sense of his words, which are clearly blasphemous. The Roman Church is the local name for the universal Church. In this sense the Bull is simply re-iterating the truth of *nulla salus*. Although the Church's only Head is Christ, and it can have no head on earth, there is a sense in which the pope has headship because he governs the Church. This authority can be recognized, provided that the pope is predestinate and performs his office faithfully (19). The pope and the college of cardinals are first in dignity provided they closely follow Christ. Otherwise they are a nest of heretics (88).

Wyclif's significance is that he openly and fearlessly challenged not only the abuses and corruptions of the late mediaeval Church, but also the structures of spiritual authority that supported them, those of the bishops, cardinals and popes. If Wilks is right, Wyclif had been a convinced papalist himself in his early years; he knew the arguments better than the papal publicists. His denunciations were aimed not at the shortcomings of individual hierarchs, nor even particularly at the contingent inadequacies and abuses of clerical practice, but at the institution that bred them both. Wyclif was not interested in reforming the structures of Christendom to make them more efficient and then continuing with the inherited framework. Unlike, say, the Augsburg Confession of 1530 or the Henrician legislation in England in the 1530s, he was not interested in the continuity of the institutions of authority based on an episcopally structured Church, albeit liberated from the papal monarchy and acting in alliance with the civil power. The whole ecclesiastical hierarchy was the product of the Donation of Constantine: although Wyclif accepted the authenticity of the Donation, he regarded it as a satanic device to corrupt the Church systematically.

Wyclif's rejection of the papacy pre-dated the Great Schism which occurred towards the end of his life. Though initially Wyclif welcomed the election of Urban as a reforming pope who castigated his predecessor for his corruptions (Wyclif 1886: 37), when the schism occurred it merely confirmed his jaundiced view of the papacy as an institution. Wyclif logically deduced that one or even both of those claiming to be pope must actually be the Antichrist. 'The conclusion Wyclif drew from this intolerable quandary was brutal in its simplicity and directness' (Farr 1974: 27). It was that Christ must have ordained precisely this schism in order to demonstrate to the faithful that it did not belong to the substance of faith to believe that either of them was his vicar on earth. Towards the end of the fourteenth century, in England, the disorientation generated by the Great Schism and the fear of subversive Lollardy, Wyclif's legacy, played into each other: some suspected that they were connected at some deep subterranean level (Harvey 1983, 1987).

Moreover, Wyclif's revolutionary theology, intensified by a maverick metaphysic, was even more subversive than this. It would have ultimately eliminated the tangible structures of the visible church as an effective institution. If, as I suggested at the beginning of this book, the institutional aspect of the Church dominated the mystical aspect by late mediaeval times, the reverse is true of Wyclif's ecclesiology. He bucks the trend and stands received assumptions on their head. The Church is not a political community for Wyclif, not a cohesive society spread out in space and enduring in time. The Church is essentially dispersed; it is found here and there, wherever the faithful gather in submission to the truth of Scripture. The Church is a function of the Bible and the Bible is the heart of the Church. The mystical Church – predestined to salvation, evoked in Scripture and hid with Christ in God – is all in all. The visible, empirical Church – a mixed multitude of the saved and the damned, the wheat and the tares – is contingent, shadowy and insubstantial. In the end it becomes irrelevant, except to be condemned. Wyclif demands its wholesale disendowment: material possessions are the cause of the Church's spiritual impoverishment; to be completely stripped of them will bring spiritual riches. Deprived of worldly property, churchmen could no longer trade mercenarily in holy things; the Church would live by faith and by the alms of the faithful freely given as in the days of the Apostles. But the institutional dimension of the Church would be reduced to vanishing point, taking with it its theological and devotional traditions.

Wyclif's theological dualism pushed the biblical imagery of the two cities, the city of God and the earthly city, seminally elaborated by Augustine, to an extreme that Augustine avoided. No longer was it a theological construction overlaid on an untidy empirical scene that partakes of both, as it was for Augustine in *The City of God*. The scheme became in Wyclif a concept of two entirely separate and opposed communities that should hold no commerce with each other. There is scant theological connection between the mystical Church and the visible Church: a great divorce has been effected in Christian ecclesiology.

What compounds Wyclif's heterodoxy with regard to the Church is the perfectly orthodox contention that only God knows those who are predestined to be saved and those who are not. This is a function of the metaphysically unchanging nature of God's love: the objects of that love are given metaphysical permanence also. However, we cannot know who is predestined and who not. That tenet is not contentious until it is added to a doctrine that undermines the visible Church and its authority. Only the predestined Church matters but we cannot tell where it is to be found. But then what becomes of Wyclif's exhortation that prelates who are damned should not be obeyed? Which ones are they? Strictly speaking, of course, we cannot know; but in practice they are collectively under suspicion. The clergy, from the Pope downwards, become tarred with the same brush and discredited as an entire order of society.

God's purpose of bringing the elect to salvation is not dependent on the priesthood and its sacramental ministry: God could endow a layman with sacerdotal powers at will, Wyclif believes, because all true Christians are priests (Spinka 1953: 84). The sacraments benefit only the elect anyway, and they will be saved with or without sacraments. The preached word is more important than the sacraments because it brings to bear the power of God contained in Holy Scripture. Wyclif also strips the law of the Church of its legitimation. The ordering of the Church in canon law has no divine sanction; it is all man-made and no more. Only priests and deacons are mentioned in Scripture: there are no bishops, cardinals or popes. Those who reject the commands of the hierarchy are rejecting merely human authority. Thus in Wyclif's programme the visible Church is subverted both materially (by disendowment) and juridically (by the negation of its divine authority). The combination of ideas is subversive of all authority and order: the visible church ceases to count – one might say, as Leff does, that it ceases to exist in any meaningful sense.

But Wyclif is not an anarchist (perhaps he is theologically, but not politically). The hierocratic, imperial authority wielded by pope and bishops is not part of God's plan of salvation. There is no need for the pope. Indeed, the hierarchy is Antichrist. If ecclesiastical power is to be dissolved, as it deserves to be, it must be at the hands of the king. Lay authority, in the person of the magistrate, must replace clerical authority and fill the vacuum created by its dissolution. Wyclif almost certainly had read Marsilius of Padua, though he does not mention him. The king is God's vicar on earth and represents Christ in his divinity (compared with the priest who represents him in his human nature). Royal power is absolute. The divinity that doth hedge a king means that resistance, even to tyrants, cannot be justified. The king must put in hand the complete disendowment of the Church and so return it to primitive purity. The owning of property is at the root of evils such as simony (the buying and selling of ecclesiastical offices) and this root must be severed. This was not an appeal from sacred authority to secular, but from ecclesiastical to civil within the one Christian commonwealth. Church and realm were coterminous: 'The church or realm is one body of all the inhabitants of that realm.' Wyclif rejected the monolithic, imperial concept of the Church that informed Roman policy and saw the earthly manifestation of the Church as a federation of distinct Christian territories. He could therefore speak of several 'churches militant' which were identical with the political realms described by geographical and cultural identity (Wilks 1987: 152–57; Farr 1974: 36, 40–41).

Sustained by a profound sense of a distinctive English ecclesiastical tradition (Tatnall 1969), Wyclif used historical arguments to show that the possessions of the Church had been donated by the laity as alms and then he added legal arguments to prove that where the original spiritual purpose of alms giving had been thwarted, the gift should return to the giver. His message resonated with popular resentment against the wealth of the Church: the cause of dispossession was in the air. For Wyclif the logician, endowment led inexorably to heresy and thus to treason. Endowment was heretical because it entailed an enticement to sin in the form of simony and other abuses. It was treasonable because it was an offence against the realm and its wealth. This line of argument suited Wyclif's purposes beautifully: unlike heresy, of course, treason was exempted from the ecclesiastical courts, and if it were proved, all lands and chattels were forfeit to the crown – disendowment by default. The bishops held most of their tempo-ralities from the king on a feudal basis (tenure by barony and knight service) which carried attendant obligations. So when the nobility take action to correct the clergy they are carrying out their obligations under English law and particularly according to the Magna Carta. Thus, para-doxically, Wyclif's revolutionary programme was to be implemented by responsible legal methods (Farr 1974: 95–137).

No other reformer until the Anabaptists so marginalized the visible Church. (Although some Roman Catholics accused Luther of this at the time and others have colluded with the charge since, Luther never lets go of the objectivity of the sacraments, nor does he push beyond the mixed, territorial church, nor does he flirt with ideas of ecclesial perfection.) What was driving Wyclif's remorseless theology? Workman finds extreme indi-vidualism in Wyclif's thought and little sense of the organic unity of society. Workman also accuses him of a negative, destructive approach and a lack of constructive ideas: he swept institutions and social order away, but unlike, say, Calvin, he had nothing to put in its place except a rhetorical appeal to civil authority (Workman 1926: II, 324; I, 19). But the issue goes deeper than temperament and rhetoric. Wyclif was much more than an academic loose cannon. The root is ideological, indeed metaphysical.

Wyclif's extreme ecclesiology was, if not determined by, certainly aided and abetted by an extreme metaphysic: a radical realism that invested all truth and value in the eternal, perfect and unchanging 'forms' or 'ideas' (the universals) in the mind of God (though Wilks [2000: 6–7, 59, 67] contests this, claiming that Wyclif was a dialectical thinker who found truth in the tension between positions and believed in their ultimate harmony). At any rate, Wyclif insisted that 'intellectual and emotional error about universals is the cause of all the sin that reigns in the world' (Kenny 1986: 29). Church and Bible are located by Wyclif in this transcendent realm like heavenly twins. His thought should be interpreted by reference to these two foci held together. Bible and Church are viewed by Wyclif as exempt from contingency, change and imperfection. The real Church is as it exists in the mind of God and what appears to us to be far from that glorious body is not the Church at all. The Bible (its meaning, not the bare text) is all-sufficient for doctrine and morals, without human imperfection, flawless, peerless and infallible. Bible and Church together were the complementary archetypes governing Wyclif's polemic against the Church as he knew it. The archetypes residing in God were reality to Wyclif; the empirical world was insubstantial.

It is this radical transcendent realism that shapes Wyclif's eucharistic theology also (text in Spinka 1953: 61–88). There is still Real Presence, but the bread and wine are not transubstantiated: they remain alongside, as it were, the body and blood of Christ, since accidents and substance mutually coinhere and cannot exist independently. Again we see that his theology, driven primarily by the passion for reform ('A shoddy claim for physical, sacerdotal magic, that was what Wyclif thought of transubstantiation': Keen in Kenny 1986: 14), was pushed into heterodoxy by metaphysics. But personal revulsion also comes in here: it was, as Rex puts it, the papal condemnation of Wyclif that, in revealing the papacy as Antichrist, removed the last restraints on Wyclif's radicalism, the restraints regarding the Eucharist (Rex 2002: 42–45).

Wyclif's mind, especially in his last years in internal exile at Lutterworth, from where he poured out scathing denunciations of pope and prelates, especially after the Great Schism in 1378 which completed his disillusionment with the hierarchy, was obsessive, ill-disciplined and unbalanced, albeit powerful and logical. An extreme philosophical position reinforced a destructive ecclesiology. Wyclif pushed insights about the mystical Church, predestined in Christ to eternal salvation – insights that had biblical grounding and were expounded by Augustine, Luther and Calvin, for example – to and beyond their logical conclusions. As Leff puts it: 'Wyclif's originality, like his daring, consisted in stepping in where angels fear to tread' (Leff 1967a: II, 500). His fulminating chimed in with long-standing national resentment against the papacy and its financial depradations. Heterodox though he was, he retained his liberty until he challenged the doctrine of Transubstantiation (though not the Real Presence as such), on which the whole mediaeval sacerdotal and hierarchical structure in effect depended. At that point he became a liability and had to quit Oxford for the country vicarage at Lutterworth.

Wyclif suffered multiple condemnation on various grounds: by Gregory XI in 1377, by Archbishop Courtenay in 1382 and at the Council of Constance in 1415, years after his death. What in his voluminous teaching principally elicited condemnation was the tenet that the Church was simply and solely the body of the predestined. It was the absolute form of this doctrine that gave offence because of all the consequences that flowed from it: in effect the elimination of the visible Church as the structured community of grace, mediating God in the world.

Jan Hus

The witness of Jan Hus – and it was a witness (*marturia*) in life and death, in preaching, writing and steadfast testimony to the last that was Hus's contribution, rather than any systematic exposition of theology – essentially concerned the Church. Texts: *On the Church*, trans. Schaff, 1974; *On Simony* in Spinka 1953: 196–278; *Letters*, trans. and ed. Spinka 1972; contemporary accounts and documents, trans. and ed. Spinka 1965. Studies: Spinka 1966; Leff 1967a, II; Kenny 1986. Life: Spinka 1968.

For nearly a millennium the great institution of the Church had been so immediately present to Christian people, so taken for granted, that critical dissent was at a premium. The corruptions of the Avignon papal court, followed by the great papal schism, the hunger for reform and the longing for reunification, changed that. A new critical distance from the institution became possible and enabled a flourishing of theological reflection on the nature, structure and health of the Church. We see it in Wyclif and Hus, with their denunciation of abuses; in the conciliarists as they strive for the unity and integrity of the body; and in the humanists with their exposure of false foundation documents, such as the Donation of Constantine and the forged decretals.

Hus's *De Ecclesia* (Hus 1974 [1915]) is one of the first of a new genre: theological treatises specifically on the Church. It was more influential than Wyclif's treatise of the same name which remained in manuscript form until the late nineteenth century. A century later the Hussites sent Martin Luther a copy of their master's work, recognizing a kindred spirit, and in 1520, a pivotal year of the Reformation, Von Hutten printed an edition in Mainz.

Of the thirty charges on the basis of which Hus was condemned, twenty-five concerned the Church and of these a dozen concerned the papacy (see Hus's final reply to the charges in Spinka 1965: 26–4). The thrust of Hus's writing and preaching on the Church was the opposite of theoretical or speculative: it concerned practical reform of abuses, clustering around the sin of simony, which was in Hus's eyes the root of all ecclesiastical corruption because it sucked acquisition of real estate and love of money into a purely spiritual calling. Hus identified the sin of Simon Magus with the biblical sin against the Holy Spirit: 'the sacred canons teach that simony is the first and principal heresy' (Spinka 1972: 6–7). Like Wyclif, Hus wants to subject all Church possessions to the temporal ruler: the Church has only the use, not the ownership, and can lose even this if use becomes abuse.

However, a distinctive ecclesiology underpins Hus's prophetic witness to the purity of the Church. The _De Ecclesia_ was Hus's response to eight colleagues, doctors of the theological faculty of the University of Prague who had themselves in 1413 responded obediently to the papal bull requiring absolute submission to the pope, condemning the forty-five Wycliffite articles and demanding that Bohemia be cleared of heresy, if necessary by severe ecclesiastical and civil punishments. It is Hus's theological _apologia_.

Hus drew heavily on Wyclif's _De Ecclesia_ and his _De Potestate Papae_, so publicizing Wyclif's views and in the process becoming tarred with the same brush. He defends the same principles, deploys the same quotations from the Fathers, from canon law and from the Scriptures. Some paragraphs are reproduced verbatim from Wyclif. But it cannot be said that Hus followed Wyclif slavishly. He had an independent knowledge of canon law and of Augustine, as well as of the Bible. (Of Hus's 347 quotations from the New Testament in this work, 93 are from Matthew and 67 from John.) His argument is clearer and more direct than Wyclif's and he is less severe in his judgements than Wyclif's wrathful denunciations. 'He remained a disciple of Wyclif in those doctrinal matters which did not infringe upon orthodoxy' (Spinka 1972: 65). Hus either passed over in silence what he did not agree with, or else interpreted Wyclif in a sense contrary to what the latter intended.

Hus repudiates the view, held by his opponents on the basis of good mediaeval precedents, that the pope, the cardinals and other prelates constitute the Church. Moreover, the Church is not confined to the circumscribed body of Christians over which the apostolic see has jurisdiction. ('No partial church,' Hus writes in a letter, 'is the universal, holy, apostolic Church': Spinka 1972: 99.) Rome is not the apostolic seat in the exclusive sense that without it the Church of Christ would fall, for if Rome, like Sodom, were destroyed, the Christian Church would remain (Hus 1974: 215–16). Hus has a quasi-conciliarist federal concept of the Church: he envisages several vicarial heads of particular churches, which together comprise Christendom; the Roman Church is only one of them. To claim that the Church of Rome is the whole Church brands the pope who claims it as the Antichrist (Spinka 1972: 96).

The Roman Church is not inerrant and the pope is not infallible. The authority of the pope and of other prelates is conditional on their moral rectitude. 'By their fruits' it will be known whether they are good shepherds or 'thieves and robbers'. If the pope is virtuous, he is true pope; if he is wicked he is the Antichrist (Hus 1974: 87, 136, 143). The pope may be heretical, and some popes have been, notably Boniface VIII. While Hus accepts a faithful, pure pope, to rebel against an erring pope (as Hus himself had done in refusing to obey the summons to Rome) is to obey Christ (Hus 1974: 211). No priest should be prevented from preaching the gospel, nor indeed can be (Hus had refused also to obey the injunction of the Archbishop of Prague). To obey the pope and the archbishop and cease to preach the gospel, said Hus in a letter, would be 'contrary to God and to my salvation' (Spinka 1972: 91).

Positively, Hus states that 'the holy catholic church' or 'holy mother Church' consists of the totality of the predestinate (*omnium praedestinatorum universitas*) – actually, of Christ and the body of the predestinate (cf. Augustine's 'head and members'). But this is not coterminous with the visible Church. There is one *ecclesia* or congregation of the righteous and another of the reprobate, 'the foreknown' (*praesciti*). Following Augustine, Hus holds that the foreknown enjoy present grace through the sacraments of the Church, but ultimately fall away. They are in but not of the Church (Hus 1974: 2, 21, 24–25). Augustine had written:

> While the City of God is on pilgrimage in this world, she has in her midst some who are united with her in participation in the sacraments, but who will not join with her in the eternal destiny of the saints. Some of these are hidden; some are well known, for they do not hesitate to murmur against God, whose sacramental sign they bear, even in the company of his acknowledged enemies. At one time they join his enemies in filling the theatres [where Christians were tormented], at another they join with us in filling the churches' (Augustine 1972: 45–46: CD I, 35).

For Hus, therefore, the unity of the Church is constituted by the unity of predestination and the unity of blessedness (in the Church triumphant in heaven). In the present, its unity is composed of true faith and the Christian virtues (Hus 1974: 14–15). Elsewhere, Hus says that those in the Church militant who are foreknown (i.e. as those who will prove to be reprobate) do not in reality belong to it, but (in words that Luther would echo) 'are as ulcers, phlegm, and excrements which will finally be separated from the body of the Church, in their foulness and waste, in the Day of Judgement' (Spinka 1966: 69). His accusers persistently alleged that Hus denied to the reprobate any place in the Church militant, in fact that his theology abolished the Church militant altogether. Defining the Church as the company of the predestinate has immediate consequences for the power of the clergy: a priest can only declare, in exercising the power of the keys, what God has already determined and predestined with regard to the salvation of a particular soul.

Christ, not the pope, is the head of the Church, not just in heaven but on earth. In an extraordinary turn of phrase that alludes to Boniface VIII's *Unam Sanctam*, Hus says that Christ is the true Roman pontiff, to whom all should be subject for salvation (Hus 1974: 119). True to his convictions, Hus had appealed to Christ himself, over the heads of the pope and the curia. The 'rock' of Matthew 16.18 is Christ, not Peter, and the Church is built on the faith that confesses that Jesus is the Son of God. Christ is 'the foundation of foundations' because the Church is said to be also built on the Apostles and prophets (59, 72–79). The pope should share authority with the other bishops, just as Peter did with the other Apostles. Originally all bishops were called 'popes'. Nevertheless, the Roman Church is the 'principal' church militant.

The corruption of the Church began with the Donation of Constantine. While Hus accepts the historicity of the Donation, he believes (like Dante) that Constantine had no right to bestow his temporal authority on a bishop.

Although Hus undoubtedly was attracted to the Donatistic view that an unworthy minister cannot celebrate true sacraments, he remained on the orthodox side of the line (unlike Wyclif himself). Priestly ministry may be unworthy, but does not cease on that account to be valid. By the same token – and this was dangerously subversive – kings did not worthily occupy their thrones if they had fallen into mortal sin.

Hus remained orthodox in theology. He consistently affirmed the doctrine of Transubstantiation and did not flirt with the notion of remanence (that the bread and wine remain after consecration, as Wyclif had taught towards the end of his life). Hus accepted seven sacraments and believed that one should pray to the Blessed Virgin and the saints. He did not question Purgatory and he attacked the particular manner in which indulgences were promoted, not the idea as such. But Hus is passionately convinced that the laity should receive the sacrament in both kinds. It is sheer madness to condemn the institution of Christ, the example of the Apostles and the teaching of St Paul (Spinka, ed. 1972: 179).

At his trial during the Council of Constance, Hus was not allowed to state his views clearly and his protestations that he had never held the tenets attributed to him were brushed aside. He begged not to be forced to abjure articles that he had never held. But it was against principle for the Council to argue with a condemned heretic (Spinka 1968: 260). Tied to the stake and with the wood piled up to his chin, Hus was urged to recant. His reply, recorded by an eyewitness, was:

> God is my witness that those things that are falsely ascribed to me... I have never taught or preached. But that [*sic*] the principal intention of my preaching ... was solely that I might turn men from sin. And in that truth of the gospel that I wrote, taught and preached in accordance with the sayings and expositions of the holy doctors, I am willing gladly to die today (Spinka 1965: 233).

Chapter 6

THE GREAT SCHISM OF THE WEST AND THE COUNCIL OF PISA

The Schism of 1378

The conciliar thinking that was latent in mediaeval theology and canon law was given its opportunity by the challenge thrown up by the Great Schism of the West in 1378. The schism threw the whole of Christendom into a crisis unprecedented in its severity. Although there had been schisms in the papacy before, the Great Schism was unlike earlier divisions in its far-reaching ideological implications and by virtue of the fact that was insoluble within the limits of the current polity of the Western Church. In his pioneering study in 1930 G.J. Jordan proposed that the schism was 'the most thought-provoking event in the history of the Church' between the Great Schism of East and West that came to a head in the mid-eleventh century and the Reformation itself (Jordan 1930: 13).

The schism triggered an outbreak of frustration against the constitution of the mediaeval Western Church, enshrined in doctrine and upheld by canon law, in which the pope held supreme and unchallengeable authority in relation to other sources of authority in the Church: the college of cardinals, the episcopate, the universities, the civil power, a General Council itself. Only when all these centres of subsidiary power combined together to challenge papal absolutism, as they did, in various combinations and with varying degrees of success, between 1378 and 1417, could papal supremacy be seriously called into question. The schism was generated by the challenge of oligarchy (the college of cardinals) to monarchy; in terms of its resolution and outcome, it points beyond oligarchy (for the cardinals failed to develop any coherent alternative) towards constitutional monarchy in the form of representative, constitutional governance, expressed in the conciliar principle (for narrative and analysis of the Great Schism, with documentation, see especially Ullmann 1972b).

The schism, this *magnum et horrendum scisma*, as Cardinal Fillastre later called it, would be resolved only when thinkers, drawing on traditional canonical and ecclesiological resources, where alternative ideas existed in embyro, broke out of the received framework where everything hung on the all-embracing power of the papacy. In order to attempt to reform the

Church 'in head and members', both parts of this equation had to be reinterpreted. The conciliarists invoked the authority of Christ, the true Head of the Church, inherent in his body, its members, to heal the divisions caused by the deficiencies of the earthly head of the Church, the pope.

Following the death of Gregory XI, who had returned the papal court to Rome from Avignon where it had been in exile for a century, the College of Cardinals elected, from outside their own ranks, the Archbishop of Bari as Urban VI amid scenes of confusion and popular unrest. By this time the cardinalate held a uniquely important advisory and co-adjutory position in the government of the Church, but without being able to curb papal power. The college was, according to Hostiensis in the thirteenth century, part of the pope's 'body'. The cardinals participated in the exercise of the *plenitudo potestatis* and even administered the Church during a vacancy in the papal see, but the primacy remained that of the pope alone. The sacred college thus found itself in a potentially frustrating position (Watt 1971, 1980).

In this case the cardinals soon became disaffected from their chosen candidate. Urban rapidly alienated them by his arrogance, irrational behaviour, petty vindictiveness and violent temper towards his court. A former senior curial official, a man of unimpeachable integrity and something of a puritan, Urban attempted immediately to curb the power and opulence that the cardinals had become accustomed to during the Avignon papacy, but went about it 'with a humiliating truculence and a paranoid sense of his authority' (Kelly 1986: 227). The cardinals were offended by the *rigor iustitiae* of Urban's dealings with them, claimed St Catherine of Siena. Urban's unexpected elevation seems to have gone to his head, literally tipped the balance of his mind, and the conviction spread that he was deranged and unfit. He took a sadistic pleasure in the torture of some of the cardinals whom he suspected of plotting against him and several were put to death or disappeared. Urban ranted about reform, but had no serious concept of what this would entail. Though they had treated him as pope, receiving Holy Communion from him, begging favours and carrying out his instructions, the cardinals claimed (against the evidence and against the judgement of distinguished lawyers) that the election was canonically invalid because they had acted out of fear, intimidated by the Roman populace. They proceeded to elect a second pope, Clement VII, a man with murder and massacre in his *curriculum vitae*. There was in fact no legitimate way that a pope who was out of control could be removed, except for heresy, and in that case a General Council was needed.

The fact that the same sacred college of cardinals had taken the irreversible action of canonically electing a second pope within the space of a few months sent a shockwave – whose magnitude can hardly be conceived from the retrospect of post-Christendom – throughout Europe. For the first time in the Church's history, two popes, each with his own hierarchical structure, demanded the allegiance of Christendom. The schism produced a dual system of popes, cardinals, curia and ecclesiastical allegiances, right down to the parochial clergy. It could mean that people did not know who was their rightful parish priest, bishop, religious superior or dean of cathedral. They could not tell whose sacraments were valid. Rival candidates were appointed to important offices, such as the headship of religious houses. Each side denounced and excommunicated the other.

The empire was under weak leadership and was soon to be divided itself. The schism coincided with the social and economic consequences of the Black Death. It occurred, moreover, in the year specified by various seers as that in which Antichrist would be manifested on earth. Christendom was fragmented on national lines, with France, Scotland and most of the Iberian peninsular opting to support Clement VII, while England, most of Italy and much of the rest of Europe remaining loyal to Urban VI (on national influences, from the point of view of England, see Harvey 1983; Du Boulay 1965). Had the nations taken concerted action, they could have nipped it in the bud; but their divisions and rivalries allowed the schism to fester for forty years. Little wonder that in those dark days the schism was often seen in mystical and apocalyptic terms (Swanson 1979: 20–21). Somehow the blatant fact of a divided church did more than all the scandals and corruptions of the clergy and hierarchy to undermine the divine credentials of the institution in the minds of the faithful. Oberman commented that the Western Schism, 'with its concatenation of abortive solutions..., called the sacred basis of existence into question to an extent hitherto unknown', generating both private and public evils: confusion of consciences and political conflict (Oberman in Trinkaus and Oberman 1974: 8). At the end of his survey of the Avignon papacy, Renouard concluded: 'The schism put everything in question' (Renouard 1970: 134). The traumatic impact of the Western Schism of 1378 can hardly be over-estimated: the effect on the ideological cohesion and credibility of the Roman Church was seismic. Moreover, the fault lines exposed by the schism were to become great crevasses two centuries later. The schism prepared the ground for the Reformation: as Ullmann says, the tide was beginning to move (Ullmann 1972b: 96–99; source documentation for reform in German and Latin, not available to me, are found in Miethke and Weinrich 1995, 2002).

The general clamour for a council which would reform, unite and heal the Church began to intensify. Therefore the need to forge a new constitutional instrument that would enable a council to be convened without the normal papal initiative became urgent. A council should properly be called by the pope, but that was plainly impossible. The cardinals were discredited and divided. The emperor was too weak to do so. The path to a solution was charted by two theologians of the University of Paris: Conrad of Gelnhausen and Henry of Langenstein.

The First Conciliar Theories

From the University of Paris, Conrad of Gelnhausen and Henry of Langenstein drew on earlier conciliar practice: they were aware that clergy and laity, as well as bishops, had been involved in the councils of the late Middle Ages (the Lateran, Lyons, Vienne). They had glimpsed something of the conciliar *modus operandi* of the early Church in Gratian's *Decretum*. They began to invoke the recognized principle, 'What affects all should be approved by all', and to apply it to the resolution of the schism. Conrad argues that the schism cannot be resolved within the strict requirements of church law. According to the letter of the law there is nothing that can be done. But law is not about words, but about realities. Its application must follow Aristotle's principle of *epieikeia*, equity, which requires flexibility in responding to circumstances. Understood in this way, the law should be no obstacle to the convoking of a General Council without papal authority.

Henry of Langenstein's *Letter on Behalf of a Council of Peace* of 1381 (text in Spinka 1953) reproduced much of Conrad of Gelnhausen's *Epistola Concordiae* (*A Letter of Concord*) of 1380, the first full statement of the early conciliar position. In the name of God and in the light of Judgement Day, Henry solemnly adjures the civil rulers of Christendom to convene a council just as the Christian Roman emperors had once done. As many precedents show, there are circumstances in which this could happen without the co-operation of the pope. Even though in normal circumstances a council ought to be called on the authority of the pope, this is not essential but *per accidens*. The common good takes precedence over all other considerations. It calls for the exercise of *epieikeia* (a pivotal concept of the Conciliar Movement that can be tracked through many of its most prominent exponents: see Jordan 1930: 47–58). *Epieikeia* transcends the letter of the law and looks to the intention of the legislators, who cannot envisage all contingent events. Christ is at work in his Church, making good its deficiencies and continually animating it towards renewal.

Henry invokes the Roman legal maxim that had been incorporated into the canon law by Innocent III and deployed by Marsilius of Padua, William of Ockham and all subsequent conciliarists, *Quod omnes tangit*...: 'For what affects all must consistently be dealt with by all or by the representatives of all.' While there were two popes, the bride of Christ had become a two-headed monster. A council should be preceded by a time of repentance and reconciliation to God, followed by a prolonged Ash Wednesday of fasting, weeping and prayer. A council could be constituted in one of several ways, but in any event the pope would be subject to the council. Henry laid down the fundamental axiom of conciliar theory: 'The universal Church, of which a General Council is representative, is superior to the college of cardinals and to every other particular grouping (*congregatio*) of the faithful and to every single person of whatever dignity, even to the holder of the highest dignity or precedence, the lord pope' (Henry of Langenstein in Spinka 1953: 118).

Such early conciliarists as Conrad and Henry were not revolutionaries but traditionalists. As even Jedin, the Roman Catholic historian of the Council of Trent, recognized, they believed they were restoring the ancient ecclesiastical constitution (Jedin 1957: I, 10; for Conrad see Ullmann 1972b: 176–81). In the vacuum of authority, other voices were becoming more radical: Dietrich of Niem (*On Uniting and Reforming the Church through a Universal Council*, 1410) and Matthew of Crackow were prepared to challenge the claim that Christ had bestowed the supremacy in the Church on Peter.

The Council of Pisa

Ironically, the schism was inadvertently exacerbated by the first council to be called – by the cardinals who had created the problem – to deal with the situation, at Pisa in 1409. The role of the College of Cardinals gives an insight into the nature of conciliar thought (cf. Wilks 1963: 479–81). It was aristocratic, certainly not democratic. The College was seen by some conciliar theorists as the 'weightier part' (*valentior pars*) of the whole body that had been mentioned by Aristotle and taken up by Dante, Marsilius and others. Conciliarists had debated the question: who had the authority to initiate action against an errant pope. Most had looked first to the cardinals; failing that, to the emperor; and in desperate straits, to anyone with the leverage to act. As the remedial constituency was broadened, the bishops and archbishops of national churches began to stake their claim to be more than surrogates of the pope; perhaps collectively to be the corrective to a distorted papacy.

Pisa mustered four patriarchs, twenty-four cardinals, more than eighty archbishops and bishops (with another hundred represented by proxies), a hundred abbots (another two hundred being represented by their proctors), the generals of most religious orders, including the mendicant orders, several hundred theologians and canonists, and representatives of European universities, cathedral chapters and princes.

Mandell Creighton claimed in his history of the papacy in this period that Pisa was an attempt to appeal from the Vicar of Christ on earth to Christ himself, residing in the whole body of the Church (Creighton 1892: I, 200). That is a noble idea, but its time had not quite come: the attempt was rather half-hearted and not fully conciliar. The constitution still revolved around the pope and the cardinals: a way had not yet been found of mobilizing the Church as such.

Far from being the spontaneous movement of the *congregatio fidelium* to restore the theological and practical unity of the *ecclesia*, the Council of Pisa had been from the first conceived as a constitutional process within the church ... the constitutional framework within which the council had to operate was still basically that of 1378, and rather than remedying the defects which the clash between Urban VI and his cardinals had revealed,

the council merely compounded the problem. The Council of Pisa was not revolutionary, it was intended to be fully in line with the established constitutional order (Swanson
1979: 179).

Both rival popes were deposed at Pisa and a third, Alexander V, was elected
– but he was not recognized by the other two. So now there were three
popes. Pisa had failed because it had perpetuated, indeed aggravated the
schism. It is not normally recognized as a General Council (even though
lists of popes have usually included Alexander V, the pope elected at Pisa,
and the next pope called himself Alexander VI). However, Pisa gave
momentum to the growing demand for a council that would be able to
unify the papacy and to reform the Church. It also gave an urgent impetus
to the development of conciliar theology.

Dietrich of Niem

Dietrich of Niem (c. 1340–1418) was a curial official who became a
scathing critic of the papacy he had served (see Jacob 1963: 24–43).
Dietrich's history of the schism and life of Pope John XXIII are vital historical sources. In *De Modis Uniendi et Reformandi Ecclesiae* (written after
the Council of Pisa had deposed the two rival popes and elected another;
translation in Spinka 1953: 149–74) Dietrich laments that there is not one
person left in the Church who will work for the common good in the sacrificial way shown by Christ and the saints.

Dietrich does not identify the Catholic Church with the Roman Church,
but with the universal Church, comprising Greeks and believers beyond the
frontiers of Christendom, as well as Latins. Men and women, peasants and
nobles, poor and rich constitute one body which is the Catholic Church. Its
head is Christ alone: popes, cardinals and prelates, kings and princes,
together with the common people, are members. The pope ought not to be
called the 'head', but the vicar of Christ – yet only, Dietrich adds cryptically,
'while the key does not err'. This Church administers the seven sacraments
for the salvation of the faithful and in its faith everyone can be saved, even
if the papacy were to be absent. This Church retains the power of binding
and loosing, cannot suffer schism or heresy and cannot sin, even though it
could be reduced (as Ockham insisted) to one faithful soul.

The Roman Church is a particular Church, the Apostolic Church and is
made up of all the clergy, from the pope and cardinals to the parish priests.
This Church may indeed suffer schism and heresy and may even fail
(*deficere*). It is included within the Catholic Church but is not the whole of
it. Its authority derives from the Catholic or universal Church. The task
now is to reunite and reform the Roman Church and this responsibility
belongs to all Christians, whether pope or king, priest or peasant. Every
part of the body must act for the common good. All laws (as Thomas

Aquinas had said) are properly promulgated only to this end. The common good is greater than any individual good and is a law that takes precedence over any individual right, including that of the pope and prelates. An evil pope must be quickly deposed because of his power to harm the common good. Citing Marsilius of Padua, Dietrich insists that the pope is a mere man, perhaps the son of a poor peasant, not an angel or a saint. He is subject to the gospel and to the authority of Christ. Therefore the decree that says that the pope is judged by no one is false. All Christians are compelled, under pain of mortal sin, to withdraw their allegiance from the two popes who were deprived by the Council of Pisa.

A General Council is superior in authority to the pope and he is bound to obey it in all things. It can elect, deprive and depose a pope. There is no higher appeal on earth. The powers of a council are inalienable and cannot be transferred or delegated to the pope. The common good of the Church requires that another council be called in succession to Pisa, to complete its work in unifying the papacy and uniting the Church in good laws and practices. A radical flexibility is justified because fresh remedies must be prepared for new diseases.

Henry of Langenstein and Dietrich of Niem provide a link with the spontaneous outbreak of reform in Germany, sparked by Luther more than a century later. Dietrich's treatise on how to unite and reform the Church speaks for the reformist agenda of Germany. It has been called 'the preface to the Reformation' (Jordan 1930: 190). Luther articulated (and capitalized on) the profound German resentment at papal exactions and the pent-up frustration that reform had been thwarted for centuries. The tragedy was that Luther's reform shattered the veneer of unity that the post-Basel papal triumph over the Conciliar Movement had created and widened the split within Christendom.

Pierre d'Ailly

The most notable contribution to conciliar theology in the Pisan period was made by Pierre d'Ailly (1350–1420), theologian of the University of Paris and Bishop of Cambrai. During the earlier period of the schism, D'Ailly had thrown in his lot with Benedict, the 'Francophile' pope, and had enjoyed his favour. In 1406 he risked arrest for refusing to withdraw his allegiance at the command of the king. He remained loyal to the pope until it was clear even to him that there was no hope of healing the schism; then he threw his energies equally wholeheartedly the other way. However, in both his papalist and conciliar phases d'Ailly may be said to have adhered to his dictum: 'No true union without reform and no true reform without union' (*Nec vera unio sine Reformatione nec vera reformatio sine unione*) (Jordan 1930: 142).

As a follower of William of Ockham, d'Ailly borrowed extensively from Ockham's *Dialogues* in his political and ecclesiastical thought. He also borrowed largely from the writings of John of Paris, but no direct influence of Marsilius of Padua is apparent. D'Ailly prefers to define the Church as a *congregatio fidelium*, but he also calls it a *regnum*, a *respublica* and an ecclesiastical polity. The spiritual definition has the edge over the political. It was essential to the conciliarists to continue to think of the Church as a political society. Both papalists and conciliarists worked with the model of the Church as a society that was complete in itself (*societas perfecta* – not 'a morally perfect society' but 'a politically complete' one). A *societas perfecta* is a society that is fully empowered to take responsibility for its affairs and to order its life without depending on outside assistance. Of course the mutual protagonists of the conciliar period interpreted this in very different ways, the one monarchically and hierarchically, the other in a corporate and conciliar way. Christ had perfectly ordained the Church and had left nothing lacking to its integrity as a community. If it were claimed that the principles of political society were not applicable to the Church, it would mean that Christ had founded the Church in an imperfect way. With the scandal of the papal schism and papal abuses in mind, d'Ailly argued that 'a community is not sufficiently ordered if it cannot resist its own ruin and open destruction'.

A nominalist in philosophy, d'Ailly believes that the determinate will of God is expressed in natural law which is accessible to human reason. Reason and natural law tell us that the source of all political authority is the consent of the community and that rulers rule with the consent of the ruled. The right to elect their ruler belongs by natural right 'to all those over whom any authority, secular or ecclesiastical, is placed'. Applying this to the Church, d'Ailly holds that *plenitudo potestatis* belongs ultimately (or as he puts it, causally or finally) to the whole Church as a body and derivatively and representatively to a General Council. He does not altogether deny *plenitudo potestatis* to the pope, to whom it pertains 'in a ministerial way', for it is ordained by God to an end beyond the papacy, that is to say, to the universal Church. So, if the pope abuses his power he is subject to correction by a General Council. The full authority (*potestas jurisdictionis*) inherent in the Church by Christ's institution thus belongs 'separably' to the pope, 'inseparably' to the whole body (*universitas*) of the Church, and 'representatively' to the General Council. The council is the 'image or mirror' of the universal Church and acts 'in its place or name' to reform the papacy. The right to represent the Church in a General Council belongs to those who are pre-eminent in wisdom and influence, though d'Ailly never really explains how a council is representative. It is significant that the authority inherent in the Church is not transferred to the pope when he is elected but is, as it were, delegated to him while remaining latent in the body. At every stage political authority resides within the community and cannot be alienated from it (Oakley 1964).

D'Ailly was absent from Pisa on the business of the council during the two fateful sessions which attempted the deposition of the rival popes. But his *Propositiones utiles* set the agenda for the council. D'Ailly's premise in these propositions was that the unity of the mystical body of the Church depends on its head, Christ, not on the pope. This gives the Church the power to act, in the name of Christ, who promised that where two or three were gathered together in his name he would be present in the midst.

> From Christ, the head, his mystical body which is the Church, originally and immediately has its power and authority, so that in order to conserve its own unity, it rightly has the power of assembling itself or a general council representing it (Oakley 1960 = Crowder 1977: 52).

D'Ailly went on to claim that a General Council could be convened without the pope under certain circumstances: in the event of a vacancy for pope; if the pope were insane or heretical or refused to co-operate with demands for a council; and if there were rival claimants to the papal throne. D'Ailly was also a dominant influence in the early sessions of the Council of Constance (which he regarded as the logical continuation of Pisa), preaching the opening sermon on 2 December 1414. But there his influence was eclipsed by that of his pupil, Jean Gerson.

Jean Gerson's Early Conciliar Thought

Jean Gerson (1363–1429), Chancellor of the University of Paris, was a major influence at Pisa and the dominant theological voice at Constance. For relevant aspects of Gerson's multi-faceted achievement see Morrall 1960, Pascoe 1973 and Ryan 1998. For detailed exposition of Gerson's developing position see Meyjes 1999. Translated texts are available in Spinka, 1953: 140–48; Crowder 1977; Gerson 1985; and O'Donovan and O'Donovan 1999: 517–29.

Gerson turned to conciliar principles comparatively late in his academic career when he realized (c. 1408–1409) that conventional methods of resolving the schism were proving futile. Though his conciliar stance was slow to develop and he was a reluctant convert to the conciliar solution, Gerson's conciliarism was not a pragmatic, political response to an intractable situation: he consistently evinced concerns that were typical of 'apostolic', reforming and renewal movements of the Middle Ages. But ideas that have their provenance in the Conciliar Movement are found in Gerson's thought from an early stage. For him unity was the greatest good. His first extant academic work *Pro Unione Ecclesiae* (1391) argued that doctors shared with bishops in the governance of the Church. After the episcopate, the university enjoyed the greatest authority in matters of faith. Furthermore, a layperson has the right to reprove the pope when he is in error (Gerson had in mind no ordinary layperson, but the King of France). At this stage he sees no realistic possibility of a council.

In 1403 Gerson's Pentecost sermon *Emitte Spiritum Tuum* develops a spiritual and mystical vision of the Church (as opposed to an institutional and canonical one), profoundly influenced by Bonaventure's mystical sense of earthly and heavenly hierarchy. He evokes the Church as the body of Christ on which the Holy Spirit is outpoured. Such a Church obviously has the authority and the power to reform itself and to heal its wounds. A few years later (by 1406) Gerson's emphasis on divine authority and the evangelical law of liberty led him to propose that the canonical provision that papal presidency was necessary for a General Council should be abandoned.

In *De Schismate* (c. 1403) Gerson argued that because Benedict had not yet been deprived of the papal office, nor accused of *pertinacia* (obdurate persistence in schism, tantamount to heresy), no council should be called against him. If the issue was, who was the true pope?, a council was an uncertain solution, since councils were infallible only in matters of faith, not in questions of fact. In other works of this period Gerson protested in vain that, in spite of the schism, it was still possible to live in peace and harmony and that one should not resort to excommunicating those who took a different view of the issue; after all, no one can be sure what is the best course of action. Against the proposal to call a council of one obedience, Gerson insisted that reform was the concern of the whole Church, so the whole Church needed to be involved. Although Gerson had not yet embraced the idea of a General Council, he had accepted a decisive premise of the *via concilii*.

Another plank of the conciliar platform was put in place in Gerson's sermon *Apparuit Gratia Dei*, preached on behalf of the University of Paris, in the presence of Pope Benedict on New Year's Day 1404. Gerson is turning away in despair from the fruitless legalistic, uncompromising approach to establishing who was the true pope. Positive law must give way to natural law (*lex aeterna*), equity (*aequitas*) and humaneness and moderation (*epeiekeia*) in the application of law. Unrelenting legalism will bring the destruction of the Church. Here and elsewhere Gerson attacks the dominant juridical way of thinking, promoted by the canonists, and the uncritical and excessive use of appeal to divine law or revelation (*ius divinum*) which is properly concerned only with matters of salvation, combined with the tendency to make positive law omnicompetent and all-embracing. Canon law should be subject to theology. The goal of every ecclesiastical polity and of the laws that support it is the God-given peace that brings salvation. The authority of the hierarchy exists to maintain that peace. There is an appeal to the whole (hierarchical) body of the Church and for a harmonious division and distribution of responsibilities throughout the episcopate. The question of how to resolve the schism is not a matter of salvation. The Church is fallible when it comes to adjudicating on facts. It is possible to be uncertain who are the actual schismatics in this case. The combined duration and distress of the schism were forcing Gerson to seek a solution outside of the existing provisions of Church law. He was beginning to realize that the schism was not simply an unfortunate, fortuitous event, but evidence that the structures of the Church were deeply flawed. If the hierarchy had tackled the abuses, the schism would not have happened. It is a judgement on the corruptions of the Church.

In works written immediately prior to Pisa and in preparation for it Gerson advocated exclusively the *via concilii*. At this stage we have the first clear references to Henry of Langenstein and Conrad of Gelnhausen, the earliest explicit advocates of the conciliar solution. In *De Auctoritate Concilii* (1408–9) Gerson considers the circumstances in which the whole Church can call a General Council without the authority of the pope. Both the whole mystical body of the Church and its hierarchical structure have been instituted by Christ. The Church therefore comprises a *congregatio authentica*. The episcopate corporately will not fall into heresy. A General Council is infallible on faith questions. A council is the assembled Church and as the Vicar of Christ has full authority, even to depose both popes. Gerson does not go as far as to claim that a General Council has ordinary jurisdiction over the pope(s), but only the right to subject the legal titles of the rivals to scrutiny.

Gerson's address to the English delegation en route to the Council of Pisa contains in embryo a number of his conciliar principles (for what follows, Gerson 1985). Whereas Christ's intention was to gather into one the children of God who were scattered abroad (John 11.52), we now see a Church turned by schism into an appalling two-headed monster. However, a potentiality for self-preservation and renewal, 'an infinite fruitfulness', lies within the whole body of the Church. The Church will not be left by God to dwindle to laypeople, or even (as Ockham speculated) to a solitary woman; there will be faithful bishops and priests until the end of time. These orders, successors of the Apostles, derive from the primitive Church, where they were sown by Christ as the seed of the hierarchical Church that developed later. The pope does not have the power to abolish them.

The key to right judgement in the situation lies not in a legalistic approach, which is sensual and unspiritual, but in the application of *epieikeia*, equitable interpretation. *Epieikeia* points to following the *via concilii*.

Although the Church does not have the power either to institute the papacy or to abolish it, it can vary the method of appointment to the papacy and can remove and replace a pope. With good reason the Church can convene in General Council without the presence of the pope and without his authority. This is clear, not only from the Acts of the Apostles but also from the principle of association which we see commonly at work in civil society. If the Church were ultimately dependent on the permission of the pope in order to act to deal with a threat, its very existence could be put in jeopardy. The see of Peter could be vacant; a pope could be insane, heretical or depraved in his behaviour; he could lose the obedience of the faithful. In such circumstances the whole Church, by virtue of the divine seed diffused throughout its whole body, must be free to act.

Gerson's *Tractate on the Unity of the Church* (1409) is replete with appeals to natural law and exhortations to seek the common good (Spinka 1953: 140–48). Arguments based merely on positive law – such as: a council can be called only by the pope – must give way to divine and natural law which tend purely to the common good of the Church. No human laws can prevent the Church assembling in a representative manner to restore her visible unity under one undisputed vicar of Christ. 'For the mystical body of the Church, perfectly established in Christ, has, no less than any civil, mystical, or truly natural body, the right and the power to procure its own union' (Spinka, ed. 1953: 142). Since a pope may die or fall into heresy at any time, the life of the Church cannot be suspended for lack of a true pope. The well-being of the whole is supreme: natural law dictates that the part should surrender its interests for the sake of the whole. Guided by divine and natural law, a council will not be afraid to tackle the disunity of the Church. Its remedy will be shaped by equity and *epieikeia*, the power to interpret, adapt and if necessary abandon positive laws.

Gerson and the Council of Pisa

Before the Council of Pisa (at which he was not present) Gerson had argued for caution, patience and moderation. He drew comparisons with the events that came to a head in 1054, the decisive separation between West and East. At that time, he believed, the Latins had raised the stakes unnecessarily by making controversial points into dogma. If the issue had been left as a dispute about the power of the pope, eventual agreement might have been possible. But now the schism of East from West was irreparable, for each side had condemned the other as heretical. Therefore, Gerson concluded, the Church should take doctrinal decisions only when absolutely necessary.

The convoking in 1409 of the Council of Pisa, in which his master d'Ailly played a leading role, stimulated Gerson to produce a spate of writings that directly addressed the question of the schism and the conciliar response. He offered a detailed agenda for church reform, from the papacy to parish level. Charity and unity were the imperatives, not the observance of ecclesiastical law. Theologians, not church officials, were the best people to decide on the solution to the schism. Divine, biblical law was identical with natural law and enshrined the principle of *epieikeia*, justice applied with humanity and flexibility. Ecclesiastical law could not bind the conscience and breaching it was not a mortal sin. Only the evangelical law found in Scripture could bind the conscience of the faithful. Gerson stands with

Ockham and Luther in his stress on evangelical liberty. This emphasis on the evangelical law of liberty led to Gerson's being somewhat disillusioned by the legalism that was prevalent at Constance.

During the Council, particularly in *De auferibilitate sponsi ab ecclesia* (literally, of the taking away of the betrothed – or perhaps bridegroom – from the Church; cf. Matthew 9.14–15; Mark 2.18–20; Luke 5.33–35), Gerson began, from a distance, to bolster the council to exert its authority, just as he would do at Constance (Meyjes 1999: 166–68). The Church has the promise of the Spirit and will receive his *influxus* from above in time of need. The Church lacks nothing to provide for its well-being. It is a *societas perfecta*, a complete society: it will always continue in its integrity and in the completeness of its members (*Manebit ergo semper ecclesia cum suorum integritate et perfectione membrorum*). Taking issue with Ockham's speculation that the Church could be reduced to a single woman, Gerson insists that the Church could not even be reduced to all women, or even to laymen, because that would deprive her of the hierarchy and therefore of the sacraments. A pope may be deposed in several circumstances: if he is a prisoner among the heathen and there is no hope of his release; if he becomes insane; if all the cardinals should be wiped out after the canonical election in conclave, but before the result has been made known to the Church; if the Greeks (the Eastern Churches) were prepared to accept reunion under a new pope; if a pope refuses to carry out the terms of his electoral oath. As far as the present circumstances were concerned, the Church has the inherent power to depose two rival claimants to the papal throne who are accused by good and serious men of schism, perjury and possibly heresy.

Chapter 7

THE UNIFICATION OF THE CHURCH AND THE COUNCIL OF CONSTANCE

The Council of Constance

It was Alexander V's successor in the official line, the criminally minded John XXIII (he is not counted in the official list of popes, which is why there was a notable Pope John XXIII in the twentieth century) who, under pressure from the emperor, Sigismund of Hungary, called the Council of Constance in 1414. This time the council had firm imperial support which proved decisive. John XXIII's plan to triumph at the council by exploiting the huge numerical preponderance of Italian bishops was scuppered when the council decided to organize itself into five 'nations' (that is to say, combinations of nationalities), each with a single vote. John believed that he would undermine the legitimacy of the council by prudently withdrawing, but in the event the council, inspired by Gerson, rose above this setback and articulated the doctrine of the ultimate superiority of a council to a pope.

The council's purpose was threefold: to restore the unity of the Church by unifying the papacy, now split three ways; to purge the Church of erroneous doctrine by dealing with the 'heresies' of Wyclif in England and Hus in Bohemia; and to reform the Church 'in head and members' (that is to say, starting with the papacy and the hierarchy). The council succeeded in the first task by deposing the three rival popes (John XXIII being arrested, tried and condemned for the crimes of perjury, simony, etc., not – significantly – for heresy or schism) and electing another pope whose claim was virtually undisputed. It did indeed condemn Wyclif and it executed Hus. Texts of the Council of Constance are most conveniently available in Latin and in facing English translation in Tanner 1990: I.

Gerson at Constance

The Council of Constance was stiffened in its resolve by Gerson's sermon *Ambulate* of 1415 after John XXIII had fled the council and a number of the envoys considered that this had *ipso facto* dissolved the council. Appealing to the text 'Walk while you have the light, lest darkness come upon you' (John 12.35), Gerson spurred the council to action – to defeat 'the darkness of divisions and schism, the darkness of so many errors and heresies ... the horrible darkness of so many vices that pour out of the Church's wretched body on a limitless tide' (Crowder 1977: 77). Gerson, who had been taught by d'Ailly, then asserted the authority of a General Council over the pope:

> The Church, or a general council representing it, is so regulated by the direction of the Holy Spirit under authority from Christ that everyone, of whatsoever rank, even papal, is obliged to hearken to and obey it (Crowder 1977: 81).

Gerson went on to give what has become a classical definition of the conciliar ideal:

> A general council is an assembly called under lawful authority, at any place, drawn from every hierarchical rank of the whole catholic Church, none of the faithful who requires to be heard being excluded, for the wholesome discussion and ordering of those things which affect the proper regulation of the same Church in faith and morals (Crowder 1977: 81).

Gerson avoided the extreme anti-papalism that would become characteristic of conciliarism in its next phase, at the Council of Basel. He did not condemn the church's enjoyment of temporal possessions nor its authority in temporal matters – provided that these had been bestowed, as a matter of human law, by the civil rulers themselves – and he did not deny *plenitudo potestatis* to the papacy, for it had been bestowed by Christ 'supernaturally', yet solely for building up the Church. Yet a council could limit and restrain the use of papal authority, ensuring that it was exercised constitutionally, in accordance with the laws of the Church and for the edification of all. Gerson distinguished between passing incumbents of the seat of Peter and the institution of the papacy itself (*Papa fluit, papatus stabilis est*) and this enabled him to argue that though the place of the papacy in the ecclesiastical constitution remained secure, a General Council, as representative of the whole Church, could intervene to remove an individual pope (Ryan 1998: 168).

Gerson produced one of the most balanced and comprehensive treatments of conciliar theology in his treatise on Church authority (*De Potestate Ecclesiae*, 1416–18), presented to the Council of Constance (see Meyjes 1999: 247–86). It was Gerson's view, following his master Pierre d'Ailly, that the Church has the authority to convene in General Council in certain specific circumstances: (a) when there is no pope; (b) when the pope is heretical, insane or captive; or (c) when the pope contumaciously refuses to call a council after sufficient requests. A General Council was superior to the sole power of the pope in every way, claimed Gerson: 'in vastness of extension, in infallible guidance, in reformation of morals in head and members, in coercive power, in final decision on difficulties with regard to matters of faith; greater finally because more numerous; for it embraces at least virtually every kind of authority and every political regime'. Power of jurisdiction is granted directly by God to the (hierarchical) Church as a totality and thus to a General Council. As Augustine had said: 'The keys of the Church were given to the whole Church' (*claves Ecclesiae datae sunt unitati*). The pope should make use of the *plenitudo potestatis* only when lower levels of the hierarchy failed. Gerson thus made a General Council part of the permanent governmental machinery of the Church.

Following Gerson's lead, the Council of Constance claimed in the historic decree *Haec Sancta* (6 April 1415) that the authority of the whole Church – to which not even the pope was superior – resided in a General Council:

> This holy synod, constituting the general council of Constance, for the purpose of erad-icating the present schism and of bringing about the union and reform of the Church of God in head and in members, lawfully assembled in the Holy Spirit, to the praise of Almighty God, ordains, defines, enacts, decrees and declares as follows ... that lawfully assembled in the Holy Spirit, constituting a general council and representing the catholic Church militant, it holds power directly from Christ; and that everyone of whatever estate or dignity he be, even papal, is obliged to obey it in those things which belong to the faith and to the eradication of the said schism and to the general reform of the said Church of God in head and members (Crowder 1977: 83; Latin text in Alberigo *et al.* 1962: 385-87).

In this decree, stated Gerson, the council 'has liberated the Church from this pestiferous and most pernicious doctrine [i.e. that of papal absolute monarchy], the continuance of which would have led to the persistence of the schism which it had nurtured. For it has of course been declared and decreed that a General Council can be convoked without the pope and that in certain cases the pope can be judged by the Council.' Even discounting the rhetoric, Gerson was right. It was widely held that persistence in schism constituted heresy and that an heretical pope could be deposed by a council. Had not all three popes shown themselves 'heretical' by refusing to heal the schism?

Zabarella at Constance

Cardinal Zabarella (1360–1417) was among the greatest and weightiest of the scholars gathered at Constance. On Zabarella see Ullmann 1972b: 191–231; Tierney 1955: 220–37; Morrisey 1973, 1978, 1981; Swanson 1979: 151–53. Zabarella opposed *Haec Sancta* in its earlier drafts, but was instrumental in stripping the text of extraneous anti-papal rhetoric and in giving legal precision to the final version. It was canonical orthodoxy that a General Council was superior to a pope in matters of faith and that is why an heretical pope could be deposed by a council. Zabarella, who had grown up under the schism and knew from experience its dire effects, regarded the schism itself as a matter touching the faith. Zabarella had worked cautiously but tenaciously at the problem of the schism since early in the century. His *De Schismate* (1402–1408) set out his proposals for dealing with the schism. It collated all the conciliar elements in the canonical glosses of the preceding two centuries, 'fusing together in one system of thought ideas which had formerly seemed unconnected or even incompatible' (Tierney 1955: 220). Although he had been awarded a cardinal's hat by John XXIII, Zabarella remained at Constance when John fled the council.

Zabarella elaborated constitutional constraints on papal authority (first the episcopate as such, then the College of Cardinals within the episcopate, finally a General Council quite broadly constituted), to seek to ensure that the papacy served the common good or well-being of the Church (*status ecclesiae*). He criticized the late-mediaeval papacy for aggregating authority to itself and for over-riding the rights and authority of lower prelates. Bishops received only the conditions of their episcopal authority from the pope, not that authority itself. The keys were given to Peter within the college of the Apostles. The pope should act on the advice of the cardinals whose rights and roles should be safeguarded.

Zabarella was no populist, however; responsibility to take action lay with duly constituted authority, structured hierarchically. First it rested with the cardinals, who should excommunicate an heretical pope. Second, it lay with a council, convened by the cardinals. Third, if cardinals and council proved impotent, responsibility reverted to the emperor who should step in. But, fourth, *in extremis* any competent party could act. When a General Council was convened it should have wide and effective representation: cardinals, bishops and other prelates (abbots), clergy, judges, theologians and lawyers, eminent laypeople. A council without the pope lacked the authority of a council with the pope, but ultimately a council was superior to the pope. The pope held *plenitudo potestatis* on behalf of the whole body of the Church: it was a limited and derivative authority accorded to the head by the members. Zabarella realized probably more clearly than other conciliarists that the key to resolving the situation was to find a way of giving legal effect to the mystical unity of the *congregatio fidelium*.

The Contested Status of Haec Sancta

In all probability there was no true pope at the time that *Haec Sancta* was enacted. As Tierney has pointed out, if there was one, it was quite impossible for contemporaries – as it is for us – to tell which of three it was. The only possible way out of the impasse of a three-headed papacy was for some qualified body to credibly assert jurisdiction over all three claimants. 'The historical event which broke the deadlock of the Great Schism and made possible the restoration of a legitimate papacy was the enactment of *Haec Sancta*' (Tierney 1969: 361).

It was this decree *Haec Sancta* that Figgis described rather excitedly as 'probably the most revolutionary official document in the history of the world', because it attempted to restrain by constitutional consent the virtually untramelled divine authority of centuries (Figgis 1916: 31). Interestingly, Gerson insisted that *Haec Sancta* was not derived from the canonical tradition but from higher authority, being grounded in the nature of the gospel and of the Church: it enshrined an evangelical and ecclesial principle (Ryan 1998: 61). This was tantamount to making it an expression of divine law.

Constance took measures to consolidate its achievement. *Haec Sancta* was followed in 1417 by the decree *Frequens* which prescribed that General Councils should be convened at least every ten years – which was tantamount to setting up an ecclesiastical parliament to regulate the life of the Church and to exercise a continual curb on the power of the papacy (text of *Frequens* in Crowder 1977: 128–29; Latin text in Alberigo *et al.* 1962: 414–16).

There is no question that Constance was a General Council (that is to say, a General Council of the Western Church; the Eastern Churches do not accept any councils subsequent to the schism of 1054 and good practice is to distinguish between Ecumenical Councils prior to that schism and General Councils of the West subsequent to it). However, the canonical status of the various decrees of Constance are disputed (in addition to authors cited immediately below, see the discussion in Oakley 2003: 81–99, 252–60). Only those decrees later ratified by Martin V, the undisputed legitimate pope, count officially as conciliar. Therefore Denzinger, the definitive digest of official Roman Catholic teaching, does not include Constance's decisions about conciliarity itself, only its condemnations of Wyclif and Hus (DS 315–25). However, the whole point of *Haec Sancta* was that it was so framed as not to require papal ratification. Küng argues strongly for the binding authority of *Haec Sancta* (Küng 1964: 240–58), but Tierney points out that the decree does not meet some of the usual criteria for irreformability: it is not cast in the form of a dogmatic definition; it is not concerned with faith and morals; and it does not carry anathemas (Tierney 1969: 363). If *Haec Sancta* is binding, is *Frequens*? Is anyone seriously suggesting that a General Council should be held every ten years? The significance of the decree, Tierney suggests, is not that it legislates for all future councils – it clearly has in mind the present emergency and once normality had been restored the pope would be an integral part (to put it at its lowest) of any council – but that it effectively vetoes the more extreme late mediaeval claims for papal power. As Tierney says: 'If *Haec Sancta* had not been enacted, the Great Schism could not have been ended; *Haec Sancta* could not have been licitly enacted if the more extreme mediaeval theories of papal power were valid' (Tierney 1969: 365).

However, there is rather more to the question than that. If *Haec Sancta* was not an authentic conciliar decree, Martin's incumbency of the papal throne was not secure. Yet the line of popes since then stems from him. In deposing John XXIII the Council treated him as the true pope, as did Martin's own papal registers (Oakley 2003: 86–87). And if *Haec Sancta* was an authentic conciliar decree, why was *Frequens* not so? The Roman Catholic theologian George Tavard has stated the issue nicely:

> One cannot deny that the unified papacy as it was restored in 1417 was grounded in the principles of conciliarism [the superiority of a General Council to the pope] ... Pope Martin V's legitimacy depended precisely on the legitimacy of the council of Constance and its decrees. The later condemnation of conciliarism that was implicit in the definition of papal infallibility in 1870 was itself made possible, historically, by conciliarism. The Roman Catholic Church is, therefore, in the paradoxical situation that its most specific doctrine, the definition of papal infallibility, presupposes – not doctrinally but historically – its opposite, the superiority of the council over the bishop of Rome. Papalism presupposes conciliarism (Tavard 1992: 109).

From whatever angle we consider it – even if we concede for the sake of argument Jedin's claim that *Haec Sancta* was an emergency measure to deal with particular circumstances – the General Council of Constance intended to establish the principle of the ultimate superiority of a General Council over a pope.

Assessment of Constance

The Council of Constance lasted three and a half years (for contemporary accounts see Loomis 1961). It was a vast and momentous occasion for mediaeval Europe: 100,000 people had descended on one small city. At its height the membership of the council included five patriarchs, thirty-three cardinals, forty-seven archbishops, 145 bishops, ninety-three suffragan bishops, 132 abbots, 155 priors, 217 doctors of theology, 361 doctors of canon and/or civil law – not to mention more than 5,000 other priests and scholars. Ullmann said of Constance that it represented 'the decisive victory of conciliarism and the utter and most convincing defeat of the papal-hierocratic system' (Ullmann 1972b: 299).

The condemnation of Wyclif's heresies (he had died in 1384) was the vehicle for the condemnation of Jan Hus. Wyclif's indictment included his claim that the Emperor Constantine and Pope Sylvester had 'erred' in making the 'donation' of the western Roman empire to the pope (Constance still accepted the authenticity of the 'Donation'). The first doctrine condemned in the list of heresies attributed to Hus was the identification of the Church as the body of the predestined (*Unita est sancta Universalis ecclesiae, quae est praedestinatorum universitas*). Though this is a characteristic Wyclifian teaching, he was not condemned for it. Hus retorted that this was the teaching of St Augustine, thus implying that the Council was also condemning a Church Father and Doctor (Tatnall in Cuming and Baker 1971).

However, while Constance succeeded in unifying the papacy and in condemning the 'heresies' of Wyclif and Hus, it failed to make more than trivial reforms in the administration of the Church (for an account that plays up the success of the reforms see Stump 1994). The Council was split over priorities: the Emperor Sigismund, together with the German and English 'nations' at the Council, wanted to tackle reform first and only then to proceed to elect a new pope; the cardinals, with the support of the Italian, French and Spanish 'nations', were concerned to put the unity of the Church first, to chose a new pope and then to implement reform (Gill in Cuming and Baker 1971: 186). The latter agenda prevailed. Mandell Creighton commented on the failure to effect reform:

> During the abeyance of the papacy, while Europe was smarting under the exactions which the maintenance of two papal courts had involved, while everyone had before his eyes the ruin wrought in the ecclesiastical system by papal usurpations, a splendid opportunity was offered for a temperate and conservative reformation. The collective wisdom of Europe after nearly four years' labour and discussion was found unequal to the task (Creighton 1892: I, 418).

Chapter 8

THE ECLIPSE OF CONCILIARISM AND THE COUNCIL OF BASEL

The Shaping of the Council

The Council of Constance had decreed that General Councils were to be held at least every ten years. So in 1431 Pope Eugenius IV was reluctantly compelled to convoke a council at Basel (Basle), which had been first called by his immediate predecessor Martin V. Martin had mandated the council to reform the clergy and the entire ecclesiastical estate, as well as to lead back the Eastern Church to the fold and to extirpate the Bohemian and other heresies. The council (1431–49) was buoyed up by enormous expectations of reform that were doomed to be disappointed. 'All hopes for the renewal of the church devolved upon the Council of Basel. The reform legislation which was subsequently enacted at Basel ... constituted the fulfilment of the hopes for church reform which had originally centred on the Council of Constance' (Stieber 1978: 11).

If Pope Eugenius could suceeded in dissolving the council on his own authority or transferring it to Florence, he would thereby negate the provisions of *Haec Sancta* and *Frequens* which provided that a council could be transferred or dissolved only on its own authority. In effect, Eugenius treated the council as though Constance had never happened, while in return the council studiously ignored his fulminations (Stieber 1978: 13–15, 19). His attempt to dissolve it before it had begun and, when this failed, to undermine its authority by purporting to transfer it to Florence, polarized opinion and drove conciliarists either to a constitutional extreme, which aimed to neutralize in practice the power of the papacy, or firmly back into the papal fold.

Eugenius went on the offensive against the council. In June 1436 he issued his *libellus apologeticus* in which he defended his conduct and denounced the council, attacking it particularly for renewing the Council of Constance's decrees *Haec Sancta* (even though the legitimacy of his title to the papal throne depended on that decree, which was the ground for the reunification of the papacy) and *Frequens*. Eugenius attempted to portray the reformist programme as the revolt of the inferior clergy (who were dominant at certain stages of the council) against their rightful lord, the pope, and as therefore constituting a sinister precedent for the rebellion of subjects against their kings. Eugenius asked pointedly, 'Why do they hasten to bring down this monarchy [the papacy], which God established by his own word, to a popular state and to a democracy?' (Stieber 1978: 27–34).

Basel was the most radical of the fifteenth-century reforming councils. Where Constance had been divided into nations (a move intended to curtail severely the dominance of the numerous Italian bishops and which had given the English a disproportionate influence), Basel had a committee or 'deputation' structure, with a number of consortia working on issues of faith, reform, peace in the Church, and 'common matters' (a step intended to curtail the dominance of the higher clergy as a whole over the 'inferior' clergy). In a provocative move, motivated by hostility to Eugenius' manoeuvrings, the council attempted to reform the curia and to replicate in itself the entire structure of papal administration and justice – hearing appeals and issuing bulls. It assumed the authority to issue a plenary indulgence. The council now saw itself as no mere emergency measure but as the ordinary way of governing the Church (though, as Stieber stresses, not at the expense of the judicial supremacy of the pope: Stieber 1978: 52–56, 346).

Remarkably, Basel permitted the Hussites to participate and to speak and gave them permission to practise communion in both kinds (a decision condemned by Eugenius). The council, bolstered by no less than the papal legate Cesarini, decreed that it could not be dissolved except by itself. It laid down that every pope would have to swear an oath of office to bind himself to observe the decrees of Constance and Basel and not to make any major changes without the written consent of the College of Cardinals. The sacred college was to be limited to twenty-four, none of whom was to be related to the reigning pope, and not more than one-third of whom were to be from any one nation. New cardinals would have to be approved by the majority of the existing college (Stieber 1978: 33). Here was a blatant challenge of oligarchy to monarchy.

Nicholas of Cusa

The outstanding figure at Basel was undoubtedly Nicholas of Cusa (Cusanus) and his *Catholic Concordance* was the outstanding conciliar document of the age. Text: Nicholas of Cusa 1991. Studies: Sigmund 1963; Watanabe 1963 and see further below on particular points. He was a member of the deputation *pro fide* which had the task of examining the points of contention with the Hussites. Nicholas addressed these issues in his *Episolae Bohemos*.

In *The Catholic Concordance*, written in 1433, Nicholas offered what is probably the most complete exposition of conciliar theology (Nicholas of Cusa 1991: references are by page number hereinafter, except when large tracts of text are indicated by section). Augustine is the most quoted author; Hugh of St Victor, Bonaventure, Raymond Lull and Jean Gerson are also significant authorities. The ideas of sacred hierarchy are shaped by the Neo-platonist Proclus and by Pseudo-Dionysius. In tension with these ideas are Aristotelian ideas of participation and consent ('What concerns all ...') mediated directly to Nicholas by Marsilius of Padua who, however, is not acknowledged as the source (Watanabe 1963: 58; Sigmund 1962). Nicholas's theme is concord, harmony, order, agreement, and he insists that this can only come about when all individuals and groups recognize the scope and limits of their power and subordinate it to the common good, according to laws that are in keeping with natural law.

Cusanus begins with an elaborate outline of the hierarchical structure of the cosmos and the Church. All rational creatures – angels and men – are set in hierarchical gradations. The Church itself is 'a concordance of all rational spirits united in sweet harmony in Christ ... who is the spouse of the Church'. The Church exists in three forms: triumphant in heaven, sleeping in purgatory, and militant on earth, and each is divided into three 'choirs'. Particular guardian angels watch over the *cathedra* – the ruling and teaching authority – of the Church. In the present time of distress Christ will come on the clouds of heaven to the Church. Cusanus breaks out into fervent prayer:

> O God, if only we could lift up our heads at this time and see that our redemption is at hand, for we see that the Church has never fallen as low as it now is. God grant that his elect may meet in the holy synod of Basel, and gathered there amid such adversity and perplexity, may manifest the coming of his majesty in the heavens (36–37).

Cusanus upholds the supreme authority of the pope but he interprets this in a collegial sense. When Christ promised Peter that the gates of hell would not prevail against the Church, Peter was representative of the Church. The unity of the *cathedra* is Cusanus's uncompromising presupposition. The angel given to a church is not assigned to one that is not in union with the chair of Peter. All Christians must be united to the chair of Peter. That chair signifies 'the power to rule the Church'. It is shared by the patriarchs of Alexandria and Antioch 'and all the subordinate bishops along with them', though the bishop of Rome is highest (38–40).

The pope enjoys the primacy in order to articulate decisions on matters of faith, but in this he is subject to the council of the Church, which cannot itself define a matter of faith without considering the pope's views. On matters of faith the pope, with his patriarchal council, cannot err. The distinctive characteristic of a synod is concord: 'those who disagree among themselves do not form a council'. A council cannot ordinarily be held without the pope and is incomplete without the other four patriarchal sees. All those present at a council should be able to state their views freely and in public. 'If anything is then defined by general agreement it is considered to be inspired by the Holy Spirit and infallibly decided by Christ who is present among those gathered in his name.' As Cusanus rather oddly puts

it: 'the greater the agreement, the more infallible the judgement' (43–69) –
as though there could be degrees of infallibility.

Cusanus then moves on to state the fundamental principle underlying his
theory of the authority of pope and council: that of consent expressed by
election. The authority of a council – and of the pope in the context of the
council – stems not from hierarchical power descending from above, but
from consent emerging from below: 'The authority of councils does not
depend on its head but on the common consent of all.' When the pope
defines and legislates for the Church he does so on the grounds, not merely
of the advice, but of the consent of the faithful. Here Cusanus is applying
to ecclesiastical structures a general principle that he takes to be self-
evident. No law has force until it is accepted into usage: 'The force of a law
comes from the concordance of the subjects who are bound by it.' 'All legislation is based on natural law. Since by nature we are all equally free, all
coercive power is derived from the election and consent of the subjects.'
'The binding force of every law consists in concord or tacit consent.'
Consent expressed through election is a 'spiritual marriage'. 'All power,
whether spiritual or temporal and corporeal, is potentially in the people' –
though it still needs to be activated from above for that is its ultimate
source (76, 82–83, 86, 98, 101, 124, 128). However, Nicholas's understanding of consent is not that of popular democratic rights, but that of the
harmonious acceptance of God's will as revealed by the Holy Spirit.
Consent is in accordance with natural law and is not in conflict with hierarchical unity (Watanabe 1963: 46–48, 187).

How does this position leave the power of the papacy? In the *Catholic
Concordance* Cusanus denies the pope *plenitudo potestatis* and immediate
universal jurisdiction: he is not the universal bishop but the first among and
in a sense above his equals. A province can provide for its needs without
the pope. He is superior in jurisdiction to all synods except a universal
council. The decrees of a council need the approval of the pope even
though the council's authority is not dependent on the pope. There is no
doubt, Cusanus maintains, that a truly representative universal council 'is
over the patriarchs and the Roman pontiff' (88, 97, 102, 104, 111). In his
thought, the power of rulers, both spiritual and temporal, is constrained by
the supremacy of law (ultimately natural law) and the consent of the
governed. In this sense Cusanus is a constitutional thinker. He fuses
together the theological vision of mystical unity and the political and legal
concept of the corporation (Watanabe 1963: 59, 71).

A council would not wish to deprive the papacy of those privileges that
have been granted by earlier councils, but would act simply to correct
abuses:

> But because those who sit in that see are human beings subject to error and sin, and espe-
> cially because at present – with the world moving towards its end and evil on the increase
> – they abuse their power, using what was granted for the building up [of the Church] to

destroy it, who of sound mind can doubt that without any diminution of the true power and privilege of that see the universal council has power both over abuses and over the one who commits them ....? A univeral council that represents the Catholic Church has power directly from Christ and is in every respect over both the pope and the apostolic See (113, punctuation altered).

The pope can be judged by the council for heresy and other faults such as negligence. Infallibility resides primarily in the whole Church and the pope is on safe ground when he articulates the mind of the Church. 'The more certainly and truly that synod represents the Church, the more its judgement tends towards infallibility rather than fallibility ... this judgement is always better than the individual judgement of the Roman pontiff who represents the Church in a very uncertain way (*confusissime*) ... Hence the individual judgement of a pope should be presumed to be less stable and more fallible than that of the pope along with others' (116, 118, 121).

What does Nicholas of Cusa have to say about the role of the laity in councils? All 'qualified learned churchmen' – laymen or clerics – should be involved in decision-making for the good of the whole Church. Since laity (presumably rulers) have to witness the decrees of a council by their signa- tures, they are entitled to a say in how the proceedings are conducted (106–107). The emperor is the pre-eminent layman, the vicar of Christ and defender of the faith, and should certainly address the council. (Nicholas believed that the Donation of Constantine was apocryphal, not for literary- critical reasons, but because the emperor is not dependent on the pope in the way postulated by the Donation; political authority is natural, original and independent: Watanabe 1963: 97–114.) Otherwise, if canonical matters are being discussed, laymen should be present only when invited and princes may merely listen in to matters of clerical concern – though any layman accused before the council of a crime must have the right to defend himself (Bk III, chs 5, 7, 8). Clearly Cusanus limits the influence of the laity on the substance of conciliar debate, but in giving them a presence as witnesses he pre-empts any clerical monopoly of councils.

Cusanus Changes Sides

The Catholic Concordance remains the grandest expression of conciliar theology, but Nicholas did not remain wedded to its principles. Disillusioned with the Council of Basel, he switched sides to support Eugenius IV. For Cusanus a General Council, by definition, was marked by the virtues of harmony, concord and unanimity. The personal rivalries, quarrels and even violence that marked the Council of Basel – exacerbated by its attack on the papacy, when it sought to arrogate the latter's powers to itself and to depose the single universally acknowledged pope – discredited

Basel in Nicholas's eyes. It could not longer be regarded as a true council. While the council was becoming ever more extreme and divided, the pope was concluding an agreement with the Greeks for the reunification of the Church. By their fruits you shall know them. Nicholas's love of classical literature may also have played a part. The works of ancient authors had been preserved in the East; the pope was wooing the Greeks; therefore the pope was proving himself the patron and guardian of humanist learning. The humanist Ambrose Traversari no doubt appealed to Nicholas's humanist sympathies in trying to persuade him to support Eugenius.

The motives for Cusanus's *volte face* remain mysterious; he did not reveal his mind. Some scholars have postulated a crisis of identity, a conversion experience and a reorientation of thought. Others have suggested, more plausibly in my opinion, that Cusanus remained consistent in his principles but, in the light of his experience at Basel, drew different conclusions from them about the well-being of the Church. The centre of gravity of his ecclesiology shifted from the dispersed expressions of the whole Church, which came together in a council, to the unified representation of the whole, the pope. His Platonic realism enabled him to see the pope as the representative or embodiment of the *ecclesia*. Acton pointed out that Cusanus well knew that the Greeks would not accept the developed system of papal monarchy and that, if Eugenius really wanted an agreement, one that would hold, he would have to compromise on issues of authority: no doubt he saw this as an opportunity to bring the pope round to his own views. Because Cusanus never had an intention of abandoning the papal primacy, he could assent to the decrees of the Council of Florence, but he did not thereby renounce his principle, enunciated in the *Catholic Concordance*, of the ultimate supremacy of a General Council over a pope (Acton 1952: 249; Parker 1965: 139; cf. Sigmund 1963: 227–35; Watanabe 1972; Bieckler 1975; McDermott 1998).

Nicholas now begins a progressive retraction of his conciliar views in his post-Basel writings. In theory, a unanimous council remains superior to an erring pope, but 'where any part of the council adheres to the Roman pontiff, even if a much greater part opposes him, that part united to the pope makes up the Church, and hence the council'. The pope is now designated the head (*caput*) of the Church and council. The pope together with the cardinals constitute the infallible apostolic see (*sedes apostolica*). All power in the Church stems from the pope as head of the hierarchy and is distributed to the Church through him. Nicholas even reverts to that ancient crux the *plenitudo potestatis*: it gives the pope power to transfer a council and power over a council. Sigmund comments: 'The *plenitudo potestatis*, which he earlier would grant only to the whole Church, now inheres in the pope as the source and the fulfilment of all power in the Church hierarchy' (Sigmund 1963: 270). Although Nicholas of Cusa had become, to all practical intents and purposes, an exponent of papal monarchy, he had not lost his desire for reform; the publication of his

Reformatio Generalis in 1459 signalled this continuing concern.

The Post-Basel Eclipse of Conciliarism

Mandell Creighton commented that 'the Council of Basel asserted against a legitimate pope, who was universally recognized, the superiority of a General Council against the papacy' (Creighton 1892: II, 71). In the Pragmatic Sanction of Bourges, France gave twenty-four decrees of Basel the status of law (though it did not endorse the council's suspension of Eugenius) and the German Electors did similarly in the *Acceptatio* of Mainz. Thus they gave impetus to the conciliar tradition by re-affirming *Haec Sancta* and *Frequens*. As Jedin points out, the two most powerful nations of Christendom were willing to regulate their ecclesiastical affairs without reference to the pope (Jedin 1957: I, 20). But in spite of defining the proposition 'the General Council is above the Pope' as a dogma of the Catholic Faith, the council failed in its bid for a power *de facto* greater than that of the pope. Cusanus and other eminent figures, including Cesarini, defected to the papal side. Eugenius trumped the Council of Basel by calling a rival council at Ferrara and then Florence, which achieved the propaganda coup of the putative reconciliation of the Eastern Churches in return for illusory western promises of protection against the Turks.

The council fathers who remained at Basel purported to suspend and then to depose the pope as a heretic and to elect an antipope. These actions – mimicking the blunder of the cardinals in 1378 and the botched attempt at Pisa to unify the papacy, and so effectively renewing the dreaded schism – discredited the council which steadily lost the support of the participating nations to Eugenius. Since the princes won certain prerogatives in return for their support, it could be said that the chief beneficiary of this turn of events was the incipient modern state (so Jedin 1957: I, 21) – but it was the state over against the Church. Eugenius' concessions inflicted long-term and irremediable damage on papal sovereignty. They played into the royal and episcopal claims that had been asserted for centuries and fed the sources of Gallicanism and the Reformation in Germany respectively. The cause of church reform was further fuelled and the papacy was confirmed in its role as the opponent of reform because it was seen as the enemy of representatively constituted councils. What the papacy got out of these accommodations was the theoretical acknowledgement of universal jurisdiction even while some of its substance was being given away. The Pragmatic Sanction was abrogated a century later by the Concordat of Bologna (1516). Thus the conciliar decrees of Constance, re-affirmed by Basle, were repudiated in return for substantial powers for the King of France to appoint to bishoprics, abbacies and benefices. This was just another swing of the pendulum in the ongoing Gallican tussle with Rome. What sealed the defeat of conciliarism was the readiness of the popes to offer concordats and the eagerness of princes to enter into this kind of alliance with the papacy at the expense of conciliar loyalties which they had formerly seen as the best route to their national ambitions.

The status of Basel among the General Councils is not entirely clear – it had a chequered relation to the papacy, which it needed to validate its decrees – but the work of the first twenty-five sessions is now generally accepted as conciliar.

The Council of Ferrara-Florence re-affirmed the papal *plenitudo potestatis* and decreed that the pope was indeed the successor of St Peter and the vicar of Christ. Jedin calls these decisions 'the Magna Carta of the papal restoration' (Jedin 1957: I, 20). Eugenius' biographer celebrates him as the saviour of monarchical catholicism from the radical constitutionalism of Basel (Gill 1961). Pius II, who (as Aeneus Sylvius) had been active at the Council of Basel and an eminent theorist of conciliarism, submitted to Eugenius in 1445 and, following his own election as pope in 1458, condemned the familar gambit of appealing to a General Council and threatened anyone who did so with excommunication in the bull *Execrabilis* (his actually favourable account of the Council of Basel is translated in Aeneas Sylvius Piccolominus 1992).

There was thus a short-term victory for papal monarchy and a defeat for the reform agenda. The longer-term consequences were rather different. Acton saw a line running from Cusanus to the Protestant Reformation. Cusanus was, he said, 'a prophet and precursor of the Reformation'. 'The causes which most naturally account for that event are most clearly displayed in the history of his mind and life.' Acton drew the moral: 'When development is obstructed or paralysed, revolution is the natural outcome' (Acton 1952: 246).

Chapter 9

THE LEGACY OF THE CONCILIAR MOVEMENT

From the Council of Basel to the Reformation

Conciliarism remained a living theological tradition after the debacle of Basel. It continued to find able defenders in the University of Paris, notably Jacques Almain and John Mair (Major). On the later history of conciliar theory in the Roman Catholic Church see Black in Wood 1991: 409–38; Skinner 1978: II, 42–47. See Spinka 1953: 175–84 for translation of Maier's 'A Disputation on the Authority of a Council: Is the Pope Subject to Brotherly Correction by a General Council?' of 1529. For Almain and Mair texts see Burns and Izbicki 1997.

Even certain champions of papal power such as the Spanish Cardinal Juan de Torquemada (not he of the Spanish Inquisition) in his *Summa de Ecclesiae* (c. 1453) were not absolute opponents of conciliarism. Though councils held routinely constituted a danger to the unity and peace of the Church, Torquemada claimed, a General Council remained 'the Church's last refuge in all her great needs' (Jedin 1957: I, 27; Küng 1965: 271–73). Torquemada attacked the Baslean notion of the authority of a council to express the mind of the Church, based on communal sovereignty, asserting: 'An association does not have a mind.' Only individuals can be ordained; only individuals can bind and loose. The council's notion of an authoritative corporate entity was a fiction. Torquemada astutely directed his attack on the council's most vulnerable point: its notion of a social unity that lacked an adequate theory of representative authority (Black 1970: 54).

The ideologues of papal monarchy drew on the centralizing thrust of Roman law, on the monarchical elements in the recently translated *Politics* of Aristotle, and on the hierarchical framework of Neo-Platonism that was mediated to them through Pseudo-Dionysius and St Thomas Aquinas. On this basis they postulated a transcendent source of absolute power residing in God, a power that mediated its authority to earthly rulers through the various gradations of the great chain of being. They developed a parallel between the sacred and the secular: pope and emperor hold the place of God in their respective spheres. As Torquemada put it: 'The pope has fullness of pontifical power, just as a king in a kingdom has the highest power and sovereignty (*principatus*) over the whole kingdom; that power resides in one man alone, the prince.' Neo-Platonism, with its hierarchical cosmology, enabled the supporters of the papacy of Eugenius IV to evolve a notion of sovereignty that was 'abstract, total and universally applicable' (Black 1970: 57–59, 95, 81).

Just as, it was said, the power of kings and princes is delegated to them by the emperor, so the power of bishops descends to them from the pope. The implication of this is that the pope can intervene 'immediately' in any subordinate sphere. As the supreme judge and the earthly fountainhead of spiritual and temporal jurisdiction, the papacy is above the law – immune from the judgement of any inferior body, including a General Council (Black 1970: 73).

In 1473, in the period of papal resurgence after the abortive reforming councils, Augustinus Triumphus produced his treatise on ecclesiastical power, the *Summa de Ecclesiastica Potestate*, dedicated to Pope John XXII, Ockham's *bête noire*, a work that Neville Figgis described as 'the most complete and uncompromising expression of the papal claim to be sovereign of the world', before the early seventeenth century (Figgis 1916: 25). Augustinus Triumphus postulated the whole Church subsisting, as it were, in the papacy and, as a result, he produced a perverse inversion of the doctrine of the common good: 'Since the good of the Church does not exist except because of the good of the pope, the pope's good is greater than that of the whole Church.'

The papacy defended itself against conciliarism by promoting a general theory of sovereignty which had wider application. At the same time as it was extolling sovereignty as a divine principle, it cultivated an alliance with the secular powers whose reward was to have the same dignity applied to them. Less than a century later, however, at the Reformation, the secular powers – their claims thus enhanced – would be lining up on the other side. 'In preferring royalism to Conciliarism, the fifteenth-century papacy contracted a dangerous alliance' (Black 1970: 129).

At the same time, the legacy of the Conciliar Movement remained strong. Gallicanism remained a stronghold of conciliarism, with the University of Paris continuing to promote it. The liberties of the French Church had been robustly upheld from early mediaeval times, by Charlemagne, Hincmar of Rheims and Philip the Fair. The Gallican tradition, episcopal and political in equal measure, maintained the independence of the French Church in temporal affairs; the superiority of a General Council over the pope; the need for the consent of the episcopate to binding papal decrees and teachings; and the power of the king to limit the prerogatives of the clergy. The *Declaration of the Gallican Clergy* of 1682 was drafted by Bossuet (see Martinmort 1953). It distinguished between the infallibility of the See of Rome and the fallibility of individual popes. Episcopal Gallicanism represented the most significant survival of conciliar thought within the Roman Catholic Church and became the only viable alternative to Ultramontanism. It fed back into official Roman Catholic ecclesiology through Congar at Vatican II, but has since suffered some reversal.

There were two abortive attempts to convoke councils in the quarter century leading up to Luther's reform. The first was a continuation of Basel in 1482, but no bishop or university heeded the summons. The second was a more serious attempt at Pisa in 1511, which had the support of a section of the College of Cardinals and of the emperor, to suspend Julius II for failure to reform the Church. Julius trumped the embryonic council by calling one of his own, the Lateran Council of 1512 which gained the general support of Christendom (Jedin 1957: I, 101–103; 106–108; for texts from this period, particularly Cajetan, see Burns and Izbicki 1997).

In the second half of the fifteenth century Gabriel Biel emerged as an exponent of a modulated conciliarism. In his *Defensorium Obedientiae Apostolicae* (1462), while defending the papal *plenitudo potestatis*, he envisaged a council acting in a time of crisis, as it did at Constance (Biel 1968).

When Huguenot political philosophers, such as Mornay, developed a doctrine of the right of resistance to tyranny, based on principles of natural law and natural right, they drew a parallel between conciliarism in the Church and constitutionalism (in the form of popular, representative sovereignty) in the commonwealth. Drawing on scholastic sources, directly or through the mediation of Lutheran and Calvinist thinkers, the Huguenots emphasized that the consent of the people was required before humankind could move out of its condition of primaeval liberty in order to create a commonwealth and appoint a ruler (Skinner 1978: II, 318–38).

Principles of Conciliar Thought

The Conciliar Movement had drawn on the ample extant resources of the western canonical and ecclesiological tradition. The college of cardinals had given conciliarism its opportunity at Pisa, but it had asserted itself against both cardinals and popes to give a voice to all estates in the Church: inferior clergy, academics, civil rulers. It had been especially hospitable to growing national aspirations and represented the highest point of the influence of academic theologians on ecclesiastical policy before the Reformation. But by setting the papacy in order it had succeeded in strengthening it and thus sealing its own defeat. It brought about its own eclipse by over-reaching itself in a mood of *hubris*. However, the ideals of the Conciliar Movement would be invoked again at the Reformation and would become entrenched in Protestant church polity, both Lutheran and Reformed, though in different ways. Those ideals would gradually be realized also in Anglicanism, as it developed, by the early part of the twentieth century, from a mode that was episcopal and Erastian to one that was episcopal and synodical. The conciliarists held a comprehensive view of unity, authority and reform in a mystical perception of the Church as the body of Christ, endued and filled with the Holy Spirit. Several key principles can be drawn out of their writings (cf. Petrie 1962).

First, conciliarism held that the Church means the whole Church, not simply the hierarchy (it was not unusual in the Middle Ages for the clergy and even the pope to be called the *ecclesia*). It is the whole Church, the community of the faithful (*congregatio fidelium*) that is the source of authority. Its authority comes to expression in a representative way through councils, above all through a General Council. Tierney asserts that 'the foundation of all conciliar thought in the age of the Schism was a conviction that the community of the church could not be destroyed by any failure of its [earthly] head' (Tierney 1982: 92).

For their conception of the whole body (*universitas*) of the Church the conciliarists were indebted to corporation theory which facilitated the development of late mediaeval cities and universities. As Panormitanus wrote: 'When it is said that the pope has fullness of power, this should be understood as referring not to him alone, but to him as head of the *universitas*: so that the power itself is in the *universitas* itself as foundation, but in the pope as principal minister, through whom this power is applied' (Black 1970: 10). This aspect of conciliar theory was particularly prominent at Basel which comprised a unique gathering of clergy from the mediaeval ecclesiastical corporations and this complexion no doubt had an influence on the radical direction taken by the council.

The Council of Basel had a seal made for its documents showing God the Father sending down the Holy Spirit on pope and emperor sitting in council surrounded by cardinals, bishops and doctors, and bearing the legend *Sigillum sacri generalis Concilii Basileensis universalem ecclesiam representantis*. The ecclesiological emphasis had shifted from the hierarchy to the whole body of the faithful. The conciliarists insisted that the Catholic Church, whose unfailing head is Christ, does not consist of the college of the pope and cardinals: it comprises the congregation of the faithful in the unity of the sacraments.

Second, conciliar theory gave due weight to new national ambitions and susceptibilities. The papacy had consistently underrated the national factor ever since Gregory VII had referred to the kings of Europe as 'kinglets' (*reguli*). Mediaeval political thought can be read as a history of the tussle between the pope on the one hand and the secular rulers (emperor, kings, princes) on the other. The proto-national feelings that emerged through the development of political and social structures were reinforced – partly positively, by the Aristotelian principle of the integrity of the natural, the human and the this-worldly, and partly negatively, by reaction against papal excesses and insensitivities. 'More and more did the papacy come to be looked upon as just another foreign power' (Ullmann 1972a: 292). In England the statutes of Provisors and Praemunire, that would be invoked by Henry VIII against those who disputed his claim to headship of the English Church, represented a long-standing resistance to the financial depradations of the papacy. Figgis said that Praemunire was 'the death-knell, though it sounded two centuries beforehand, of the Church as a non-national universal state' (Figgis 1916: 23). The Council of Constance was organized by 'nations' (though not entirely in the modern sense) and they vied one against another for status, especially the English and the French. The conciliar period also saw the first concordats with nation states (notably France).

Third, conciliarism was not fixated on General Councils but advocated synods at all levels in the Church. Gerson promoted provincial and diocesan synods. Cusanus set a high value on national synods, arguing that General Councils are only necessary for strictly universal legislation. There is an anticipation of the modern principle of subsidiarity here: that decisions should not be taken at a higher level than is necessary.

Fourth, the scholarly input at the reforming councils was decisive. Although Pisa failed, it was significant that the cardinals had issued numerous invitations to universities across Europe and that it was the universities, as the sole surviving institution with a claim to universality, that in the end furnished the Church with the conceptual tools – the theological constitution – to heal the schism (Swanson 1979: 204). Gerson in particular exalted the vocation of theologians as an order in the Church. While the pope is the successor of Peter, the theologian is the successor of Paul and, as everyone knows, Paul had to rebuke Peter to his face when he went astray. Theologians, according to Gerson, are the intellect of the Church while bishops are the will of the Church. Bishops are there to implement the teaching of the theologians (Pascoe 1973: ch. 3). While, at Pisa, the cardinals were in control, at Basel 'neither cardinals nor bishops counted for much; it was the mass of doctors and masters who claimed to represent the Church universal and who dominated the conciliar scene' (Gill 1971: 171–73). The theological centre of gravity became steadily stronger with the progression from Pisa through Constance to Basel (Black 1980).

Fifth, recognition was given to the role of the laity in the vital affairs of the Church. Marsilius of Padua and William of Ockham had given laypeople the right to convene councils in an emergency and to participate in them. Both regarded the magistrate (the civil ruler) as the representative of the laity. Ockham is the more radical here: if the hierarchy became corrupt, laypeople alone could constitute a council and even women could take part if required. The question of a lay voice at councils was on the agenda of conciliarism, but a consensus was still against it. Gerson, for example, had a highly prelatical view of the Church. Laity and women in particular do not possess hierarchical power (Gerson saw the ecclesiastical hierarchy as the mirror of the celestial hierarchy of angels and archangels, etc.) and are thus less fully the Church than bishops and presbyters. Nevertheless, Gerson pointed out, Christian perfection is not the prerogative of the religious only (with their vows of poverty, chastity and obedience), but was open to the laity also (through the virtues of faith, hope and charity) (Pascoe 1973: 32, 165–67). Gerson allows the laity merely a consultative voice at councils. Cusanus restricts their contribution to specified matters. The Council of Basel did not consider the rights of the laity as such; it banned vernacular translations of the Bible and objected to laypeople discussing articles of faith. The political aspirations of the laity could not expect to find a direct voice at the councils since they were represented by civil rulers who were ideologically akin to the higher clergy. But the concentration on the authority of the *tota communitas Christianorum* (Pierre d'Ailly's phrase) that conciliar thought exhibited undoubtedly helped to give laypeople a purchase on the decision-making structures of the Church in the long run, that is to say, via the Reformation.

Sixth, conciliarism invoked natural law against the positive (human, contingent) law that could offer no way out of the impasse of the schism. Human laws could not be allowed to perpetuate a situation that was destroying the Church's effective mission. Ultimately necessity knows no law. The extent of the appeal to the authority of natural law varied among conciliar and quasi-conciliar thinkers: Zabarella barely mentions it; the first wave of conciliarists – Conrad of Gelnhausen, Henry of Langenstein and Dietrich of Niem – make some use of it; but it is central to the argument of John of Paris, Pierre d'Ailly, Jean Gerson and Nicholas of Cusa, as well as to the work of later conciliarists such as John Major (Mair) and Jacques Almain. Natural law led to principles of constitutionality and consent: Nicholas of Cusa stated that 'by divine and natural law' the rulers within every ecclesiastical order 'must be established by consent' (Oakley 1981: 797–98). It was the principle of natural law that enabled conciliarists to appeal to the common good of the Church and to imply that only the whole Church could discern wherein its good lay.

Finally, conciliar thought developed certain principles of governance that have become all but universally recognized since then. They were fundamental not only to the emerging models of conciliar authority in the Church at the Reformation, but also to the further development of parliamentary forms of government in various nations (see, e.g., Oakley 1962, 1965). As Black has commented: 'The idea and practice of representation, if not born in the Christian church, was made a regular, inherent and sanctified part of it as of no other organisation' (Black 1992: 169).

In England the assertion of constitutional writers in the fifteenth and sixteenth centuries that the king was under God and the law tacitly implied a principle of consent. Sir John Fortescue insisted that 'the kings of England do not establish laws nor impose taxes on their subjects without the consent of the three Estates'. Laws require 'the consent of the whole realm' (even if the whole realm is represented in 'the prudence of three hundred select men' in Parliament). When laws need to be amended, they 'can be reformed immediately with the consent of the Commons and Lords of the realm, with which they were first made' (Black 1992: 168).

Customary law codes were seen as reflecting the immemorial customs of the realm of England and not as the specific enactments of legislative bodies. The common law, the principal form of positive law (which alone could constrain the power of kings) originated in customary law. In its early form it long pre-dated the emergence of Parliament, but by the sixteenth century Parliament was seen as embodying the consent of the nation (Loades 1997: 1–6). This consent, which applied equally to spiritual as to temporal affairs, was effected through a crude system of representation, while the constitutional balance of power ebbed to and fro until a resolution decisively in favour of parliament was reached by the end of the seventeenth century.

The three interlinked concepts of representation, constitutionality and consent were refined in the conciliar period. They go back long before it: as we see, for example, in the Justinian adage that what affects all requires the consent of all and in the fact, adduced by Tierney, that every major work on law and political theory written around 1300 refers to the principle of consent (Tierney 1982: 42). These political principles had an ongoing history after the conciliar period, especially, for example, in the controversies about tyrannicide in the sixteenth and seventeenth centuries. The subsequent ecclesiastical and political histories of the ideas of representation, constitutionality and consent have their common source in a period when the sacred and the secular, Church and State, were not opposed to each other but were bound together in a unified world-view.

It was only with the work of Marsilius of Padua in the fourteenth century that the idea of representation in the sense of delegation rather than that of mystical embodiment, linked to the idea of consent, came to occupy a prominent position in political thought (Quillet 1988: 558). Clearly, the principle of representation in the sense of mystical embodiment can be employed to defend a monarchical model: because the pope embodied the faithful, he could act in their name and without consulting their views. However, even on this account, representation implies that pope or king is obliged to study the welfare of his subjects and to act in their interests (Black 1992: 165). But the alternative idea of representation as delegation is the crux of the conciliar controversy and runs through this period, even though the fifteenth-century councils lacked a clear theory of representation. Constance was adamant that it represented Christ and was gathered in the power of the Holy Spirit. Its representation was, so to speak, vertical and direct. Basle also did not have a worked-out theory of representation: it tended to assume the identity of the council and the *universitas*: it did not have a mechanism for this (Black 1969). But once representation ceases to be mystical and involves the consent of whatever and whoever is represented, notions of constitutionality become necessary. What are the roles and the rules, the scope and the limits, the checks and balances that are involved in the proper and acceptable exercise of representative authority? A hierocratic head or (in the mystical sense) 'representative', is entirely self-directing: answerable to no one, accountable to no one. Even today, six centuries after the conciliar epoch, there are no formal, constitutional constraints on what the pope says or does. The pope can unilaterally make the

canon law of the Roman Catholic Church and still does so. In terms of
episcopal appointments, the pope can and does 'hire and fire' and there is
no appeal.

There is a metaphysical backdrop to these issues, concerned with the
relation of the whole and the part. Are ideas of the whole body of the
Church simply rhetorical metaphors or are they to be taken in a realist
sense? Is the pope (together with the hierarchy) the plenary representative
of the Church as the Vicar of Christ? Is the whole body virtually present
when it is represented by a part of the body, or does every individual part
have to be consulted separately? Realists, standing within a resilient
Platonic heritage (Klibansky 1982), began with the whole and then considered the parts. Nominalists looked at the issue the other way round (for
an examination of the issues at stake in diverse uses of figurative language
such as metaphor and symbol, and advocacy of a critical realist position,
see Avis 1999).

Cusanus echoes Marsilius (as well as Aristotle) when he insists that laws
that are intended to promote the common good must be made by those
who will be affected by them – or by 'the greater part' (*valentior pars*) by
virtue of their election by the rest. But it has been plausibly suggested that
Cusanus repudiated conciliarism because he was drawn by the gravita-
tional pull of his Platonism to re-affirm that the hierarchy was truly representative. Ockham, on the other hand, as a nominalist regards the idea of
the whole as merely metaphorical (in the reductionist or ornamental sense,
not the realist and incremental sense of metaphor: see Avis 1999) and
therefore as philosophically improper. For Ockham representation and
consent must be awarded by all the individuals who make up the collectivity (for that is all it is) (Quillet 1988: 563).

Representation, constitutionality and consent hang together and as fundamental principles underpin the working of parliamentary democracy as
well as the conciliar structures of Anglican and Protestant churches. So, for
example, to answer the question why synodical government in the Church
of England works as it does, it is not adequate to say, as some do, that it
apes parliamentary procedure. Both synods and parliaments draw their
constitutional inspiration from this common source. That is not, of course,
an argument for inertia with regard to reform of the procedures of either
synod or parliament.

The Reformation as a Perpetuation of Conciliar Ideals by Non-ideal Means

The Reformation is part of the legacy of the Conciliar Movement. For
some, particularly in the Roman Catholic Church, that claim, if substanti-
ated, would be enough to damn the Conciliar Movement. For others, particularly Protestants and Evangelicals, that thesis may sound subversive of
principles that they hold dear. Those fears, held at opposing ends of the

reception of the Reformation, are unnecessary. On closer acquaintance with the conciliar contribution to Reformation thought, they may be dispelled and be replaced by a sense of a tradition that bridges the Roman Catholic–Reformation divide and holds promise for the future unity of the Church.

Three-quarters of a century ago the Reformed church historian J.T. McNeill drew attention to the conciliar aspects of the Reformation in his pioneering book *Unitive Protestantism* (McNeill 1930). McNeill traced the attempts of such Reformers as Cranmer, Melanchthon and Calvin to gather Protestant leaders together in order either to overcome the differences between the German and Swiss traditions (Lutheran and Reformed) or to present a united front to the Roman Catholic Church. McNeill pursued the conciliar theme further in his contribution to the official history of the Ecumenical Movement, bringing out the catholicity of the magisterial Reformation (Rouse and Neill 1954: 27–69) in connection with the various attempts to heal the divisions of Christendom. With a striking breadth of ecumenical vision and catholic sympathy, McNeill expounded both intra-Protestant conciliarity and the conciliarity that aspired to mediate between Protestant and Catholic in the sixteenth century. He pointed out that the Reformers were 'in a large sense the heirs of the Conciliarists'. While 'Conciliarism was a frustrated revolution', its central principle of representative authority lingered in the mind a century later. Even Luther's stress on the authority of Scripture and his denial of the infallibility of councils did not mark a departure from essential conciliarism, according to McNeill. Calvin too 'frequently affirmed the ideals of the Conciliarists' and severely criticized the papal domination of councils. Cranmer also 'was a Conciliarist in his view of the Catholic Church' (Rouse and Neill 1954: 32–33, 56).

The elements of continuity and discontinuity between the Conciliar Movement and the sixteenth-century reform movement bear a careful examination – and they do not often receive it. For example, the four-volume *Oxford Encyclopaedia of the Reformation* (Hillerbrand *et al.* 1996) contains no entry for Councils, General Councils or Ecumenical Councils (though there are entries and references to Constance, Trent, etc.). Oakley's article in the encyclopaedia on 'Conciliarism' (I, 394–97) does not discuss the relation of the Reformers to the conciliar tradition. What the Reformers have to say about councils, both in general and in particular, would probably fill the four volumes of this major reference work several times over!

Among standard histories of the Reformation, Cameron certainly does justice to the pervasive conciliar background (Cameron 1991: 49–51), while Hazlett (2003), though perceptive in many ways, gives it hardly a mention. A shining exception to the general neglect is MacCulloch's one-volume synthesis of Reformation history, thought and culture which frequently ties sixteenth-century developments back into their conciliar roots.

MacCulloch points out that conciliar ideas continued to shape ecclesiology and legal thought, if not practical politics, well beyond the eventual debacle of the Council of Basel: 'the work of the greatest conciliarists was too fertile to ignore' and raised too many questions about how the Church should conduct its affairs in accordance with the will of God, though 'there was much that was incoherent or unresolved in the bundle of ideas that carried the conciliarist label' (MacCulloch 2003: 38–41, at 40). In truth the events of the conciliar period, from the Great Schism, through the execution of Hus, to the failure of Basel, were never far from the Reformers' thoughts.

The Reformation should be seen as at one and the same time a reaction to the failure of the Conciliar Movement and a perpetuation of conciliar ideals by other means – and partly, one must recognize, to other ends. Cameron aptly suggests that the Reformation was a cousin to the Conciliar Movement, rather than its direct descendant (Cameron 1991: 51). The power struggle between the centralized and the distributed modes of church authority, between the papacy and the Church at large, the earthly head and the universal body, swayed this way and that. Many of the sixteenth-century Reformers, from Luther onwards, echoed the cry of the conciliarists during the previous century and a half for a General Council that would reform the Church in head and members. The demand for reform was now irresistible. Civil rulers – the only viable rival source of authority to that of the papacy now that conciliarism was in retreat – took matters into their own hands, supported by the theological legitimation that the Reformers provided.

Chapter 10

THE CONTINENTAL REFORMATION AND CONCILIAR THOUGHT

Martin Luther as Conciliarist?

In spite of McNeill's apologia, it is implausible to claim Luther as a fully-fledged conciliarist. Luther sat far too lightly to all ecclesial structures, relativizing and even negating them by the intensity of the gospel, to be a proper conciliarist. Luther did not award to councils either the hierarchical dignity or the canonical authority that the conciliarists claimed for them. His sense of the body of the faithful (*corpus fidelium*) – a key conciliarist tenet – was dynamic, contingent on the power of word and sacrament to hold it in being, rather than structured by received principles of political philosophy such as the corporation (*universitas*) concept of the later Middle Ages. Luther did not think of the Church as a political society. He was not interested in ecclesiastical polity (though he had a political philosophy for the civil sphere, according to the doctrine of the Two Kingdoms, *Zwei Reiche Lehre*, to which we shall return almost immediately). Luther's attitude to church structures is radical and paradoxical. On the one hand, he does not challenge the legitimacy of the episcopal-diocesan structures and is content to work within them, and even to accept the papacy under certain conditions. He has no quarrel with bishops provided that they preach the gospel and tolerate the reform movement. On the other hand, these outward structures are of marginal relevance to the true Church and to the mission of the gospel; they are frankly matters indifferent (*indifferentia, adiaphora*: for Luther's use of this concept see Verkamp 1977: 96–97, 142).

We see both sides of the coin in Luther's 1520 treatise *On the Papacy in Rome* (LW 39: 57–104; WA 6: 285–324). Fundamentally, the Christian community is not a physical, visible entity, but exists wherever there is faith, hope and love in the hearts of Christian people. Christendom is an assembly of all those who believe in Christ, 'a spiritual assembly of souls in one faith'. It is not defined as a physical location, but is a 'spiritual place'. All Christians throughout the world are bound together in one community, and therefore comprise an assembly that cannot physically be collected together into one place. Each local community of Christians 'is assembled in its own place'. But this place is not no place at all; the Church is not rarified into non-existence: it is indicated and signified by the visible marks of baptism, the sacrament of the altar and the preaching of the gospel.

However, as well as this 'spiritual internal Christendom' (Luther continues in the same treatise), there is the 'physical, external Christendom' of parishes, bishoprics and the papacy. Just as there is soul and body in a human person, so there is spiritual and physical in Christendom – 'not that we want to separate them from each other', any more than soul and body should be divided. Once the primacy of the true, spiritual, inward church is secured (by analogy with the primacy of the soul over the body), one can be relaxed, even pragmatic about the outward structures. Thus with regard to the pope, one should recognize that the pope's authority over the bishops has come about through divine providence (perhaps a wrathful providence!). Provided that two conditions are met, one should 'let the pope be pope'. The first requirement is that he should not make new articles of faith and impose them on Christian folk, condemning all those, such as the Russians and Greeks, who are outside his jurisdiction; the second is that the pope should accept the authority of Scripture and submit himself to its rule and judgement. 'If these two things are granted, I will let the pope be.'

In both of the statements produced in 1537, with a view to the calling of a council, that deal with the subject of the papacy – Luther's *Smalkald Articles* and Melanchthon's *Treatise on the Power and Primacy of the Pope* – the central challenge is directed at the papal claim to universal episcopal jurisdiction by divine right. The pope's authority has neither the support of direct divine institution nor the mandate of Scripture. It is a human construction and when judged on its merits is found wanting. Even if, Luther speculates, the papacy were to relinquish its prerogatives and adopt the platform of the Council of Constance (a ministerial headship for the sake of unity), this would be less effective than a collegial episcopate, with 'all the bishops equal in office ... and diligently joined together in unity of doctrine, faith, sacraments, prayer, works of love, etc.' (Tappert 1959: 298–301; 320–35, at 300). As the Lutheran confessional writings insist throughout, episcopacy is essentially a ministry of word and sacrament and of pastoral care of pastors.

One of Luther's last writings is a vitriolic attack on the papacy: *Against the Roman Papacy, an Institution of the Devil* (1545: LW 41: 263–376). Years of papal persecution of the reform had irrevocably embittered Luther's spirit. Here is no adiaphorism – no 'take it on its merits, provided it does not oppress the conscience and we have the freedom to preach the gospel' approach – with regard to the papacy, but an impassioned attack on Antichrist. Nevertheless, the conciliar element in Luther's thought is still prominent: the Council of Constance is invoked; the words 'free, Christian, council' are waved provocatively in front of the pope. One of the glories of Constance was that it deposed three popes and elected another, thus vindicating its assertion of the superiority of a council to a pope (265–67). Luther exposes the vulnerability of papal claims: the papacy would accept neither that it was instituted by temporal authority (royal and imperial power), nor by spiritual authority (the universal Church, through its councils), but insists on direct divine institution by Christ in the gospel. But this can be challenged through historical study of the first centuries and by biblical exegesis, leaving the papacy without foundation (300–301). The 'rock' of Matthew 16.18 is indeed part of the gospel and therefore must be understood not juridically and in terms of law and works performed in obedience to authority, but spiritually and evangelically. The rock can only be Jesus Christ himself, the true foundation of the Church (309–10). The pope should be content to be simply Bishop of Rome and to tend Christ's sheep there, just as bishops of Rome did for centuries before they were popes (354–55).

Melanchthon makes a similar distinction between external structures and internal spiritual life, pointing out that one must distinguish between 'episcopal polity, bound to place, person and due succession, offices, human regulations', and 'the ministry of the gospel, instituted by God and continually restored by his great mercy, which perpetually serves the Church and is not bound to certain places, persons and human laws' (CR 5: 627; cf. 559). The succession of bishops is nothing if it does not preach the gospel (CR 24: 402). The Church cannot exist without its pastors and salvation cannot be received except through their ministry. The ministry of word and sacrament is divinely instituted as essential to the Church (CR 8: 430; 12: 490; 14: 892; cf. Lieberg 1962). For Melanchthon, as for Luther, the freedom of the gospel, expressed in word and sacrament, is the litmus test of church structures.

In spite of his casual attitude to episcopal and conciliar structures – the Gersonian concept of the sacred hierarchy cut no ice with Luther – the conciliar elements in Luther's thought are substantial and his affinity with the conciliar tradition should be taken seriously. He has been credited with a 'moderate conciliarism' in the early 1520s (Thompson 1984: 139). Luther's consistent invoking of the authority of a council, premised on the responsibility of the universal priesthood for the well-being of the Church, shows how deeply the language and ethos of the Conciliar Movement had soaked into the theological consciousness of Christendom. The trauma of the Great Schism reverberated in the memory of late mediaeval and early modern churchmen. It was a General Council that had resolved that apparently intractable problem. But no council had so far succeeded in reforming the abuses and distortions of a papacy bloated by centuries of self-aggrandizement and centralization.

Luther: The Two Kingdoms

Before turning in more detail to what Luther had to say about councils, we should note the significance for conciliarism and authority generally of his sophisticated concept of the two kingdoms, regiments or rules. This pivotal concept in Luther's theology is relevant here in two respects: first, the question of authority; second, the distinction between temporal and spiritual spheres. The Two Kingdoms is a minefield in Luther interpretation: see especially Thompson 1984, 1969; Carlson 1946; Holl 1948; Schwiebert 1943; Spitz 1953; Rupp 1953: 286–301; Cranz 1959; Wingren 1957; Althaus 1972: 43–82; Whitford 2004.

The first aspect of Luther's concept of the *Zwei Reiche* that is relevant to the conciliar question is its view of authority. While Luther certainly does think in terms of two kingdoms, they are not separate entities, dualistically conceived, but, like Augustine's Two Cities, they comprise a distinction of values and activities that runs through each individual. Life as a whole is shot through with them both. The kingdoms are twin sources of authority, rule or governance (*Regiment*) for the two dimensions of human existence: the word of God, ministered by the clergy, in spiritual matters affecting the heart and the inner life; the laws of the magistrate, the civil ruler in temporal matters, affecting outward behaviour in social and economic life. Luther's conceptual scheme was in a sense a reversion to the integral early mediaeval framework where the emperor ruled men's bodies and the pope their souls within the one Christian commonwealth. The emperor wielded the power of the sword, the pope the power of the keys. The first could bestow temporal benefits; the second could open the door to eternal life. Luther operated with this concept of the *corpus Christianum* with its two complementary sources of authority, but in place of the pope he set the gospel, the word of God. The spiritual authority of the word governs the soul and is persuasive, not coercive. It relates to the first table of the Decalogue. Christ's Kingdom is spiritual and is entered by faith. The power of the keys is purely the authority enacted in preaching the gospel, absolving or retaining sins, and administering the sacraments (Augsburg Confession XXVIII [5]; Tappert 1959: 81).

The temporal authority of the magistrate, by contrast, is for Luther authority over the bodies and goods of Christian people, not over their souls and consciences. It is coercive, rather than persuasive. It cannot result in saving righteousness in the heart, but only in external, civil righteousness in outward conduct in the community. It relates to the second table of the Decalogue. 'Temporal power is concerned with matters altogether different from the gospel. Temporal power does not protect the soul, but with the sword and physical penalties it protects body and good from the power of others' (Augsburg Confession XXVIII [11]; Tappert 1959: 82).

The second way in which Luther's doctrine of the Two Kingdoms impinges on the conciliar question is his insistence on the distinction of spheres. True evangelical theology respects the distinction between the kingdoms. It is a matter of life or death that the two regiments do not trespass on each other's territory. Just as the temporal authority has no say in matters of doctrine, for that would be to seize a divine prerogative, like Lucifer (Luther WA 51: 240), so the Church has no jurisdiction in worldly affairs. If certain bishops have temporal authority in their dioceses, that is not because they are bishops but because they combine that pastoral office with other responsibilities of civil administration, given to them not by the Church but by the emperor or king (Augsburg Confession XXVIII [19]; Tappert 1959: 83–84). On this principle Luther appealed to the German nobility in 1520 to initiate reform through a council. And when in 1527 he and the other Wittenberg Reformers invited the Elector of Saxony to undertake a visitation of the parishes, Luther stressed that the Elector would do this, not as the magistrate, the temporal ruler, but as an emergency bishop (*Notbischof*), a sort of lay chief pastor. One of Luther's bitterest objections to the contemporary papacy was to its claim of temporal jurisdiction, developed in the first half of the second millennium, claims to the temporal as well as to the spiritual sword, for this had been profoundly destructive to the souls of Christians. The two kingdoms or regimes should never be mingled or confused (Augsburg Confession XXVIII [19]; Tappert 1959: 83–84). That was Luther's answer to the legacy of the contest between pope and emperor.

Both of these aspects, the identities of the two spheres and the necessity of keeping them separate, are brought together in his *Open Letter on the Harsh Book against the Peasants* (1525) in which he attempts to justify his earlier impassioned and outraged call to the civil authorities (*Against the Robbing and Murdering Hordes of Peasants*, 1525) to suppress the peasants' revolt, an uprising that appealed to his teaching on the freedom of a Christian man. God's kingdom, Luther states, 'is a kingdom of grace and mercy, not of wrath and punishment. In it there is only forgiveness, consideration for one another, love, service, the doing of good, peace, joy, etc.' The kingdom of the world, by contrast, is 'a kingdom of wrath and severity'. In it there is 'only punishment, repression, judgement and condemnation to restrain the wicked and protect the good'. Whoever confuses these kingdoms, Luther continues, as the fanatics (the theological agitators who stirred up the peasants) do, want to put wrath into God's kingdom and mercy into the world's – and that is to put the devil in heaven and God in hell (LW 46: 70–71).

Luther and Councils

Luther himself appealed for vindication to a General Council as early as 1518 ('Appeal of Brother Martin Luther to a Council': WA 2: 36–40). His deliberate echoes of the language of the Council of Constance in this 'Appeal' is a highly significant link with the conciliar tradition: 'A sacred council lawfully assembled in the Holy Spirit, representing the Holy Catholic Church, is superior to the pope in matters that concern the faith.' In the following year, in a tract on the Eucharist, he expressed the hope that a General Council would restore the cup to the laity (LW 35: 50). The papal bull *Exsurge Domine* (1520) that condemned Luther, also condemned conciliarism (DS 1478, 1479). At the Leipzig Disputation in 1519, Luther was outmanoeuvred by Eck. When pressed by Eck on the authority of councils, so much weightier than the views of one individual, Luther burst out that councils could err. By defending Hus and denying the infallibility of councils, Luther had been defined in the eyes of the authorities as 'an enemy of the whole western Church' (MacCulloch 2003: 127). The fact that Luther was able to appeal to the canonist Panormitanus (Nicolaus de Tudeschis, 1386–1445, pupil of Zabarella, and later Archbishop of Palermo), for his opinion on the fallibility of councils (WA 59: 480) reveals the diversity and absence of consensus within the canonistic tradition on this question. Moreover, Luther's denial of papal infallibility at an early stage in his career 'was nothing unusual at all by contemporary canonistic and theological standards' (Schuessler 1981: 67–68). In the course of the disputation at Leipzig Luther clarified and moderated his position, affirming that, while councils were not infallible, neither councils nor the whole Church erred in those things that pertained to faith (*in his quae sunt fidei*: WA 59: 547; Lohse 1999: 124). It testifies to the pervasiveness of conciliar ideas that both in 1518 and in 1520 Luther drew on the appeal of the theologians of Paris to a General Council against the Concordat of Bologna of 1516, for the legal arguments in his appeals.

Recognition that councils have erred, provoked by what the Council of Constance had done with Hus, was a watershed in Luther's theological progress and marked a major departure from the mediaeval tradition. Pelikan claims that 'this admission, more than either the ninety-five theses of two years earlier or even his excommunication of two years later, initiated Luther's Reformation' (Pelikan 1964: 54). In *The Babylonian Captivity of the Church* (1520) Luther repeated that councils may err, for to err is human, and the Council of Constance erred most wickedly of all (that is, in its treatment of the Hussites: its canonical ban on communion in both kinds and its encompassing the death of Jan Hus and Jerome of Prague) (LW 36: 108; 38: 182). Luther recognized in Jan Hus a kindred spirit and fully expected to share his fate. He wrote two prefaces to editions of Hus's letters from imprisonment at Constance (WA 50: 23–25; 123–25). However, Luther believed that neither Wyclif nor Hus went to the root of the problem of the mediaeval church: they had merely attacked its failures in practice, but these stemmed from theological errors: he had gone deeper. As Luther held forth at the dinner table in 1533 (LW 54: 110):

> Doctrine and life must be distinguished. Life is bad among us, as it is among the papists, but we don't fight about life and condemn the papists on that account. Wycliffe [*sic*] and Hus didn't know this and attacked [the papacy] for [on account of] its life ... That doctrine should be attacked – this has never before happened. This is my calling. Others have censured only life, but to treat doctrine is to strike at the most sensitive point, for surely the government and the ministry of the papists are bad. Once we've asserted this, it's easy to say and declare that the life is also bad.

Luther warmed to the theme, elaborating the crucial distinction between theology and Christian living:

> When the Word remains pure, then the life (even if there is something lacking in it) can be molded properly. Everything depends on the Word, and the pope has abolished the Word and created another one. With this I have won ... that I teach aright. Although we are better morally, this isn't anything to fight about. It's the teaching that breaks the pope's neck.

In 1521 Luther finally appealed to a General Council against his excommunication and against the enforcement of this edict by the Diet of Worms. Here Luther was following a well-worn path: 'to some degree it represents a stock legal gambit' (Thompson 1984: 140). It was now routine for anyone condemned by the pope to appeal against his sentence to a General Council. However, the familiarity of the tactic merely reinforces the point about the pervasive legacy of the Conciliar Movement and the prestige of the idea of General Councils after Constance.

In 1519 Luther had insisted that the issue of whether the laity should receive the sacrament in both kinds, as the Hussites had demanded, should be resolved by a General Council. Laypeople would be wrong to take the matter into their own hands: they should wait for proper authority. Over the next few years, however, Luther became increasingly incensed by the scandal of denying the blood of Christ to his people: it was such a flagrant contradiction of the words and actions of Jesus at the Last Supper that he abandoned his earlier caution: '...the use of both kinds in the sacrament is right and Christian and evangelical; and whoever says otherwise denies and blasphemes God, whether it be pope, emperor, princes, or even the devil. So we must also assert and preserve our liberty to take the sacrament with our hands or with our mouth...' (LW 36: 247: *Receiving Both Kinds in the Sacrament*, 1522).

In his *Appeal to the German Nobility* (1520: LW 44: 123–217) Luther provided a conciliar rationale with an evangelical thrust for the authority of a council over the pope, outlined the conditions necessary for calling a council and listed the issues that it would have to tackle. This work is not, as it is sometimes portrayed, an appeal to the German princes to set in hand the reform of the Church, but rather an appeal to them to take the lead in summoning a General Council which would have the authority to undertake reform. Like Joshua at Jericho, Luther set out to demolish the 'three walls' that protected papal power. In doing so he invoked the familiar Justinian adage that had formed a major plank of conciliar thought: only with the consent of the whole community could any individual claim for himself what belongs equally to all.

The first wall was the claim, familiar from centuries of mediaeval debate, that the spiritual was superior to the temporal. It followed that the temporal authorities had no right to act in reforming the Church. Luther challenged this assertion with the doctrine of the priesthood of all the baptized: through their baptism all Christians are 'spiritual', all are priests, all are 'religious'. What distinguishes Christian folk one from another is that they are called to do different kinds of work. The dichotomy of spiritual and temporal was false. Kings, princes and knights, together with ordinary laypeople, *were* the Church and it was properly their responsibility to reform it.

The second wall was the claim that only the pope could definitively interpret Scripture. It followed that Luther's interpretation, that pointed to radical reform of doctrine and practice, was invalid and that the groundswell of demand for reform in the light of Scripture could be ignored. Luther countered this claim by insisting, as certain canonists and conciliarists had done before him (and as Erasmus had recently argued), that Peter's keys to bind and loose were given to the whole Church. Since all were priests, all believers had a responsibility to judge the meaning of Scripture.

The third wall was the claim that only the pope could summon a General Council. This was of course a reversion to papal claims as they stood before the Great Schism of 1378 and the calling of the councils of Pisa and Constance by the cardinals and the emperor respectively – claims that had been reasserted with a vengeance after the debacle at the Council of Basel. It followed from the papal power to convoke a council (let alone to preside at one and to ratify its decisions) that it was extremely unlikely that a council could ever become the vehicle of any reform of the Church that would take in hand the corruptions that benefited the papacy. Moreover, it rendered Luther's own appeal to a council nugatory. Luther attacked this 'wall' with the argument that there was no historical justification for it. A council could be called by the Church as a community, as the first council, at Jerusalem (The Acts of the Apostles, ch. 15) had been, or by the emperor, as Nicaea had been. Whoever sees fire break out in a town should sound the alarm. Natural reason alone taught that no one had the authority to do evil or to forbid evil from being resisted. Finally, Luther applies the criterion of the gospel: no Christian authority whatsoever can be valid if it is exercised contrary to Christ.

Luther then proceeded to enumerate the issues that a council would need to tackle. First, the pomp and worldliness of the papacy (the current incumbent being the Medici Leo X, the opulence of whose court surpassed that of Henry VIII). Second, the devouring power of the cardinals who were being rewarded with monasteries and churches, even in Germany. Third, the bloated system of papal administration of taxes (such as annates) and benefices. The Romanists, Luther expostulated, traffic in livings more disgracefully than the Gentiles at the foot of the Cross trafficked in Christ's garments.

In full reforming flow, Luther then listed twenty-seven proposals for ameliorating the sorry state of Christendom. Many of them reflect concerns typical of the Conciliar Movement and touch on issues of authority, including aspects of subsidiarity. The Church at large should no longer be drained of wealth, energy and resources in favour of the centre. Annates should be withheld, no more benefices should be transferred to Rome and new bishops should not go to Rome for the Pallium. No civil matter should be referred to Rome and cases reserved for papal judgement should be resolved locally. The papal court and bureaucracy should be cut back and the episcopal oath of obedience to the pope should be abolished. The temporal jurisdiction of the pope, that is to say his authority vis-à-vis the emperor, based on the fraudulent 'Donation of Constantine', should be denied and he should quit the Italian states that he had forcibly occupied. Every parish should have its own pastor and the money spent on pilgrimages to Rome would be better spent on caring for one's family. The universities should be reformed and the Bible should be studied instead of Aristotle. Not least, canon law should be blotted out.

In *The Babylonian Captivity of the Church* (1520) Luther repeated his call for a General Council to free the Church from the tyranny of the pope over the cup (LW 36: 28). Attacking the Aristotelian captivity of theology – in particular the concept of Transubstantiation – Luther asserted that the opinions of the Thomists, even if approved by pope or council, would not become articles of faith even if an angel from heaven were to decree them, because they are devoid of support from Scripture and reason. Moreover, councils are not what they were: they may have numbers and power but they lack scholarship and saintliness (29, 106). *The Babylonian Captivity* explicitly invoked the conciliarist principle of consent: 'Neither pope nor bishop nor any other man has the right to impose a single syllable of law upon a Christian man without his consent; if he does, it is done in a spirit of tyranny' (70). So all the prayers, fasts, donations and other exactions that the pope compels the faithful to observe are an infringement of their Christian liberty.

Later councils, Luther believed, were too preoccupied with enacting merely human laws that oppressed Christian souls when faithful attention to Scripture would have solved many problems (LW 37: 14). By 1534 Luther was revelling in the progress of the reform: the revival of the gospel at his hands had achieved more than the papists might have done with five councils. It had removed indulgences, abolished pilgrimages, put a stop to papal bulls and checked priestly covetousness (LW 38: 231–32).

Luther and his close colleagues expected to be called to testify at a council. The Smalkald Articles of 1537 were drawn up for the abortive council at Mantua, and Luther's preface reveals profound ambivalence: so much stands in heartbreaking need of reform, but will any good come of a council convened by the pope? (Tappert 1959: 288–90). On reading the decree of the Council of Constance that a safe-conduct given to an heretic is not binding, Luther vowed that he would put all his cards on the table at the first meeting: he would release the thunderbolt of the doctrine of justification by faith and that would shatter all the apparatus of the papacy, even if he and Katherine his wife were burnt at the stake like Hus (LW 54: 215–16). A council meets in order to defend pure doctrine and to banish heresy, to put out a fire. If councils must concern themselves with ceremonies, they should leave them free as far as the conscience is concerned (LW 54: 333).

With a papally convoked council in prospect for some time (after two false starts it was called for Trent in 1542 and began work in 1545), Luther researched the history of councils for his work *On the Councils and the Church* (1539: LW 41: 9–178; cf. Pelikan 1964: 56–76). He felt highly ambivalent about the impending council: he had been calling for one for twenty years, but suspected the pope's motives in this sudden conversion to the cause of a council, after consistently resisting it. He noted that early councils of the Church had been conspicuous for conflicts of personality and lack of unanimity. This council should be drawn from the Christian nations, not from the pope's lackeys and should include representatives of the temporal powers. Any council would need to give priority to the word of God over all human laws. It would have no authority to innovate in doctrine and its decisions would only be binding in so far as it reaffirmed the faith of the Church. It would not enjoy infallibility; even the Fathers were fallible and went astray and the decisions of the Council of Jerusalem in Acts 15 had not proved to be the last word on the matters that it addressed. A council should be convened not by the pope but by the civil magistrate, like Nicaea and Constance (to take ancient and modern examples); it should not meddle in civil laws and temporal government. Every council has one primary purpose, one urgent matter that it is called together to address, and in its concentration on that issue – not in any peripheral rules and regulations that it might pass – it finds its authority.

The Augsburg Confession (1530) is prefaced with an offer to participate 'in full obedience, even beyond what is required, ... in such a general, free and Christian council as the electors, princes and estates have with the highest and best motives requested in all the diets of the empire' (Tappert 1959: 26).

There is paradox, but no contradiction, in the fact that Luther steadily appealed to a council to vindicate his stand and to bring unity to the divided Church while at the same time insisting that councils could err and could not guarantee the truth of their teaching. Councils represented the Church, but the Church was greater than a council. The truth of a council's decisions is a function of its faithfulness to Scripture, to the gospel, and its humble dependence on the guidance of the Holy Spirit (WA 39I: 189–91; Lohse 1999: 282; Althaus 1966: 340–41).

John Calvin and Conciliarism

Luther still stood within the late mediaeval framework that had been shaped by such profound factors as schism in the Church, the unheeded cry for reform, the conciliar ideology leading to the councils of the first half of the fifteenth century and then, by reaction, the resurgence of papal absolutism. Calvin, by contrast, stands on the other side of the watershed of the Reformation. He largely addresses the matter of councils and their authority, not as one who urgently seeks vindication at the hands of a council, but by reaction to attacks on the reform and on the integrity of his own theology. His comments on the role and authority of councils span his career as a reformer.

In 1539 Calvin penned a refutation of Cardinal Sadoleto's letter to Geneva, from which Calvin had recently been forced to flee, in which the cardinal attempted to woo the city back to the Roman fold by demolishing the pretensions of the reformers, who (he alleged) opposed the venerable authority of the early Fathers and General Councils with their merely human fancies. Far from disparaging all authority in the Church, Calvin retorts, we honour the ancient councils – so far as they accord with the Word of God (Calvin 1958: I, 66).

In 1542 Calvin wrote an 'antidote' to the articles of faith, published by the University of Paris, that re-affirmed the authority of councils. Councils that are gathered in the name of Christ are guided by the Holy Spirit, but there are many gatherings that are not under his sway (Calvin 1958: I,108). Two years later Calvin published scathing remarks on the letter of Pope Paul III to the Emperor Charles V who had announced his intention of calling a council. Against the pope's claim that only he could convene a council, Calvin pointed to the precedent of the Emperors calling the councils for five hundred years before the papal prerogative became established (Calvin 1958: I, 260–61).

Calvin's 'Antidote to the Council of Trent' of 1547 reviewed the early sessions of Trent. Councils, such as Trent purported to be, Calvin began, are deservedly held in reverence; they are the best remedy for doctrinal disputes. But Trent is not representative of the Church: for example, there are very few French bishops in attendance and they are either unlearned or ungodly or both. The council is being manipulated by the pope and consists more of outward show than inner substance (Calvin 1958: III, 30–32).

In the definitive 1559 edition of the *Institutes* Calvin devoted a chapter to councils and their authority (IV, ix: Calvin 1962: II, 402–12; cf. IV, viii, 10: II, 395–96). He immediately takes issue with the conciliarist gambit that everything that is said of the Church applies to General Councils, but he pauses to make an *apologia*: his apparent harshness in tackling this error is not due to any disrespect for councils: 'I venerate them from my heart and would have all to hold them in due honour' (403). The truth of faith does not always depend on the clergy; the Church is bigger than its pastors. The Church does not reside in meetings of the pastors; and councils are not always the bulwarks of faith that they are thought to be. Councils have no automatic guarantee of truth, but should be examined at the touchstone of Scripture. Many councils have been marred by human failings, especially rivalry and conflict. They are subject to error and must be viewed with discrimination. On the other hand, a council is the best forum for interpreting doctrine and for resolving doctrinal differences, though it has no power to make new doctrines (as some councils have presumed to do). The indefectibility of the Church is not dependent on councils: truth does not perish in the Church, even though a council should oppress it, but 'is wondrously preserved by the Lord to rise again, and prove victorious in his own time' (411).

Calvin on the Papacy

Calvin's view of the papacy is unrelentingly hostile: chapters 6–11 of Book IV of the *Institutes* constitutes a sustained demolition, on historical, theological and moral grounds, of the contemporary claims of the Roman See. The papacy is the foil to all that Calvin expounds positively about the nature, authority and ministry of the Church. There is little or no suggestion, such as we find in the earlier Luther, Melanchthon and the Augsburg Confession, that a reformed universal primacy might be acceptable. Calvin drops the condescension of the consummate humanist scholar who will not quibble about minor points that marks much of his discussion on other issues: he is implacable. While he recognizes that 'Rome was formerly the first of churches', he denies that the hierarchy now has the nature of a church ('I am not now speaking of the people, but of the government'): 'She is not a mother of churches who is not herself a church ... he cannot be the chief of bishops who is not himself a bishop.' 'Would they then have the Apostolic See at Rome? Let them give me a true and lawful apostleship. Would they have a supreme pontiff, let them give me a bishop.' There are marks of authenticity of a church and the ministry of a bishop is to teach the word of God, to administer the sacraments and to exert holy discipline. Which of these things does the pope even pretend to do? (Calvin 1962: II, 387, 383).

The Reformed ecumenist Lukas Vischer points out that Calvin not only denounced the corruptions of the papacy, but 'called into question the institution of papacy as such'. In Reformed eyes, says Vischer, the papacy is not in keeping with the tenor of the New Testament and is excluded by the Reformed understanding of the Church. Positively this is because that tradition stresses that the governance of the Church is carried out by representative bodies (conciliarity) and because it insists that no particular church can have authority over another. Negatively it is because the Reformed tradition has an underdeveloped theology of the universal Church and an ingrained suspicion of personal leadership. In Vischer's opinion, ecumenical experience and dialogue expose the inadequacies of that stance and challenge the Reformed churches to achieve a broader and more flexible view (Vischer in Puglisi 1999: ch. 9).

If Calvin's view of the papacy seems rather extreme in this ecumenical age, we need to remember that his criticisms of its errors and corruptions can be matched from a wide range of Roman Catholic sources – mediaeval, sixteenth-century, modern and contemporary. Moreover, equally devastating indictments came from a battery of Anglican divines, not merely during the Reformation, but throughout the next three centuries (one of the most effective being by Isaac Barrow: see More and Cross 1935: 59–65 for a sample), including scholars as High Church as you like, even the Nonjurors. And we need to remember also that, however ferocious the attack on divine right, universal immediate jurisdiction, infallibility, etc., the question of the primacy of the Roman See and of its bishop has remained a separate, legitimate question in the eyes of many non-Roman Catholic critics to the present day.

Zwingli and Bucer on Conciliarity

Before leaving the Continental magisterial Reformers, it is worth touching briefly on the views of Zwingli and Bucer on conciliarity. Zwingli was always his own man and with regard to councils, as in other matters, he stands apart from the magisterial Reformers. Zwingli's view of General Councils was rather jaundiced. Although he was a serious patristic scholar (and in particular a devoted student of Augustine), Zwingi firmly relativized the authority of Fathers and Councils over against the word of God in Scripture. 'To cry for councils,' he insisted, 'is nothing but to cry for the word of God to be imprisoned again and imprisoned in the power of the swaggering bishops' (Stephens 1986: 52).

Martin Bucer, the Reformer of Strasburg and one-time mentor of John Calvin, hoped, worked and prayed for a General Council that would resolve the Catholic–Protestant conflict. But, meanwhile, he insisted that all efforts should be made to reform the churches according to the pattern of Jesus Christ, as exemplified in the early Church. Bucer made specific proposals for a council in 1533, and in 1540 he and Johann Gropper drew up the so-called Regensburg Book to be the basis of discussion at the forthcoming Diet of Regensburg (Ratisbon). Bucer stressed that the authority of General Councils lay not in their constitution – the fact that they were convened on the authority of the pope or the emperor and were composed of various prelates – but in their faithfulness to Scripture, which might or might not be the case. In previous times it had made sense for councils to be made up of clergy, but with the advent of an educated laity and the decline into ignorance of many clergy, it was now appropriate for laypeople to play their part. Bucer held no programmatic view of the best church structures: like Luther, he conceded that the pope and the bishops could remain in office, provided that they lived up to their calling and allowed the gospel free course. In his proposals for a council he went far towards recognizing the inherited structures of

Christendom and was prepared to settle secondary matters on the authority of the early Fathers (Matheson and Augustijn in D.F. Wright 1994). In lectures given in Cambridge, Bucer appeals to Cyprian on the unity of the episcopate: 'the episcopate of the universal Church is one'; all bishops have equal authority. Cyprian's teaching is a transcript of Catholic opinion which was followed up to the time of Gregory [I]. The consensus of the Fathers is that the keys, though delivered to Peter first, were subsequently given to all the Apostles. The Fathers accorded pre-eminence to the Roman Church and to its bishop as first among the patriarchs, but they did not ascribe universal jurisdiction to him with the power to intervene at will in dioceses under the care of other shepherds. The Church has no single earthly head, except Christ who is the universal bishop and monarch of his Church. The word of God is above the Church, and even before the word was consigned to writing in the form of the Scriptures it was being preached, for the word of God is eternal and is active in every age (Wright 1972: 213–15; 236–51).

The Reformers and Natural Law

The philosophical idea of natural law affirms that the way that the world and human nature are inherently constituted (the natural order) and the way that we ought to live (the moral order) are intrinsically connected. (For the nuances and qualifications required here in order not to fall headlong into the naturalistic fallacy – attempting to read off values from facts – see the fuller discussion of natural law in the final chapter). The task of moral philosophy and moral theology is therefore to correlate the natural order and the moral order. In theological concepts of natural law, nature and ethics are seen as correlated by divine intention, ordered the one to the other in the plan of creation and in divine providence. When our individual lives and the organized life of society conform to natural law they fulfil their original God-given purpose, expressing a harmony intended by the Creator and inscribed in the texture of the created universe. (In modern philosophical accounts of natural law, created nature is replaced by underived, self-evident human goods and the intention to acquire them: again, see the later discussion.)

The Reformers, just as much as the mediaeval schoolmen, accepted this set of theological assumptions. Natural law is frequently and explicitly invoked by the Reformers and its principles shape not only their attitudes to questions concerning Christian behaviour, social mores and civil codes but also their approach to issues of authority in State and Church. The old adage, *Quod tangit* ..., 'What affects all must be proved by all' (or variations on this theme), was deployed by the Reformers, just as it was by the conciliarists and by the canonists before them.

The natural law approach includes three closely related and overlapping ideas. (1) The basic notion of distributive justice: giving everyone their due.

(2) The Roman principle of equity (*aequitas*): fairness that is transparent and evident to all and is the antithesis of arbitrary rule. (3) The Greek concept (derived from Aristotle's *Nichomachean Ethics*, V, 10 and *Rhetoric*, I, 10 [1374a]: Aristotle 1953, 1991) of *epieikeia*: applying positive law with flexibility and humanity in the light of circumstances – there is no single adequate equivalent in English. These three connected principles have their provenance in the natural law tradition. In what follows, we are concerned to draw out the Reformers' views on natural law only in so far as it impinges on questions of authority and the relation between authority, unity and freedom.

A Necessary Revisionism

The extent of the Reformers' indebtedness to this natural law tradition, stretching back through mediaeval philosophy and jurisprudence to the patristic and classical periods of European civilization, was obscured in modern historical interpretation, especially in Germany (cf. Haikola 1967). Luther was read in the light of Kant's Categorical Imperative, with its premise that there is no necessary correlation between 'is' and 'ought' and that we are not to look for an empirical correlative of ethical demands. The moral imperative is purely a matter of will; it loses its unique authority if it is seen as grounded in being. Luther could not, therefore, (it was assumed) have recognized a natural moral law, written in the hearts of all peoples at all times. Although Luther and other Reformers may have used the language of natural law, it did not carry the same ontological freight as for the scholastic writers – or so it was generally assumed.

   Karl Barth's onslaught on natural theology, understood as a knowledge of God grounded in a general revelation in nature and conscience, in the name of the revelation of God given solely in the person and work of Jesus Christ and accordingly intersecting the human world vertically from above – a theological version of Kant's Categorical Imperative – also swept away as a consequence the idea of a natural knowledge of the moral law. Revelation in Barth was grounded in the God who could not be known by reason and conscience but only by a revelation for which one could not dispose oneself in advance. Barth was reacting, first, against the liberal Protestant collusion with late nineteenth and early twentieth-century German cultural and political hegemony and, second, against the Nazi ideology, an implicit theology, that located sacred, transcendent value and its ethical consequences in a theory of racial supremacy (for a critical analysis of this aspect of Barth's theology see Avis 1986b: ch. 3). It has been widely assumed that any significant appropriation of the natural law tradition by the Reformers would have been incompatible with their sup- posedly dualistic, transcendent, interventionist theology of grace. So even Skinner rashly claims that Luther's political thought 'involved no appeal to the scholastic concept of a universe ruled by law, and scarcely any appeal even to the concept of an intuited law of nature' (Skinner 1978: II, 19). Presumably for these sorts of reasons the *Oxford Encyclopedia of the Reformation* (Hillerbrand, *et al.* 1996) contains no entry on natural law, no section on this topic in the entry on law in general and no reference to it in the index! Even the illuminating Jean Porter, the *doyenne* of contemporary Thomistic natural law exponents, confuses natural law with natural theology when she pronounces: 'Since the Reformation, this doctrine has been seen as an expression of human pride, an effort to establish human righteousness apart from God's law and God's grace' (Porter 2005: 40). The truth is rather different, as we shall see.

Luther on Natural Law

The tradition of Luther interpretation with regard to natural law is, then, wildly divergent. The extremes are represented by Karl Holl's patently unsustainable view that natural law played little part in Luther's theology, on the one hand, and F.X. Arnold's approach, which virtually assimilates Luther to Thomas Aquinas on the matter of natural law, postulating too much bland continuity between nature and grace, on the other. A further complication is provided by Troeltsch's theory of absolute and relative notions of natural law: absolute natural law referring to its origins in the pristine state of things before the Fall of Man (prelapsarian); relative natural law denoting the accommodations required by the Fall and human sin (post-lapsarian). According to Troeltsch, Luther is a prime exponent of the relative concept of natural law, because for Luther the primary purpose of the moral law and its expression in positive law is to keep human depravity within bounds (Holl 1948; Arnold 1937; Troeltsch 1931: I, 259–62, 343–49; II, 503–506). However, nearly a century ago Lang signalled that there was fresh work to be done in this area (Lang 1909). In 1941 the always perceptive American Reformed historian J.T. McNeill signalled a turn of the tide in the assessment of Luther's view of natural law, insisting that 'natural law is determinative for Luther's political thinking' (McNeill 1941: 227).

More recently, the revisionist Finnish school of Luther interpretation, stemming from the work of Tuomo Mannermaa, has provided the essential theological basis for a reappraisal of Luther's use of natural law. Mannermaa has reclaimed the ontological dimension in Luther's theology; he has shown that in Luther justification was never merely forensic and external (extrinsic), but always involved moral transformation by the indwelling presence of Christ which was nothing less than the content of faith (*in ipsa fide Christus adest*). Mannermaa and others have argued that Luther's concept of justification/sanctification, as a single act, is analogous to the Orthodox idea of *theosis*, divinization, sharing by grace in the life of

God. These Finnish scholars have helped to overthrow the common assumption made by Protestant (not least Lutheran) scholars and Roman Catholic scholars alike that Luther was the prisoner of a sharply dualistic nominalism that polarized grace and nature, justification and sanctification, natural law and the divine command. On the contrary, they have argued convincingly, Luther was no dualist in ethics, any more than he was in justification: the scope of natural law embraced creation and redemption, the temporal order and the Church, faith and reason, the nature of God and the calling of the Christian. There is one law and principle of self-giving sacrificial love that runs through the order of creation and the order of salvation. The Finns have vindicated the instinct of many non-specialist readers of Luther who always knew that his wonderful sense of the intimacy and inwardness of Christ's presence and of the freedom of a Christian to stand before God and the neighbour, fully united with Christ, and fulfilling the law of love was fundamentally incompatible with the extraordinary dualism so often attributed to Luther. Mannermaa 2005; essays in Braaten and Jenson 1998, esp. Raunio 1998. For other basically sound accounts of Luther's view of natural law and related questions see Althaus 1966: 89–91, 251–52; 1972: 25–30; Gerrish 1962: 10–27; Wingren 1957.

Luther's notion of natural law is practical, rather than theoretical. With all the Reformers he rejected the Pelagian tendencies in late scholastic ideas of natural law which elevated it to the status of an autonomous element, mediating, as it were, between God and the world, and a symbol of the power and dignity of human nature (d'Entrèves 1951: 70). Luther appeals to natural law as a rule of thumb in social, economic and political matters, and uses it as a hefty stick with which to beat Roman legalism and the exactions of canon law. He also brings it to bear on the question that exercised the Reformers, but has been little considered by modern scholars, whether the judicial (that is to say the political, as opposed to the moral or the ceremonial) laws of the Pentateuch are binding on Christian governments. Finally, and significantly for our theme, Luther sees natural law as underlying the proper exercise of authority with gentleness and humanity (*epieikeia*). Luther's commitment to natural law is so often overlooked, so little understood and yet so decisive for his political (as well as his ethical) thought, including his views on authority, that it is worth setting out fairly substantially here.

According to Luther, natural law is given to all peoples at all times. God has created it as a light for all humanity (LW 54: 293). It is naturally and indelibly imprinted on the minds of all human beings (LW 25: 19, 180 [*Lectures on Romans*]). The Ten Commandments are in part declarations of natural law. But in so far as they express the natural law, they do not derive from Moses; they have ruled in all people from the beginning and still do (LW 47: 89–90). 'There is one law which runs through all ages, is known to all men, is written on the hearts of all people ... [and] which the

Holy Spirit dictates unceasingly in the hearts of all' (LW 27: 355). This leaves all people without excuse for their sin and under the wrathful judgement of God.

Natural law is sometimes invoked by Luther in a descriptive sense, as what we observe to be commonly (and therefore properly) done. But, rightly understood, natural law has imperative authority – the office of law is to command – and is therefore not found in animals, but only in humankind. 'Law is what ought to happen', not what does happen. Natural law is reasonable, not instinctive (LW 54: 103 [*Table Talk*]). The rationality of natural law means that arguments based on sound reason and imperatives based on natural law inter-penetrate. 'This light lives and shines in all human reason', for all human beings 'carry along with them in the depths of their hearts a living book' which, if heeded, would guide them in all they do (WA 17 II: 102: Althaus 1972: 27n). Luther speaks of 'love and natural law with which all reason is filled' (LW 45: 128). Reason is 'the soul of law and mistress of all laws' (Gerrish 1962: 13).

Natural law stands above human laws in the form of civil positive law and the Church's canon law and judges them: if they fall short of justice, fairness and equity they are not true and worthy laws. From the beginning of his career as a Reformer – from the moment in 1520 that he burned the books of canon law along with the papal bull *Exsurge Domine* denouncing him – Luther condemned the oppressive piling up of canon law. He condemned burdensome legalism not only on behalf of the freedom of a Christian man under the gospel, but also in the light of natural law. Experience, historical chronicles and the Scriptures themselves, he said, teach this principle: 'The less law, the more justice; the fewer commandments, the more good works' (LW 35: 79). Luther blames the proliferation of sects and the swarms of religious charlatans and hypocrites on the legalistic mentality inculcated by canon law: their pestiferous activities were driven by a misguided zeal to perform meritorious works (80). The Pope may make canon law, but he cannot dispense from natural law. Luther repudiates the claim made by the papacy to give dispensations from divine law, that is biblical injunctions that were underpinned by natural law, for example regarding marriage vows, making it one of his indictments against the papacy in the *Babylonian Captivity* in 1520 (LW 36: 80).

For Luther, the Scriptures, especially the Decalogue, are infused with natural law. The law of Moses applies to Christians only when it expresses the natural law. The judicial and ceremonial laws of Moses have been abolished, though some strands of Anabaptism and separatism invoked 'the judicials of Moses' and the Reformers generally accused the Roman Catholics of 'judaizing', that is to say, imposing the Old Testament ceremonial laws to do with external purity and fasting (for this issue in Reformation debates see Avis 1975). According to Luther, some aspects even of the Decalogue are not supported by natural law and are therefore not binding. In *How Christians Should Regard Moses*, Luther argued that we read Moses, 'not because he applies to us, that we must obey him, but because he agrees with the natural law' and we are not to follow him except where he does (LW 35: 172–73). The commandments forbidding murder, adultery and stealing are not simply Mosaic laws, but belong to the natural law, written in each man's heart, and as such remain valid (LW 40: 98). Even the Sermon on the Mount is an expression of natural law. In fact, the whole of the 'transmitted law' is the natural law, speaking of love of neighbour, and is therefore one with the law of Christ. The love of God is poured into our hearts, fulfilling the law of Moses and of Christ. 'Indeed, it is a law without a law, without measure, without end, without limit, a law reaching far beyond everything that a written law commands' (LW 25: 180, 187 [*Lectures on Romans*]). It can be summed up in the Golden Rule: at the very least to do to others as you would they should do to you and beyond this to love your neighbour as yourself (LW 27: 56–57).

Temporal peace and stability, Luther's great concern in turbulent times, depend on following natural law. In his response to the demands of the insurgent peasants in 1525 Luther makes it clear that social stability rests on the natural law, 'which even the heathen, Turks and Jews have to keep if there is to be any peace or order in the world' (LW 46: 27). The peasants have confused the Two Kingdoms or Regiments, imagining that evangelical freedom means the abolition of social and political constraints. But in the kingdom of the world, natural law teaches obedience and submission – and Christians gladly embrace these with their attendant sacrifices because Christ himself suffered under political authority.

Natural law has implications for the exercise of authority for Luther, just as it did for the conciliarists. It requires that the consent of the subjects of positive, enacted law be sought. In the *Babylonian Captivity* Luther says: 'I lift my voice simply on behalf of liberty and conscience, and I confidently cry: No law, whether of men or of angels, may rightfully be imposed upon Christians without their consent, for we are free of all laws' (LW 36: 72). Natural law requires the exercise of *epieikeia*. Luther particularly admired Aristotle's treatment of this quality in his *Ethics* (Aristotle 1953: 166–68). Natural law is 'a practical just principle in the sphere of morality'. When positive law is administered, circumstances should be taken into account (LW 54: 293). One biographer of Luther has suggested that *epieikeia* had concerned Luther more and more in his administration of the reformed churches 'until at last it grew into his most poetic, and perhaps his most important vision' (Haile 1980: 345). His preferred German equivalent was *Gelindickeyt*, gentleness and this led Luther to assimilate *epieikeia* to Christian charity, which allows for extenuating circumstances and takes the intention into account. It moderates severity in the application of the law. The law of love, the Golden Rule, the abiding value of biblical law and natural law hang together in a world constantly addressed by God and called to emulate God's generosity and gentleness.

Zwingli: Law and Natural Law

Zwingli makes considerable use of the idea of natural law, but in his thought it tends to become assimilated to divine (that is to say, biblical, revealed) law. Zwingli refers to Matthew 7.12 and Romans 1 and 2, backed up by Cicero, to prove that the heathen recognized the law of nature: essentially the Golden Rule, with love as the guide and touchstone. The Christian language for this is the will of God or the *imago Dei*. Even in the most evil men the divine image has not been completely obliterated. Zwingli diverges radically from Luther when he makes law the perfect expression of the will of God (*Lex nihil aliud est, quam aeterna dei voluntas*). All we need to know and do is expressed in the law of God. Divine law and natural law coincide, but only the Christian believer is able fully to acknowledge the natural law. The law of nature, written by God in the heart of man, is renewed by the grace of Christ through the Holy Spirit. Then this natural law is fulfilled in true religion, divinely inspired (*Lex naturae est nihil aliud quam vera religio. Das gesatz de Natur ist nüt anders den lüter geist gottes*: CR 90: 707; Zwingli 1929: III, 137–38; Stephens 1986: 140–41).

God has 'sweetened' the law of nature with the love revealed in Christ. To the Christian, law is part of the gospel because it accords with the Christian's inner desire to conform to Christ. God puts into our hearts the love that rejoices to keep his law, even though the flesh still resists. As far as the inner spiritual life is concerned, the law is eternally valid. God's will becomes second nature to the believer and loses its legal character. For the faithful, we might say, law becomes as gospel. Zwingli pointedly referred to certain eminent men (i.e. Luther) who had not spoken with sufficient care of the law of God, saying only that it terrifies. Zwingli believed that his integration of gospel and law should put an end to the intra-Protestant argument about law and gospel. Justice and mercy in God should be held together in faith and theology, not opposed to one another, as Luther had done (Locher 1981: 196–201).

Zwingli's thoroughgoing biblicism led him to interpret certain positive laws of the Old Testament (those concerned with adultery, witchcraft and offences against property and against parental authority, for example) as expressions of the law of nature. He did not consistently reject the validity of the judicial laws of the Pentateuch. Zwingli did not operate with the category of *adiaphora*; nothing was indifferent; everything had to find its sanction in Scripture regarded as a book of commands and precedents (cf. Walton 1967).

Zwingli brought biblical revelation, rather than natural law, to bear on abusive practices that had the sanction of long use. At the first Zurich Disputation, he affirmed: 'We want to speak of the truth ... [of] a divine law that has long been set aside by men. For we believe ... custom should yield to truth' (Locher 1981: 111). As Locher comments, in an age when to find truth was to look to the past, Zwingli's statement 'caused a stir throughout the whole traditional world of thought'.

Melanchthon: Natural Law and Social Fabric

Phillipp Melanchthon (Witte 2002: 121–140) agreed with his master Martin Luther that God has written his law on the hearts of all people, that the same law is inscribed in Scripture, and that the natural reason can discern how that law guides us in matters of earthly government. The early Melanchthon set out ten principles, beginning with the requirement to worship and obey God and going on to prescribe various social obligations, that were taught both by the Bible and by classical writers, both Greek philosophers and Roman jurists. The fact that sacred and profane authorities spoke with one accord lent support to the universal and timeless principles of the natural law. The Decalogue is the supreme statement of the natural law: it continues to guide the behaviour of the individual Christian (the third use of the law – *tertius usus legis*, a departure from Luther's position) and should shape the laws that regulate society. The 'first table' refers to our duties toward God, the 'second table' sets out our duties to our neighbour. But the Christian ruler, the magistrate, is bound to provide for both: the law of the land should support the true faith and divine worship, as well as ensuring moral behaviour in the interests of the common good.

Melanchthon's position on the binding force of biblical law is difficult to pin down: there is both ambivalence and development. He can be found to say that all law, even the Decalogue, is abrogated in Christ. The Decalogue binds Christians no more than the laws of Solon: its only remaining validity is as an expression of the natural law (*quia in natura scripta est*). Yet he came to accept the third use of the law (*tertius usus legis*) as a guide to Christian living (CR 21: 102; 12: 473–74). In the *Common Places* (*Loci Communes*) Melanchthon divides all law into natural, divine and human. Concerning natural laws, he says, 'I have seen nothing worthily written either by theologians or lawyers.' Because human reason is so enslaved and blinded by sin, it struggles to draw out the teaching of natural law and its dictates are often distorted. But Paul teaches in Romans 2.15 that there remains a law of nature written on the heart. This law of nature is 'a common judgement to which all men give the same consent'. God has engraved it and impressed it on the minds of all as a guide to morals. 'There are certain common axioms and a priori principles in the realm of morals; these constitute the ground rules for all human activity' (Pauck 1969: 50).

Like Luther, Melanchthon defines natural law as what is distinctive to humans, the prescriptive, conscience-based imperative to follow right and eschew wrong. It does not include what humans have in common with the animal creation, the instinct of self-preservation and procreation. These are simply certain natural dispositions (*affectus*) implanted in all living beings. The natural laws that pertain to humankind, however, are threefold: God is to be worshipped; we are not to harm but rather to help one another (e.g. 'What is more foreign to nature than slavery?'); all God's gifts are to be shared – because we are bound and joined to one another in a life that is essentially social. Goods should be shared to the extent that public peace and the safety of the group permit; the higher law, that we should not do harm to one another, overrides the lower law, that there should be common use of all things (Pauck 1969: 50–53).

The teachers and legislators of Lutheran Germany followed Melanchthon rather than Luther: law was needed to regulate the lives of Christians; institutions that promoted the common good were necessary. It was a Christian duty, one that flowed from the gospel, to provide good laws, stable marriages and excellent schools, for example. Johannes Eisermann and Johann Oldendorp developed the Melanchthonian appeal to the natural law and put in place laws, structures and institutions that were intended to promote the common good (details in Witte 2002).

Bucer: Natural Law and the Kingdom of God

Martin Bucer's first book, published in 1523, was entitled *That No-one Should Live for Himself but for Others* (Bucer 1952; cf. Greschat in D.F. Wright 1994: 29–30). Bucer, who had been imbued with the thought of Thomas Aquinas during his ten years as a Dominican, here invoked a law implanted by God in the whole creation, the law of interdependence and of mutual service. Through grace the Christian is once again able to live out this law in a fallen world. In his mature work Bucer frequently invokes natural law, employing several virtually synonymous expressions: *ratio legis* (the reason or rationality of law), *ratio pietatis* (the reason or rationality of piety), the Golden Rule, the love commandment (*Liebesgebot*). Bucer's theological rationale for this principle echoes Aquinas: *Spiritus enim Christi, naturam non tollit, sed restituit* ('For the Spirit of Christ does not destroy nature, but restores it': Koch 1962: 74–75; cf. 69, 219). While natural law remains valid in spite of changing times and persons, the validity of positive law depends on contingent times and persons and is subject to change and abolition. Where positive laws, such as some of the judicial and ceremonial laws of the Pentateuch, merely express natural law, they remain valid. Natural law is therefore the criterion of positive, enacted law.

Bucer saw divine (revealed, biblical) law as one with natural law and was inclined to find it in the imperial law also. There is a sense in which, for Bucer, law is more fundamental than gospel: the gospel of Christ explicates and clarifies the law of God (*Verbum Dei, Euangelium Domini nostri Jesus Christi hoc est, lex Dei explicatior et dilucidior*: Koch 1962: 67). Both Old

Testament Israel and the Constantinian Christian empire had been instantiations of the Kingdom of God. Through the rule of right laws, laws that conformed to both natural and divine law, the Kingdom could come in Christian nations – in Strasbourg and in England. His *De Regno Christi*, which Bucer presented to Edward VI, was the most detailed blueprint produced in the sixteenth century for the moral and social ordering of a Christian society. In this work (Pauck 1969: e.g. 322, cf. 377) Bucer frequently appeals to the law of nature, seeing it expressed in imperial and canon law, as well as in Scripture. A striking example is the way that Bucer invokes multiple expressions of law to support his argument that couples getting married should give their consent to each other – no arranged marriages against the will of the parties: 'According to the norm, therefore, which the very law of God ordains and the law of nations and of nature teaches, and which we see all pious and honest men follow as established custom, written laws to the contrary notwithstanding...' See also Avis 1975; Müller 1965: 150–53; Lang 1941: 25–28; Pauck 1928: 21–23, 33–34; Hopf 1946: 107–108, 122–23; Stephens 1970: 93–95. For the love motif in Bucer see Torrance 1956: 82–84, 87–88. For the background in Bucer's ecclesiology and reform programme see Wright 1994.

Calvin: Natural Law and Equity

There cannot be any doubt that Calvin, like the other Reformers, operates with a concept of natural law. For discussions of Calvin on natural law see Bohatec 1937: 27–30; Baur 1965: 47–50, 71–73; Lang 1909; Doumergue 1917: V, 465–67; Wendel 1963: 206–208; Cochrane 1966; Little 1968; Höpfl 1982: 179–84: each of these accounts should be approached with critical discrimination. For the related issue of natural revelation, natural knowledge of God and natural theology (with which natural law is often confused) see Barth and Brunner 1946 and discussion in Avis 1986b: ch. 3.

Calvin is constantly invoking 'nature', 'reason', 'natural reason' and 'natural law'. He does not feel the need to analyse what is meant by this: like all his contemporaries, he is working within a received tradition of discourse, a given intellectual universe. To that extent, Höpfl's criticism that Calvin does not give the idea 'any serious examination' is misplaced (Höpfl 1982: 184). In Calvin natural law is largely deployed polemically, to add force to his primary authority of Scripture and to vindicate the patent truth of biblical teaching. To that extent, Little is correct to say that Calvin's theory of natural law is subservient to his theological and moral design grounded in revelation (Little 1968: 185–86).

But Calvin also uses the appeal to natural law or natural reason as a hermenutical criterion in the interpretation of Scripture, both in his exposition of the Decalogue and in his exegesis of Pauline commands. 'What?', he expostulates, 'Is religion placed in a woman's bonnet, so that it is unlawful for her to go out with her head uncovered? Is her silence fixed by a decree which cannot be violated?' (Calvin 1962: IV, x, 31). In these matters, custom, modesty and humanity guide the application of general revealed principles in the light of circumstances.

Those scholars who stress that Calvin's appeal to natural law and similar ideas is radically subordinated to his appeal to the word of God are of course correct, but to harp on about a matter of emphasis is to miss a sense of the whole. Therefore I cannot agree here with the usually highly reliable Wendel that this element in Calvin's theology is 'somewhat of a foreign body', which can be assimilated to his system only with difficulty (Wendel 1963: 208).

In his exposition of the Ten Commandments in *Institutes* II, viii, Calvin states that 'the very things contained in the two tables [of the Decalogue] are, in a manner, dictated to us by that internal law, which ... is in a manner written and stamped on every heart. For conscience ... acts as an inward witness and monitor', reminding us of our duty to God, distinguishng between good and evil and convicting us when we depart from our duty (Calvin 1962: I, 317). Reason has some competence in arriving at the precepts of the second table, which is 'more closely connected with the preservation of civil society', though reason is weak when it comes to resisting the force of desire (concupiscence) (II, ii, 24). But reason is unable to attain the full truth of the first table, concerning the worship and service of the one true God. With regard to God, 'the end of the natural law is to render man inexcusable', as Paul shows in Romans 2.14–15 (II, ii, 22). For, as Calvin shows in his exposition of the moral law in *Institutes* IV, xx, 15, the moral law, comprising the worship of God and the love of humankind, is nothing other than 'the true and eternal rule of righteousness prescribed to the men of all nations and of all times, who would frame their life agreeably to the rule of God'. For, continues Calvin, 'his eternal and immutable will is, that we are all to worship him and mutually love one another' (Calvin 1962: II, 663).

Although the human perception of what is right and the ability to perform it are woefully damaged by the Fall and the presence of sin, so that reason is weak in every respect, especially with regard to the things of God (Calvin 1962: II, ii, 25), God graciously continues to pour the light of truth upon humanity. In reading non-Christian ancient writers, 'the admirable light of truth displayed in them should remind us that the human mind, however much fallen and perverted from its original integrity, is still adorned and invested with admirable gifts from its Creator'. Since the Spirit of God is the fount of all truth, we will embrace truth wherever it is found. How can we deny the fact that divine truth shone upon those ancient lawgivers who arranged civil order and discipline with so much equity? Philosophers, dialecticians, physicians and mathematicians, and all those with technical and artistic skills, are the evidence of the Creator Spirit who indwells, moves and energizes all things (II, ii, 15–16).

Calvin invokes natural law in support of the reform. While positive law varies according to time and place, what unites all true law is *aequitas*, equity. 'It alone ought to be the aim, the rule, and the end of all laws', no less in the Church than in the civil realm (Calvin 1962: IV, xx, 16). Innumerable rules and regulations of the Roman Church are burdensome, oppressive, superstitious and a torment to Christian consciences. They are not reasonable, salutary, compassionate and adapted to human weakness and are therefore lacking in equity (IV, x, passim). Equity is the heart of divine law also, because the moral law of God 'is nothing else than the testimony of natural law, and of that conscience which God has engraven on the minds of men' (IV, xx, 16). Equitable law is fulfilled in divine charity; and it is God's purpose that charity should reign supreme.

Chapter 11

CONCILIARITY IN THE ANGLICAN TRADITION

The English Reformers and Conciliar Ideas

Conciliar ideas were in the air in early sixteenth-century England. It suited Henry VIII's purposes to invoke conciliar authority when the pope would not back his matrimonial strategy to secure a male heir. Henry instructed his ambassadors to threaten the pope with an appeal to a General Council if they did not get a sympathetic hearing for his demand for a divorce. He prepared such an appeal in expectation of his excommunication. He insisted that it was not for the pope to call a council but for him and his fellow Christian princes. In any case, he blustered, he did not need the authority of a council to reform the church in his lands. He would curtail the authority and jurisdiction of the pope, while continuing to recognize a kind of ministerial primacy: 'in the whole congregation of Christian men ... [the pope was] a chief and a principal member', but he 'hath attained and forged himself such a throne and power' as was blasphemous to Christ and his Church. However, Henry's invocation of conciliar ideas could backfire. When Pope Paul III initiated moves to bring about a council (the one that became the Council of Trent), Henry was alarmed and insisted that it should be a 'free' council. Would the decrees of a General Council be automatically binding on Christian princes? Was appeal to a council consistent with the theory of royal and imperial power descending from God, rather than devolved from the people? As Scarisbrick points out, 'Thus, ironically, the Henrician personal supremacy was threatened by the same notions of the Church as *universitas* and *congregatio fidelium* possessed of authority in both head and members which had made mediaeval Conciliarism so clear a threat to the papal primacy ... Henry thus inherited both the power and the problems of the papacy' (Scarisbrick 1971: 515n; see also 343, 383, 385, 506-507).

In the intellectual climate of the time, Henry was pushing at an open door: Christopher St German, Thomas Starkey and Thomas More were students and advocates of conciliar principles, while for subsequent generations Foxe's *Book of Martyrs* probably did more than any other source to keep the councils of the previous century, along with their claims and achievements, in the public eye (Oakley 2003: 133–40). Starkey is significant because he bridges the ecclesiastical and the civil uses of conciliarity, its canonical and secular applications. Though he was one of those who advocated taking Henry VIII's divorce case to a General Council, he did not accord ultimate authority to General Councils and rather played down their importance. Instead, and drawing directly on Aristotle and the English common law tradition (notably Sir John Fortescue), rather than on the conciliar tradition in general and Marsilius of Padua in particular, Starkey advocated a sort of secular analogy of conciliarism. The king would be advised and directed by a system of representative councils, the greatest of which was Parliament. His senior advisers would be like the college of cardinals that surrounds the pope (Mayer 1989).

Conciliar ideology is clearly at work in the official formularies of Henry VIII's reign, a period when the Lutheran Reformation was still repudiated in England. *The Bishops' Book* (1537) and *The King's Book* (1543, 1545) both insisted on the integrity and equality of national churches as parts, portions or members of the Catholic Church, differences of rites, cere-monies and opinions notwithstanding. The unity of the Church is 'a mere spiritual unity', unaffected by 'diversity of nations and countries' (Lloyd 1856: 55–56, 246–47). (Perhaps it is necessary to say that 'a mere spiritual unity' here does not mean an invisible unity, one merely of the heart, as some pietists, ancient and modern, would have it, but certainly implies a universal visible communion of particular churches. The formularies are still speaking the language of Christendom. 'Spiritual unity' certainly includes doctrine and sacraments and equally certainly excludes universal jurisdiction. Here it is uniformity of rites and ceremonies, decreed by Rome, that is being challenged.)

If the ecclesial centre of gravity was shifting from an imperial papacy to 'national' churches, there was also a redressing of the balance of authority between clergy and laity. Late mediaeval papal policy had rashly over-looked the upsurge of educated and capable lay piety, infused with mysticism. The Reformation saw the coming of age of the Christian laity and their liberation to take greater control of the Church – both its property and its policy. Luther had called on the nobility of the German nation to set in hand the reform of abuses through a council: his doctrine of the universal priesthood of the baptized entitled them to do so. But the role of laypeople was particularly decisive in the English Reformation. The *devotio moderna* signalled the awakening of lay piety. Lollardy contributed to the conscientization and instruction of the laity through vernacular Scriptures. The energy and zeal of lay folk, to which 'revisionist' historians have rightly drawn attention, would find a channel in reform (which is not to say that most of them wanted it to go in the directions that it did). Elton characterized the progress of the English Reformation as 'the unquestioned triumph of the laity over the clergy' (Elton 1972: 336). R.W. Dixon deplored the fact that reform, necessary though it was, was managed by bad instruments, being taken out of the hands of the clergy and entrusted to the tender mercies of the laity (Dixon 1878: I, 7–8). No doubt this

Anglo-Catholic historian was mindful that Henry VIII's ambitions and policies were fuelled by a consuming anti-clerical bias. However, Dixon overlooked the point that any programme of reform that had emanated from the clergy would have needed papal approval and so would have been still-born. The clamour for reform had been resisted for centuries. The only alternative source of authority for reform (that is to say, centre of jurisdiction), was the lay one of the godly prince, and to this the Reformers turned. The Elizabethan settlement was forced through by Parliament against the resistance of the Convocations (the Marian episcopate could hardly have supported it).

The flow of power from clergy to laity is not the whole picture. As Scarisbrick has pointed out, the abolition of lay guilds and fraternities, the employers of chaplains and mass priests, reduced the power of lay patrons and transferred power to the hierarchy (Scarisbrick 1984: 39, 43, 165–67). But this was swimming against the tide: as Cross points out in a book that is significantly subtitled *The Triumph of the Laity in the English Church*, the emancipation of the laity was already symbolized in the 1530s by the legal right to own and study a Bible in the vernacular (Cross 1999: 59). The Elizabethan Act of Supremacy gave Parliament (with the Convocations assenting) the authority to judge heresy (by the standards of Scripture and the early councils). 'To the limits of their capacity, laymen were trying to ensure that never again would the clerical estate have the power to enquire into religious beliefs in the way it had done during the Marian persecutions' (Cross 1999: 112). It is clear from the failure of the Laudian reforms in the next century that the lay ascendancy would not again be reversed: Laud's downfall and the destruction of his policy is largely attributable to lay opposition. Under the impress of the Reformation and its long aftermath the Church of England became – what it remains to this day – very much a layperson's church.

The English Reformers continually appeal to the conciliar tradition to support their claim that a General Council may be summoned to depose a wicked pope (PS Fulke: II, 160). They assert that a General Council is not restricted to bishops, but includes inferior clergy and laymen, and that historically the pope has not always presided (PS Jewel: I, 412; III, 206–207; IV: 1003; Jewel's view of ecumenical councils is described in Fenner 1974). They also echo the conciliarists in deeming a council 'the representative Church' (PS Whitaker: 22). They are convinced that provincial (i.e., in effect, national) synods have, as a matter of fact, decided many things independently of the pope (PS Fulke: II, 160–61). Philpot stands for all the English Reformers in calling for a council that should be free and fair – not like Constance which executed Jan Hus and Jerome of Prague, like the Two Witnesses of the book of Revelation, in spite of a safe-conduct:

> Grant us a council to be where Christ with his disciples may sit as judge, and not the pope with his flatterers; I mean where sentences may be given by holy scriptures and not

by man's constitutions: appoint us some sure and free place to come unto, where the practice of your council of Constantine [Constance] might not be dreaded, in the which council ye murdered two witnesses of the Lord, by common consent, for their open faith sake; and ye shall understand that we will never hide ourselves, nor refuse the authority of councils (PS Philpot: 396).

The Council of Constance, which had not only compassed the executions of Jan Hus and Jerome of Prague, but had refused the Hussites' demand that the cup at Holy Communion should be offered to the laity, was – needless to say – not particularly admired by the English Reformers. They favoured the Council of Basel because it was the most explicitly anti-papal of the councils. Basel had declared that many popes had fallen into error or even heresy; it had insisted that the pope is not greater than the Church, and it had asserted that a General Council is above the pope (see for example: PS Jewel: I, 400; III, 345; IV, 704, 922, 927, 1110).

Cranmer can with confidence be claimed as a conciliarist – and in his case it is patently not merely an anti-papal ploy. In the 1520s, while still far from conversion to Protestantism, Cranmer mentally distanced himself from Fisher's full-blooded papalism in a conciliar direction (MacCulloch 1996: 29). Over the matter of the royal marriage Cranmer advised Henry on his appeal to a General Council. During Henry's reign, he was in correspondence with Melanchthon to convene a Protestant council and he continued to canvas the continental Reformers about calling a council that would formulate a Protestant consensus on doctrine (not least eucharistic doctrine about which there was, Cranmer felt, distressing disagreement among the Reformers). In its concentration of learning and godliness it would rival Trent and would emulate the unity of the primitive Church. Under Edward, Cranmer attempted to persuade Calvin to meet with the Reformed theologians then sheltering in England in order precisely to resolve the eucharistic controversy among Protestants. Calvin professed that he was prepared to cross ten seas to bring about such a council, but Cranmer's plans were thwarted by the premature death of Edward and the accession of Mary (PS *Original Letters*: 14, 17, 24–25; McNeill 1930: ch. 6).

Article XXI of the Thirty-nine Articles of Religion, *Of the Authority of General Councils*, makes three points. The Latin original dates from 1563; the English text was published in 1571. The Articles are printed at the back of the Book of Common Prayer, 1662. The history of various recensions, together with Latin and English texts, is given in Hardwick 1851. The first proposition lays down, against the background of the Council of Trent (the article goes back to the Forty-two Articles of 1553), that 'General Councils may not be gathered together without the commandment and will of princes'. Though this article does not insist that princes must actually convene a General Council, it makes its point against the background of the papacy's claim to convoke councils, to preside at them and to ratify their decisions. Many modern (i.e. post-Tractarian) Anglicans would no doubt regard this typical Reformation statement as a pathetic piece of sixteenth-century special pleading; to affirm it today would almost certainly carry an air of futile implausibility. However, Bishop Gibson astutely points out in his treatise on the Thirty-nine Articles (1st edition 1896–97) that governments not only have the right to be consulted as a matter of courtesy, but in practice also have the power to say whether or not an Ecumenical Council will be held (not least, we might add, whether it will be held on their territory). Gibson recalls that European governments did in fact play an important part in determining whether or not the Vatican Council of 1870 should take place. It is also a brute fact that every General Council during the period of the 'undivided church' was convened with 'the commandment and will of princes' (Gibson 1910: 532–33).

The second proposition of Article XXI insists that councils are not infallible: 'And when they be gathered together (forasmuch as they be an assembly of men, whereof all be not governed with the spirit and word of God) they may err, and sometime have erred, even in things pertaining unto God [*in hijs quae ad normam pietatis pertinent* – in matters pertaining to the rule of faith].' Though this is making a negative point, it is clear from the more expansive statement of the proposed reformed canon law (see below) that General Councils are revered by the English Reformers. Gibson makes the point that Councils 'have always been treated by the Church as liable to err', in so far as many have had their decrees reviewed by later councils and sometimes their decisions have been reversed (Gibson 1910: 534).

The third proposition lays down a scriptural test for these sometimes fallible councils: 'Wherefore, things ordained by them as necessary to salvation, have neither strength nor authority, unless it may be declared that they be taken out of holy Scripture.' It is worth noting that this is not an example of the Protestant slogan *sola scriptura*: like Article 6, *Of the Sufficiency of Holy Scriptures for Salvation* and like the explicit teaching of Richard Hooker, the hermeneutical principle 'by Scripture alone' is applied purely to the doctrine of the way of salvation, not to everything that goes on in the life of the Church.

In the draft of the reformed canon law, the *Reformatio Legum Ecclesiasticarum*, Cranmer and his colleagues in the drafting committee said of councils:

> Although we freely grant great honour to the councils, and especially to the ecumenical ones, yet we judge that all of them must be placed far below the dignity of the canonical scriptures ... we do not regard them as binding on our faith except in so far as they can be proved out of the Holy Scriptures.

Councils have erred and contradicted each other, even in matters of faith (*in fide*). So councils are to be held in honour and studied with reverence, but are to be tested by Scripture (Bray 2000: 183).

Following his degradation under Queen Mary, Cranmer presented a formal appeal from the authority of the pope to that of 'a free General Council', for such a council, he insisted, 'lawfully gathered together in the Holy Ghost, and representing the Holy Catholic Church, is above the pope' (McNeill in Rouse and Neill 1954: 56). MacCulloch suggests that Cranmer's reverence for the authority of a General Council runs like a golden thread through his theological development. 'As Cranmer's papal loyalty fell away, this deep emotional attachment to the idea of the General Council remained with him all through the uncertain ecclesiological waters of the years after 1533' (MacCulloch 1996: 29–30).

Jewel longed for a council that would be held in the spirit of the gospel: 'God grant that we may once see that day that a General Council may be called, wherein Christ may sit president, and all these matters that are now in question may have indifferent hearing, and may be decided by the word of God' (PS Jewel: II, 995). Jewel was insistent that the English Reformation had not been conducted without councils, assemblies, conferences of learned men, etc., particularly in Parliament and Convocation (PS Jewel: IV, 902).

A Modified Conciliarism

Nevertheless, the English Reformers added several provisos to their generally positive remarks about councils – though Ridley (PS: 123) seems to look askance at the idea of a universal council, as neither commanded by Christ nor found in Scripture.

First, reformation of the Church could not tarry for a General Council. In the light of the reforming councils of the previous century, wrote Jewel, 'if there were none other possible way to seek redress, then most miserable were the Church of God'. It had pleased God, continued Jewel, to plant his Church in this realm of England (presumably through Joseph of Arimathea) three hundred years before the Council of Nicea, and he was well able to reform it when necessary (PS Jewel: I, 322–23). Implied in this gambit was recourse to the godly prince as the executive of reformation.

Second, councils were subject to the Word of God and their role was merely to interpret the Scriptures. 'We allow,' wrote William Whitaker, 'that it is a highly convenient way of finding the true sense of Scripture for devout and learned men to assemble, examine the cause diligently, and investigate the truth; yet with this proviso, that they govern their decision wholly by the Scriptures.' 'Such a proceeding,' Whitaker added, 'we, for our parts, have long wished for' (PS Whitaker: 434). However, not all Anglicans were willing to circumscribe the discretion of councils by making them merely seminars for biblical exegesis, for they were well aware that Scripture does not legislate for many practical issues of Church polity and worship. 'Is it not therefore manifest,' asks Archbishop Whitgift, 'that councils, both general and provincial, by their acts, declare that touching ceremonies, discipline and government of the Church, many things are left to the discretion of the Church which be not expressed in the Scriptures?' (PS Whitgift: I, 220). This liberty is indeed affirmed in Article 34 of the Thirty-nine Articles: 'It is not necessary that Traditions and Ceremonies be in all places one, and utterly like; ... they ... may be changed according to the diversities of countries, times, and men's manners, so that nothing be ordained against God's Word.' Such discretion for particular churches would soon be established on the basis of first principles of divine law and human reason by Richard Hooker.

Third, councils might be convened only by the authority or with the permission of the civil ruler, the magistrate. It is in opposition to the papal claim to convene and preside at councils that the Reformers insist that (in the words of Article XXI) 'General Councils may not be gathered together without the commandment and will of princes'. While Cranmer believes that no single prince has the authority to call a general, as opposed to a provincial council (PS Cranmer: II, 467), the English Reformers never weary of the refrain that councils may be convened only by princes (PS Parker: 110; Jewel: I, 382, 411; III, 225; IV, 902–903, 996; Whitgift: II, 362). Let Rogers, commenting on Article XXI, speak for them all:

> Never yet hath there been a council, either general or national, or whatsoever (I only except the councils held by the apostles and apostolical men in a troublous state and time of the Church, there being then no Christian princes or emperors to countenance the truth), either begun or ended to the glory of God, but it hath been, I say not *called* only, but *confirmed* also by some godly emperor king or queen (PS Rogers: 205).

Fourth, councils – even General Councils – were not infallible. For the Reformers, only Holy Scripture was inerrant. It was the execution of Jan Hus at the Council of Constance that constituted for them, just as it did for Luther, the most vivid evidence of the fallibility of General Councils. This fallibility extended even to the interpretation of Scripture, the supreme doctrinal authority, and of dogmatic judgements concerning the rule of faith. Cranmer insisted that General Councils had 'erred, as well in the judgement of the scriptures as also in necessary articles of our faith' (PS Cranmer: II, 39). Other English Reformers echo this (PS: Fulke: II, 231; Ridley 129–30, 134; Rogers 208; Jewel: III, 176–77; IV, 1109). Article XXI means precisely this when it states that General Councils 'may err, and sometimes have erred, even in things pertaining unto God'.

Fifth, the conciliarism of the Reformers had little or no place for the papacy, where the pre-Reformation conciliarists worked within the given framework of papal primacy, albeit interpreted in various ways. The English Reformers' conciliarism was Hamlet without the prince. (For the English Reformers' view of the Roman Church and the views of Hooker and Field, see Avis 2002: 12–14, 38–39, 53–56; for the early seventeenth-century, see Milton 1995.)

Finally, the English Reformers insisted that the authority of councils should not be measured by their size. Neither numbers nor unanimity were necessarily a guide to truth. Those ancient Israelites who worshipped the golden calf were very much of one mind, as Jewel pointed out, not to mention the crowds who urged Pilate to have Jesus crucified (PS III, 69). It is the substance and content of a council that lends it credibility, not the number of bishops present, or the authority of their office, but the substantive content of their conclusions commends a council to the Church (as Cranmer was reported as saying). But as Greenslade points out, this tactic demands a doctrine of reception, which the English Reformers did not elaborate (Greenslade 1967: 108).

The Reformers, continental or English, were not pure conciliarists. There is not a direct line of continuity between the conciliar theorists of the fourteenth and fifteenth centuries and the Protestant Reformers. The Reformers did not set great store by hopes of a General Council. Councils had proved to be a broken reed. Hopes of reformation in head and members were now invested in the civil magistrate, with or without the instrumentality of a council. In practice the Church of England under Henry and Elizabeth was run not so much on conciliar lines as by the autocratic methods of monarchical Erastianism, the dominance of the civil authority. Furthermore, the English Reformers compromised the integrity of their conciliarism by their hostility to the Council of Constance, which is generally regarded as the most impressive council of the late Middle Ages, and by their enthusiasm for the Council of Basel, which was marred by anti-papal excesses and latterly dissolved into a shambles. It is a modified expression of the conciliar ideal that we find in the Reformers, but their affirmation of the conciliar principles of representation, constitutionality and consent is significant for the later emergence of a reformed conciliarity. In W.B. Patterson's view, 'conciliarism, though it left its mark on the leading Reformers and on Rome, took root in the theology of the English Church to a much greater extent than in that of Lutheranism or Calvinism – or of Counter-Reformation Catholicism' (Patterson 1997a: 288).

Natural Law and the English Reformation

Natural law arguments pervaded the polemics of the English Reformation – on both sides. The significance of natural law, writes Baumer, 'can hardly be overestimated, for it constituted the backbone of all the salient arguments both for and against the Reformation' and the concept of natural law 'represented the idiom of Tudor political expression' (Baumer 1940: 131, 133). The notion of natural law was infinitely flexible, a nose of wax, but the fact remains that, in all of its various manifestations, it represented the claims of a higher authority than human, positive law, thus relativizing in principle law-making bodies and persons and all the institutions, the structures of authority, that embodied that positive law.

The appeal to natural law is deployed, in somewhat different ways, by the three most salient political controversialists of the first half of the sixteenth century: Christopher St German, Thomas Starkey (who identified natural law with Roman law) and John Ponet (who assimilated it to the Decalogue). The ancient English legal consensus, represented by Sir John Fortescue and Bracton, which held that customary law was either an expression of natural law, or else was no true law at all, was breaking up.

The English Reformers taught that law is supreme and that natural law judges positive law. This principle applies in both Church and State. In the ecclesiastical sphere, the oppressive laws imposed by the papacy must give way to divine and natural law that promotes human freedom and well-being. In the civil sphere the king is subject to the law and so must share his rule with Parliament, which makes the law of the land. The Reformers argued for the constitutional exercise of power and for the need for constraints provided by the consent of the governed. The king is responsible to God to rule for the common good. While political theorists justified Henry VIII's arrogation of power to himself, the Reformers generally were unreceptive to the doctrines of absolute monarchy and unlimited sovereignty that were currently being propounded on the Continent by some civil lawyers under the influence of Roman law. Baumer's conclusion is that 'there can be no doubt whatever that Reformation England followed the mediaeval tradition which taught that the monarch, whatever his relation to positive law, was subordinate to, and in fact the executive of, natural and divine law' (Baumer 1940: 136). Towards the end of the century, Richard Hooker took this to an extreme, minimizing the jurisdiction of the monarch in the Church to an extent that was a far cry from the views of Tyndale or Cranmer.

To what extent, if any, did later, 'classical' Anglican divines appeal to the conciliar tradition and restate its aims and principles? To go some small way towards answering this question, let us take half a dozen pretty central thinkers of the Anglican tradition from across the span of this period but with greater attention given to Richard Hooker, as befits his stature and achievement as the unrivalled exponent of Anglican ecclesiology.

Hooker as Constitutional Thinker

The scope of Richard Hooker's (1554–1600) achievement continues to astonish us. He was not only a divine with a mastery of the full range of theological disciplines, but a major constitutional and political thinker. He had made a substantial study not only of the canon law of the Western Church, but also of the civil law of Christian nations, which together comprised the *ius commune* of Christendom. He was able to deploy the views of commentators on both disciplines. He marshalled these legal resources, amply complemented by biblical, patristic and reformed theological material, in order to demonstrate that the established ecclesiastical arrangements in England were defensible, equitable and theologically orthodox. In the course of his argument, Hooker set out the purpose and scope of law, relating natural law to customary and positive law in the Church, invoked the values of the conciliar tradition (representation, consent, constitutional authority, the common good), and argued for the involvement of laypeople in governance and the making of law. On these aspects see Helmholz 2001; Thompson 1972: 21; references to Hooker's *Of the Laws of Ecclesiastical Polity* are by book, chapter and section according to Keble's edition (Hooker 1845). The Folger edition (Hooker 1977–98) provides a critical text and commentary.

Hooker sets controversial issues of ecclesiastical polity within the framework of law. His aim is to establish the 'laws' or principles that should order the worship and governance of the Christian Church at all times and to show, in the light of those principles, that the laws that currently order the reformed English Church are salutary for a Christian nation and consonant with the will of God. Although Hooker probably looked beyond immediate controversies (Shuger 1997: 116–17) – if he did not, he far exceeded his brief and it strains credibility to see the *Laws* as purely an occasional, even *ad hominem* piece of work – his contest was primarily with the puritan reformists (sometimes referred to by commentators as the Disciplinarians, the advocates of the so-called godly discipline of church government by elders or presbyters) who urged that the reform should go radically further. They believed that the English Church should become conformed to the Genevan model designed by Calvin and Beza. They campaigned for replacing episcopacy with presbyterian government, purging the liturgy of supposed formality and repetition, stripping it of so-called 'popish' residues such as the surplice, the sign of the cross in baptism and of the ring in marriage, kneeling to receive Holy Communion, etc.

However, for Hooker, the struggle was certainly not about words or gestures, or even – more importantly – about whether there should be a single pattern of Church government, but about authority. How did God order the world for the sake of peace and harmony? What authority has Christ given to his Church to conduct its affairs in such a way that souls are led safely to salvation? For what purpose is divine revelation given and what are the scope and limits of biblical authority?

Behind the issue of authority for Hooker lies the even deeper question of catholicity: the need to know that one belongs (and, as Hooker argues in the sermon *Of Justification*, to know that one's community and ancestors also belong or belonged) to the one Church of Christ in which salvation is to be had. That Church has continued from the time of the Apostles and the early Fathers; it has endured through mediaeval times and its integrity has not been fundamentally impaired by the events of the Reformation. Hooker is convinced that the 'Laws of the Church', that have informed the rites, customs and ordering of the English Church, have remained essentially unchanged for centuries and have not been abrogated by the events of previous reigns, especially the rejection of Roman jurisdiction under Henry VIII (Hooker, *Of the Laws of Ecclesiastical Polity* [hereinafter EP], I, i, 3). It is not the doings of Luther or Calvin, Henry VIII or Cranmer that occupy the forefront of Hooker's mind when he considers the Church towards the end of the sixteenth century: they are definitely on the periphery. What fills Hooker's vision is the *una sancta*, its continuity through time and its extension in space. The Church is a divine society, a *societas perfecta* (a complete or integral society), comprised of many particular churches that are also societies in their own right, with the authority to order their own affairs by human (positive) law. The Church of England is one such, the Church of Rome another, the Church of France or of Wittenberg or of Geneva yet others.

Hooker senses that, as far as the English Church is concerned, this vision and understanding of the Church is in mortal danger; the whole visible fabric that unites her with the Church of the Fathers and their mediaeval successors could 'pass away as in a dream' (EP Preface i, 1). It is not only a theology that is at stake but a Christian culture and civilization. 'Nothing less than a way of thinking about God, the world and human existence is at issue. The radical sweeping away of social structures and traditions in the name of biblical purity threatens the very foundations of a way of thought and life, of faith and worship, that is continuous with classical, patristic, and mediaeval culture and philosophy' (Patterson 2002: 963). It is not mere rhetoric but precisely an appeal to that world when Hooker says: 'we offer the laws whereby we live unto the general trial and judgement of the whole world' (EP I, i, 3).

Hooker's celebrated method of taking controversial questions back to first principles is not simply a tactic of irrefutability and a way of belittling the much more pragmatic arguments of his adversaries. The ecclesiological issues – authority, catholicity, the cure of souls – were so fundamental that they demanded this treatment. That is why the case is argued from the nature of law, which in turn derives from the mind and being of God.

Hooker on Natural Law

Hooker's exposition of the role and scope of law takes its rise in the law of reason or natural law, but behind this there lies the mysterious realm of the eternal law that guides the working of God and which is inseparable from God's very being, for 'the being of God is a kind of law to his working' (EP I, ii, 2). This means that God is not only a law to himself, but to the whole created order as well (EP I, ii, 3). The work of God in the world is an expression of God's nature which is one of goodness and generosity. His will is, therefore, not arbitrary but rational (EP I, ii, 5). The whole of nature, including the animate creation, follows the laws that the Creator has inscribed within it. Among these laws is the significant law of sociality which binds together the members of a single body and directs them to serve each other's good and to prefer the good of the whole to their own individual good (EP I, iii, 5). All creatures instinctively seek greater participation in the divine goodness for themselves and their progeny. Humankind also is driven by desire for the good, informed by knowledge and put into action by the will (though this struggles with appetite). We speak of will, rather than mere appetite, when choice is governed by knowledge and reason. 'For the laws of well-doing are the dictates of right reason' (EP I, vii, 4). Human reason has agreed over time on certain rules of action and these have the sanction of nature and of God, indeed of nature as the voice of God: 'The general and perpetual voice of men is as the sentence of God himself' (EP I, viii, 3). The laws of nature are taught to all humans by reason and do not need to be especially divinely revealed (EP I, viii, 9). For Hooker and natural law see Thompson 1972: 26–29; Grace 1997.

Respect for natural law leads to social harmony and human flourishing, for in order to live with dignity and sufficiency 'we are naturally induced to seek communion and fellowship with others' (EP I, x, 1). But beyond that natural inclination, there is always some form of compact or agreement about how humankind will live together in community and this is the Law of a Commonweal (commonwealth), 'the very soul of a politic body', all the parts of which are held together, energized and directed to such actions 'as the common good requireth' (EP I, x, 1).

It is sometimes claimed that Hooker's use of natural law (which he calls the law of reason) distinguishes him from the magisterial Reformers, such as Luther and Calvin. But, as we have seen, this is to overlook the significant extent to which these Reformers continue the mediaeval tradition of natural law, a law that is imprinted on nature and inscribed in the human heart and which Scripture confirms and the Decalogue summarizes. Natural law and divine (revealed) law are in full agreement, though mere natural law is sufficient only in the temporal sphere, in the realm of social, political, cultural and economic activity (cf. Thompson 1972: 29–32. Kirby 1990 and 1999 is right in drawing attention to what the magisterial Reformers and Hooker have in common, but he assimilates natural law to natural theology and as a result operates with an unfocused and incoherent concept of natural law.)

Natural law, Hooker points out, has to be translated into positive, human law in various forms in order to regulate specific societies. They require both 'mixed' law (a combination of natural and positive, such as laws against murder and theft) and merely positive law (that is essentially arbitrary and could be changed by agreement, such as laws concerning property and social deference). A politic society is a defined community with a common purpose which has the inherent authority to make its own law and to administer it. Nations are obviously politic societies, but in Hooker's view, so is the Christian Church and every particular church within it (to most intents and purposes, national churches: cf. EP III, i, 14).

Hooker: The Church as a Political Society

The Church is not only a 'society supernatural', a mystical body, but also a society as such, a politic society and is grounded in the same reality as other politic societies, that is to say the natural human inclination towards 'a sociable life' combined with 'consent to some certain bond of association' inscribed in the law that governs their fellowship. What distinguishes the Church as a politic society from other societies is not the political principles that determine its social life, for these are generic, but the subjects of its fellowship: not only men, but God, angels and the saints (EP I, xv, 2).

So to politic societies general political principles apply. Among the principles that apply to politic societies are various axioms that govern the exercise of authority in the making and administering of law. Authority should be exercised in a constitutional way, so that it is limited, not absolute. In kings 'the best limited power is best', that is to say, limited by the rule of law, natural and positive; whatever power the king has, he has by law, 'the bounds and limits of it are known': EP VIII, ii, 12; viii, 9). Authority is derived from the consent of the people and that consent is given in a representative way, either tacitly or explicitly.

No one has the right to rule another without the latter's consent. There is no divine right to absolute power or unchallengeable hierarchy (EP I, x, 4). Authority resides in the community, but is vested in certain officers by common consent. By God-given natural law 'the lawful power of making laws to command whole politic societies of men belongeth so properly unto the same entire societies' that it is 'no better than mere tyranny' for anyone to presume to exercise it without consent or a direct appointment from God (such as we see sometimes in Scripture) (EP I, x, 8). Laws are not laws if they lack public approval and consent. Hooker invokes what he dubs 'the vulgar [i.e. common] axiom' of the canonists, '*Quod omnes tangit ...*', what concerns all must be considered and approved by all (EP VIII, vi, 8). Against the Presbyterians, Hooker claims that the consent of the people is taken more seriously in the Church of England: 'with us the people have commonly far more sway and force than with them' (EP VII, xiv, 10: largely on the grounds that lay patronage works on behalf of the parish community).

Hooker harps on the theme of consent: the word is constantly reiterated. But (as Thompson has shown against earlier 'Whig' interpreters: Thompson 1972: 40–43) this emphasis should not be assimilated to a

Lockean theory of social contract. Hooker's concept of the social compact (not contract) is a slightly hazy one. He suggests that communities may give their consent to being ruled in all sorts of tacit ways, including some that are now inaccessible and have to be postulated in the past on the basis of our present experience. We unquestioningly obey many laws that we were not consulted about because we inherit the obligations of our ancestors as members of the same society. In an interesting invocation of the principle of representation, Hooker says: 'we were then alive in our predecessors, and they in their successors do live still'; 'corporations are immortal' (EP I, x, 8). The implication is of course that the puritan critics of the present establishment of the Church of England are bound by the assent of their ancestors to that system.

In addition to the laws that concern humankind in a state of nature and as formed into politic societies, there is a third area of law which concerns societies as they relate to each other: the Law of Nations. This expression of law is an extension of the natural impulse towards 'sociable communion' one with another, for this leads on to the wish 'to have a kind of society and fellowship even with all mankind'. And just as there are laws to promote communion among nations, so there are laws to effect and maintain communion between Christian nations (that is to say, particular churches, constituted as politic societies). When these laws are freely embraced by the sovereign powers of the various nations we would have a basis for unconstrained catholicity of practice, in contrast to 'the tyranny and oppression' arising from the universal pretensions of the bishop of Rome, whom Hooker, following Whitaker, styles a Nimrod, that is to say a mighty hunter (or predator) of the Church (EP VIII, iii, 5; cf. Genesis 10.8–9; see also Cromartie 2000). The proper instruments for the promulgation of these laws and for their administration are General Councils (EP I, x, 14).

Hooker on General Councils

Hooker's comparatively brief discussion of General Councils is 'the most coherent treatment of this subject by any theologian in the Church of England in the sixteenth century', according to W.B. Patterson (Patterson 1997a: 294). Hooker praises the role of General Councils in maintaining and furthering communion between portions of the universal Church which Hooker portrays as like the seas and oceans of the world, contiguous with each each and often flowing into each other (see further on Hooker's ecclesiology Avis 2002: 31–51; his view of councils is described in Fenner 1974). These 'reverend, religious and sacred consultations', the General Councils, have their place among the 'laws of spiritual commerce between Christian nations'. General Councils are invoked by Hooker as the antidote to that universal papal sovereignty that in recent times had supressed them. Councils are 'a thing whereof God's own blessed Spirit was the author; a thing practised by the holy Apostles themselves; a thing always afterward kept and observed throughout the world; a thing never otherwise than most highly esteemed of, till pride, ambition and tyranny began by factious and vile endeavours to abuse that divine intention unto the furtherance of wicked purposes.' The grievous abuse to which Councils have recently been subjected (by the papacy) should not cause us to despair of them, urges Hooker, but rather should spur us 'to study how so gracious a thing may again be reduced to that first perfection'. Councils come into their own when disagreements about the interpretation of divine (biblical, revealed) law need to be resolved; when disputes about human (positive) law bring scandal and offence; when agreement is needed in doctrine or polity, order and governance in the Church (EP I, x, 14).

Hooker holds to the basic political axiom of conciliarism that power of governance is vested in the people and that their consent is therefore necessary for its exercise in all matters, whether temporal or spiritual. 'The natural subject of power civil all men confess to be the body of the commonwealth ... [so too] the true original subject of power also to make church-laws is the whole entire body of that church for which they are made.' Just as no human being may impose laws upon another without their consent, so no particular church may impose 'canons ecclesiastical' upon another church (EP VIII, vi, 1). Again: 'the whole body of the Church being the first original subject of all mandatory and coercive power within itself', the consent of the laity, as well as of the clergy and 'the highest power', is required for the making of church law (EP VIII, vi, 3, 8). The consent of the clergy is given in their convocations and that of the laity in Parliament. While bishops and clergy are best qualified to adjudicate on matters of doctrine and worship, it is 'the general consent of all', including the laity, that gives the force of law (EP VIII, vi, 11).

The most assiduous advocates of 'the bishop of Rome's inordinate sovereignty', he says (thinking of the late mediaeval and indeed contemporary papal absolutists whose ideas we have sketched in Chapter 3), strive above all against the point that power of jurisdiction belongs to the whole Church and that 'no person hath or can have the same, otherwise than derived from the body of the Church'. They see clearly, Hooker points out, that this principle carries the corollary that a council of the whole Church is above the pope. Therefore, Hooker continues, 'as many as draw the chariot of the pope's preeminence, the first conclusion which they contend for is: The power of jurisdiction ecclesiastical doth not rest derived from Christ immediately into the whole body of the Church, but into the prelacy.' In this, Hooker asserts, they err in not distinguishing between those in whom the power resides and those who may exercise it on their behalf (EP VIII, vi, 2–4). Authority is vested in the whole body of the Church, but exercised on behalf of the body by its representative officers, the bishops.

The interpretation of Hooker's political theory, like other aspects of his thought, continues to be the subject of scholarly argument. His political theory informs his ecclesiology, for he holds that churches are politic societies that are subject to general legal, constitutional and political principles and that these exclude the arbitrary or absolute exercise of power, whether by monarchs or prelates. What shines out clearly when we look at Hooker against the background of the pre-Reformation Conciliar Movement is his adherence to conciliar political philosophy and to conciliar fundamental ecclesiology. He conceives the Church in organic, rather than in hierarchical or hierocratic, terms and therefore subordinates its structures of governance to the body as a whole. What is also apparent is his commitment in particular to the conciliar principles of constitutionality, representation and consent. Underlying this is Hooker's appropriation of the mediaeval natural law tradition and, linked to this, a sense that laws and their implementation should be orientated to the common good – which can only be known by consulting the people in whom authority ultimately resides.

Richard Field on Councils

Often neglected or overlooked, Field (1561–1616) stands with Hooker as a formative shaper of Anglican ecclesiology. His rather more pedestrian and scholastic method, exhaustively thorough and aiming to be definitive and unanswerable, is the foil to Hooker's creative and somewhat idiosyncratic approach (on Field's ecclesiology see Avis 2002: 51–58). Field has a strong view of the universal visible Church, containing even heretics and schismatics, but a rather low-key view of General Councils. Their role is to resolve controverted doctrines and they do this on the basis of Scripture and guided by the rule of faith.

The rule of faith is handed down from generation to generation right back to the Apostles and 'apostolic men'. It contains nothing that is not apparent in the Scriptures or necessarily implied by them and has been held unvaried and unchanging through Christian history (Field 1847: IV, 484). Because the Church of Christ cannot fail (the doctrine of indefectibility), we must postulate a body of true believers continuing within the visible Church since the beginning and adhering infallibly ('absolutely free from all error and ignorance of divine things that are to be known by revelation' and 'absolutely led into the knowledge of all truth') to this rule of faith (Field 1847: II, 292–93) .

The biblical rule of faith comprises the fundamentals of Christianity ('those things which everyone is bound expressly to know and believe, and wherein no man can err without note of heresy' and 'upon peril of eternal damnation'). They include the triune nature of the godhead, the divine creation, fall and moral government of the world; the Incarnation and atonement of Jesus Christ, the election of the Church, the means of grace including the sacraments, and the Last Things. These doctrines, and these alone, constitute 'the whole platform of all Christian religion' (Field 1847: I, 158–61).

A lawful General Council is one at which all the patriarchates are represented and which agrees unanimously to its decisions ('with unanimous consent'). Such a council demands the acceptance and obedience of the faithful. The first six General Councils meet these criteria. If, as individuals, we are not completely persuaded of the truth of their teachings, we may privately search the Scriptures and the records of the primitive Church, in a quest for truth and assurance, but it is not open to us to challenge publicly the conclusions of these councils. We do not have certainty, but a probability of truth and this is sufficient. 'We may safely conclude that no man can certainly pronounce that whatsoever the greater part of bishops assembled in a General Council agree on is undoubtedly true.' We have no reason to assume that General Councils enjoy a unique degree of divine assistance 'beyond the general influence that is required to the performance of every good work', nor are they granted more privileged guidance than patriarchal, national or provincial synods (Field 1847: IV, 51–61). Field perpetuates the conciliar tradition as it was received by the Reformation, but in a muted form compared with Hooker.

Lancelot Andrewes: Exponent of Conciliarism

We need not turn to the polemical Latin works of Lancelot Andrewes (1555–1626) to see him in his conciliar colours. His book of personal devotions and intercessions, the *Preces Privatae*, says it all. In his prayers for the Church he prays first for 'the Catholic Church, its establishment and increase'; then for the Eastern Church, for 'its deliverance [from Islam] and union'; then for the Western Church, 'its readjustment and peace'; and finally for the British Church, for 'the supply of what is wanting in it, the strengthening of what remains' (Andrewes 1920: I, 57). Here is a sense of perspective and proportion about the Christian Church and each major part or portion within it. The Catholic Church embraces what later writers would call various branches and is broadly divided into East and West, the Roman Church being subsumed within the West and – interestingly – not mentioned by name. The consequences of the Reformation require 'adjustment' and calming down (a nicely laid-back view!). Within that overall landscape the British Church (Ireland included) finds a home: it is not perfect and has lost some things of value through the Reformation, but it has integrity and is worth strengthening. Like other seventeenth-century English divines (e.g. Field, Laud, Bramhall, Cosin), Andrewes is prepared to consider universal primacy under certain conditions, but without conceding universal jurisdiction or infallibility. See further on Andrewe's ecclesiology Avis 2002: 131–33. For views on papal primacy see the texts in More and Cross 1935: 53–72.

In his sense of the universal visible Church and of its totality as a body that nevertheless is made up of particular churches, Andrewes speaks for all the classical Anglican divines. The conceptuality goes back in English ecclesiological thinking, before the influence of Lutheran ideas, to the official statements of Henry VIII's reign that reflect the conciliar tradition and, though somewhat repressed under Edward, it emerges once again in Jewel and Hooker and is elaborated by Field. When we touch on Laud and Thorndike in what follows, to avoid repetition, we can take it as read.

In his study of Andrewes' sermons Nicolas Lossky finds in him a conciliar expression of the faith that is congenial to the approach of the Eastern churches (Lossky 1991: 339–40). The authority of a council for Andrewes is a spiritual and mystical, not a juridical, matter. It shines out where a council was faithful to the fullness of the apostolic faith and allowed itself to be led by the Holy Spirit. The authenticity of councils resides in the truth to which they allowed themselves to be subject, that is to say the presence of Christ himself.

Andrewes preached before King James I at Hampton Court in 1606 on 'The Right and Power of Calling Assemblies'. His purpose is to reassure the king that he alone has the authority to call a synod. Andrewes points out that the seven General Councils (the number is significant: the English divines varied in how many General Councils they accepted; Andrewes is at the top end of the scale) were all convened by the Roman Emperor. Innumerable national and provincial councils have been called by kings and emperors, in Spain, France and Germany, for example. But the Church may herself convoke a council in the absence of the magistrate, as it did before the time of the emperor Constantine, because in such a case 'God's order ceaseth' (Andrewes 1843: 141–43, esp. 165).

What is significant here is the way that Andrewes is able to presuppose much of the conciliar ideology. He has a sense of the long and mainly honourable tradition of General Councils. He can take it for granted that councils are the normal means for the Church to consult in times of stress. National and provincial synods are accepted practice. In an emergency the Church cannot be denied its council simply because the magistrate is not available.

Andrewes lifted up General Councils in his preaching at court, but King James I needed no convincing about their importance and potential. Soon after coming to the throne of England in 1603 James was canvassing the idea of a General Council to reconcile the warring factions of Christendom and to lead to 'general Christian union'. James had imbibed the vigorous Scottish conciliar tradition, epitomized by John Maier (Major), and had a strong affinity to the conciliar ideas of Hooker and Field. James was prepared to concede that the pope should convene such a council, provided that it were free and unconstrained and that Protestant as well as Catholic churches were adequately represented. In one sense, James knew that that was the only condition on which Rome would participate; but he also openly acknowledged Rome as the Mother of the British churches, 'though defiled with some infirmities and corruptions'. Neither did he leave out of account the Eastern churches, fostering dialogue and scholarly exchanges between the Church of England and the Greek Orthodox Church, in particular between Archbishop Abbot and Cyril Lukaris, the Orthodox Patriarch of Alexandria. James's most concrete contribution to conciliarity was his sending of an Anglican delegation to the Synod of Dort (1618–19). Though as a purely Protestant, indeed Reformed rather than Lutheran council, it fell well short of James's conciliar ideals, he saw it as a possible stepping stone to greater conciliar ambitions. If the Reformed could agree among themselves, they could then reach out to the Lutherans; and if pan-Protestant harmony could be secured, a joint approach could be made to the Church of Rome. Bishop Dudley Carleton, one of James's representatives at Dort, in his defence of the Church of England, drew on the fifteenth-century conciliarists from the era of Constance and Basel, such as Gerson and Cusa, confessing, 'We are the children of them that held these councils' (Patterson 1997b: 112; cf. 36–37, 57–60, 69, 194, 196–219).

William Laud's High Conciliarism

Laud (1573–1645) discusses councils mainly in the context of polemic (see further on Laud's ecclesiology Avis 2002: 133–37). He confesses, in defending the Reformation, that a General Council, 'free and entire', would have been the best remedy for the 'gangrene that had spread so far and eaten so deep into Christianity'. But urgent treatment for this disease was called for. The Council of Trent would never have been called in order to reform the Church, he believes, unless some provincial or national synods, 'under supreme and regal power', had already initiated reform. Laud cites Gerson when he says: 'Very grave and learned men [i.e. Gerson] ... have taught me, that when the universal Church will not, or for the iniquities of the times cannot obtain and settle a free General Council, it is lawful, nay sometimes necessary, to reform gross abuses by a national or a provincial [council].' A council, according to Laud, has the authority 'to order, settle and define differences' that have arisen concerning faith. It has this authority from the whole Catholic Church, and thus ultimately from God, even though there is no explicit dominical institution of councils to which it can appeal. The decisions of a General Council are binding. It constitutes 'the supreme, external, living, temporary ecclesiastical judge of all controversies'. Laud has something like our modern doctrine of reception when he remarks that, when a council has reached a decision, it remains for the whole Church to accept it, 'be it never so tacitly' (Laud 1849: LACT, II: 170, 291, 216).

Would a General Council, as Laud conceives it, be infallible in its teaching? Laud's answer is Yes, provided that two rather swingeing conditions are fulfilled. First, the council would have to be fully representative of the whole Church (this of course excludes all councils that have taken place since the hardening of the separation of East and West in 1054 and any that have excluded Protestants). Second, it would have to submit itself to the guidance of the Holy Spirit given through Scripture (this rules out the tradition of the Church as a source of doctrine). And then its infallibility would be confined to matters necessary to salvation. At first sight, it appears that Laud is going beyond the Reformation consensus and flouting Article XXI of the Thirty-nine Articles that states that councils may err and in fact have erred. However, since in Laud's view, the truth of salvation can never perish from the Church anyway – he holds, along with the Reformers and their seventeenth-century successors, the doctrine of the indefectibility of the Church – he is in fact ascribing to councils simply the gift of discerning essential truth that is already present in the mind (or heart?) of the Church (Laud 1849: LACT, II: 155–58).

Herbert Thorndike: The Authority of Councils

Thorndike (1598–1672), one of the most acute and solid of the classical Anglican theologians, also deals with the question of 'the constitution and authority of councils' (see further on Thorndike's ecclesiology, Avis 2002: 141–44). Councils, for Thorndike, are properly constituted by bishops, though some presbyters may be privileged to take part and even to vote in the capacity of representing their bishops. Laypeople, too, may be present, but in what capacity is not clear. Thorndike points out, with the presbyterian platform in his sights, that there were no lay elders at the Council of Jerusalem in Acts chapter 15! He believes that he can call the pope's bluff regarding the promise of a General Council and argues, as Laud also had done, that 'the pretence of the pope's infinite power remains inconsistent with the very pretence of calling a council. For why so much trouble, to obtain a vote that shall signify nothing without his consent, his single sentence obliging no less?' (Thorndike 1844: LACT, IV: 432–34).

William Palmer: Tractarian Conciliarism

William Palmer (1803–1885) of Worcester College, Oxford, may serve to represent the moderate wing of the Oxford Movement in this brief gallery of classical Anglican views on conciliarity. See further on Palmer's ecclesiology, Avis 2002: 188–95. Palmer was the solid and steady scholar of Tractarianism and author of a two-volume *Treatise on the Church of Christ*. He recognizes the first six General Councils as truly ecumenical, but those held in the West since the breach between Rome and the Orthodox Churches in the eleventh century are 'merely national or general synods of the West, and are not invested with the authority of the Catholic Church'. Palmer affirms the importance of local and national synods of bishops: they may expect the guidance of the Holy Spirit, but they are not on the same level of authority as ecumenical synods (General Councils). Palmer also has a notion of reception that seems rather modern:

> The final authority of proper ecumenical councils does not arise merely from the number of bishops assembled in them, but from *the approbation of the catholic Church dispersed throughout the world*; which, having received their decrees, examines them with the respect due to so considerable authority, compares them with Scripture and Catholic tradition, and by an universal approbation and execution of those decrees, pronounces a final and irrefrangable sentence in their favour (Palmer 1842: II, 112–14, 128, 162, 188–90, original emphasis).

Palmer does not say what the consequences would be if the decisions of a General Council were found not to square with Scripture and tradition.

Modern Anglican Views: Dixon, Creighton, Figgis

Three modern Anglican scholars – all distinguished historians and all churchmen tending to the high side – are worth quoting here for their views on the conciliar tradition. They wrote before the rise of the Ecumenical Movement in the twentieth century, but they were uncomfortably aware of the Ultramontane thrust of nineteenth-century Roman Catholicism that culminated in the First Vatican Council's decrees concerning the universal jurisdiction and magisterial infallibility of the pope.

Richard Watson Dixon was the north country parson who in the 1860s and 1870s wrote a remarkable *History of the Church of England from the Abolition of the Roman Jurisdiction* in six volumes. Dixon described the failure of the Conciliar Movement in the fifteenth century as 'the most mournful event of modern history'. He was unsympathetic to the Reformation's reliance on state support and was not partial to Lutheran or Reformed theology. He therefore attributed 'the invasion of the temporal power' into ecclesiastical jurisdiction and the 'doctrinal revolution' which overwhelmed northern Europe at the Reformation to the intrigues of Rome which succeeded in thwarting conciliar aspirations (Dixon 1878: I, 23–24; see further on Dixon: Rupp 1966).

Mandell Creighton (1844–1901), successively vicar of Embleton in Northumberland, Dixie Professor of Ecclesiastical History in the University of Cambridge and Bishop of first Peterborough and then London, was the least partisan of historians: he catalogued the iniquities of Renaissance popes without a blush in his monumental *History of the Papacy during the Period of the Reformation*. Nevertheless, Creighton privately expressed the judgement that the Renaissance papacy 'rendered a violent Reformation necessary because it refused to make a mild and wise one'. Creighton recognized the power of national aspirations during the conciliar period, commenting that 'the catastrophe [*sic*] of the Council of Constance lay in the fact that national sentiment was too strong for a joint European action; but Europe did not understand the fact' (L. Creighton 1904: I, 231, 266). In his history, Creighton states that the men of that time 'could not discover the interests of Christendom because they were overlaid by conflicting interests of classes and nations. The Council [of Constance], which expressed in the fullest manner the unity of Christendom, showed that that unity was illusory' (M. Creighton 1892: I, vi).

Neville Figgis CR (d. 1919), our third Anglican historian to comment on the conciliar ideal, was a pupil and admirer of Creighton. Figgis believed that Creighton 'was imbued more strongly than any thinker since Hooker with the genius of the Church of England'. Figgis took the view that Creighton's deep study of the conciliar period had strengthened his advocacy of the claim of national consciousness in the Church. Creighton had defended the integrity of national churches and had invoked the appeal to sound learning as the distinguishing feature of Anglicanism. This, commented Figgis, 'was eminently the cachet of the conciliar movement which represented the culminating point of university influence in the Middle Ages'. Figgis was clear that those conciliar ideas – and those ideas alone – 'form the raison d'etre of the Church of England'. They comprise the ideal of a 'reformed episcopal communion', one that recognized the validity of national aspirations and was equipped with a constitution that limited the power of central authority. The failure of the Conciliar Movement nearly a century before the Reformation, Figgis believed (rather melodramatically), was 'one of the most tragic facts in the history of the world'. The Reformation itself, he considered, was 'a catastrophe rendered inevitable' by the failure of the Conciliar Movement (Figgis 1916: 236–38: 'Three Cambridge Historians: Creighton, Maitland and Acton').

Chapter 12

CONCILIARITY, PRIMACY AND UNITY IN THE WESTERN AND EASTERN CHURCHES

The Scope and Limits of Monarchical Authority in Vatican I

The First Vatican Council (1870–71) appears to represent the remotest point from classic conciliar ideals. Vatican I can be interpreted as the ultimate defeat of conciliar, constitutional aspirations by monarchical absolutism. As Rahner puts it, 'the historical development of the papal primacy of immediate jurisdiction over the whole Church and over every single diocese ... reached its highest point ever in Vatican I, the legal structure of the code of canon law based upon it and the administrative practice of the Holy See in accordance with it' (Rahner 1969: 372).

The Vatican Council's first dogmatic constitution on the Church proclaimed 'that, by divine ordinance, the Roman Church possesses a pre-eminence of ordinary power over every other church, and that the jurisdictional power (*iurisdictionis potestatem*) of the Roman pontiff is both episcopal (*vere episcopalis*) and immediate'. The clergy and faithful of every rank and place were obliged 'to submit to this power by the duty of hierarchical subordination (*officio hierarchicae subordinationis*) and true obedience, and this not only in matters concerning faith and morals, but also in those which regard the discipline and government of the church throughout the world'. To reject this teaching was to jeopardize one's faith and salvation. The constitution goes on to condemn those who hold that it is lawful to appeal from the judgement of the popes to an ecumenical council, 'as though this were an authority superior to the Roman pontiff' (Tanner 1990: II, 814–15).

On the other hand, and contrary to what is sometimes supposed, Vatican I made some attempt to safeguard the rightful prerogatives of the episcopate:

> This power of the supreme pontiff by no means detracts from that ordinary and immediate power of episcopal jurisdiction, by which bishops, who have succeeded to the place of the apostles by appointment of the Holy Spirit, tend and govern individually the particular flocks which have been assigned to them. On the contrary, this power of theirs is asserted, supported and defended by the supreme and universal pastor (Tanner 1990: II, 814–15).

Sergei Bulgakov's celebrated comment that the bishops at Vatican I committed collective suicide could perhaps be applied to the way in which many of the 'inopportunists', such as Doupanloup and Hefele, succumbed to pressure from the highest level to accept the decree on papal infallibility (see Chadwick 1998: 181–214; for the council generally Butler 1962). But Bulgakov's quip is not applicable to the council's teaching as a whole on papal primacy and episcopal authority. Both Bishop Gasser's nuanced explanation of the infallibility decree at the Council and Pius IX's conciliatory response to the subsequent German bishops' interpretation of their jurisdiction moderated the initial impressions of absolutism. For Gasser see Butler 1962: ch. 23; for the German bishops' intervention see Logan 1961. Recent Roman Catholic scholarship (notably the work of Hermann J. Pottmeyer 1998, 2004) has endeavoured to show that, properly interpreted, *Pastor aeternus* implies the conciliar principle of episcopal collegiality and therefore excludes the sort of absolute papal monarchy that conciliarists attack.

In a judicious review of the relation between papacy and episcopacy during the second millennium, William Henn has pointed out that Vatican I not only put an end to Gallican and extreme conciliarist ideas that in one way or another would have routinely subordinated the pope to the episcopate, but also, 'by explicitly acknowledging the divine institution of the episcopacy and by affirming that the primacy in no way detracts from the authority of bishops, Vatican I may equally be said to have brought an end to the more absolutist theories of papal primacy and paved the way for Vatican II' (Henn 1998: 261). Buckley has pressed the point home by pointing out that, if primacy and episcopacy are not things in isolation but are intrinsically relational terms, 'it is not enough to say that the first Vatican Council dealt with the primacy and did not get around to the episcopate'. *Pastor aeternus* had been 'distorted in its reading' for almost a hundred years (Buckley 1998: 38–39, 45).

Thus it can be claimed that the seeds of the Second Vatican Council were sown at the First; Vatican II was the continuation and completion of Vatican I, not simply its antidote and corrective. While that intriguing piece of historical apologetic may smooth over the discontinuities and tensions a little too easily, it is striking that Pottmeyer and others can appeal to Vatican I, 'correctly' interpreted – that is to say, interpreted contrary to the trend of how it was read both at the time and for a century afterwards – against the further consolidation of centralization since then. 'Vatican centralisation cannot appeal to Vatican I for its theological justification' (Pottmeyer 1998: 74). In short, the teachings of Vatican I do not stand in the way of the reform of the papacy at the present time, which is what this internal debate, recently given fresh momentum by Archbishop John Quinn, is about (Quinn 1999: see below).

Conciliar and Monarchical Authority in Vatican II

Pope Benedict XVI is someone who has wrestled with the tension between the institutional and the mystical in the life of the Church. In an essay of 1986 on the ecclesiology of Vatican II, Joseph Ratzinger quotes Romano Guardini's prophetic words: 'An event with incalculable consequences has begun: the Church is awakening in people's souls.' The Church, said Guardini, writing after the First World War, that is to say at roughly midpoint between the two Vatican Councils, 'is not some institution that has been planned and constructed ... but a living being ... It goes on living through time, developing as every living thing develops, changing itself.' We cannot be in a right relationship to the Church while we see it primarily as an organization, an official authority structure. It is Ratzinger who comments that at that time the Catholic Church was regarded as 'a fossilized machine' that seemed to have lost its inwardness, its mystical dimension of communion with Christ (Ratzinger 1988: 1–7).

In the ecclesiology of Vatican II, monarchical and conciliar aspects are not fully reconciled: they stand in unresolved tension with each other. While hierocratic and juridical elements are forcefully present, the Council's teaching also contains elements of an organic, integrated ecclesiology. In this latter ecclesiology the unity of the Church is understood not so much juridically as dynamically, holistically and pneumatologically – and these are prime attributes of conciliar thought. Black has pointed out the similarities between the ecclesiology of the Council of Basel and that of Vatican II, particularly the idea of the corporate responsibility and competence of the church community as a whole (Black 1971). In a paper written in the light of the Council, Joseph Ratzinger attempted to hold together the institutional and the relational in the Church, arguing that 'Peter' becomes the institution and that the institution can only persist through history because it is embodied in a person and takes the form of the personal responsibility of an individual (Ratzinger 1988: 32–36).

The conciliar elements of *Lumen Gentium*, the constitution on the Church, are momentous.

> The fact that the chapter on the hierarchical structure of the Church follows the chapter on the People of God is also highly significant. This reverses the priorities and modifies the perspective of pre-Vatican II Catholic ecclesiology. The Church is primarily a people in whom God is present and through whom God acts on behalf of all humanity. The Church is not primarily a hierarchical institution, nor can it speak and act as if it were (McBrien in Hastings 1991: 89).

The collegial conception of the episcopate, which was introduced into Vatican II with the personal support of Pope Paul VI, counterbalances the monarchical doctrine of the papacy that was emphasized by Vatican I. It is a paradox that, of the episcopal communions of Christendom, it is the Roman Catholic Church that has most emphasized the collegiality of the episcopate: the aspirations of many bishops in mediaeval times and since were recognized only with the Second Vatican Council. For historical treatment of episcopal collegiality see Congar 1965 and, for Vatican II era studies, Ratzinger 1965; Rahner 1969: chs 20–22. However, the doctrine of collegiality awaits full implementation, and the Vatican's resistance to the effective expression of episcopal collegiality remains an extremely sore point with many Roman Catholics. As F.J. Laishley has commented: 'Increasingly the concept of the local bishop as the symbol embodying the unity of the local church in collegial unity with other churches, including the Roman Church, is being overridden in favour of a concept of the bishop as the local representative of the pope' (Laishley in Hastings 1991: 224). The synods of bishops, administered under tight curial control, have proved deeply disappointing and frustrating to many bishops' conferences. Ratzinger (1988: ch. 3) makes it clear that the power of deliberation of a synod of bishops is delegated to it by the pope and is not inherent in the power of the episcopal college. Bishops share with the pope in the governance of the universal Church by leading their own dioceses, not by participating in the synod. Ratzinger seems to assume that the only valid expression of conciliarity is a General Council when he claims that 'the idea of a perpetual conciliarity of the Church, as the basic form of its unity' would be merely a 'cosmopolitan debating society'. The papacy, rather than conciliarity, is the indispensable model for holding together the local and universal in the Church (92–95). Here he seems to be polarizing conciliarity (by which he means episcopal collegiality) and primacy (by which he means a version of papal monarchy), rather than attempting to bring these two ecclesiological principles into harmony.

Vatican II of course retracted nothing of what Vatican I asserted about the authority of the papacy. *Lumen Gentium*, for example, reaffirms, for the required consent of the faithful, the traditional teaching about 'the institution, the perpetuity, the force and reason for the sacred primacy of the Roman Pontiff and of his infallible teaching authority' (LG 18: Abbott 1966: 38). It goes on to insist that the college of bishops 'has no authority unless it is simultaneously conceived of in terms of its head, the Roman Pontiff, Peter's successor, and without any lessening of his power of primacy over all, pastors as well as the general faithful'. As Vicar of Christ and pastor of the whole Church, the pope has 'full, supreme and universal power over the Church. And he can always exercise this power freely' (LG 22: Abbott 1966: 43). Councils of bishops are convened by the pope, presided over by the pope, and their decisions must be confirmed by the pope. Even the meetings of bishops throughout the world require papal permission (LG 22: Abbott 1966: 44). It is stressed that the episcopal college is not a college in any juridical sense, as a body composed of equals who then delegate their authority to a president ('Prefatory and Explanatory Note' [*Nota Praevia*] to LG: Abbott 1966: 98–101). Anything remotely approaching the constitutional interpretation of the papal primacy that was advocated by some of the great conciliarists is thus intentionally excluded.

The decree on the bishops' pastoral office begins by magnifying the power of the pope over the episcopal college:

> In this Church of Christ the Roman Pontiff is the successor of Peter, to whom Christ entrusted the feeding of his sheep and lambs. Hence by divine institution he enjoys supreme, full, immediate and universal authority over the care of souls ... He holds, therefore, a primacy of ordinary power over all the churches (*Christus Dominus*, Preface: Abbott 1966: 397).

Thus, taking the two Vatican Councils together (and bracketing out the issue of infallibility), we can say that, entirely in his own right, the pope has a jurisdiction that is:

- *supreme*: over all churches – in principle including those of other traditions, not just those of the Roman obedience – and over every Christian soul within them, and from which there is no appeal;
- *full*: over every matter pertaining to those churches; there is no matter that is exempt from his jurisdiction;
- *immediate*: direct and in principle unconstrained by any intermediate structures, including the jurisdiction of the diocesan bishop;
- *ordinary*: by virtue of his office, not mandated or delegated by any supposed higher authority, such as the episcopal college or a General Council;
- *episcopal*: which means either that the universal Church is being treated as a single diocese, or that the Bishop of Rome is also the bishop of every other diocese – albeit in connection and relationship (the nature of which remains unclear or confused) with the diocesan bishop; at the least it means that the Pope's universal jurisdiction is grounded in the sacrament of orders;
- *free*: there are no constitutional constraints on the unfettered action of a pope (not even canon law, because the pope can freely make law for the Church).

While (it bears repeating) Vatican II retracted nothing of what Vatican I had decreed about the pope's primacy, his infallibility when teaching *ex cathedra*, and his universal immediate jurisdiction, it clarified an essential presupposition of its doctrine of the collegiality of bishops when it affirmed that bishops possess by consecration the fullness of the sacrament of orders and are not simply an extension of the priesthood. The episcopate is the definitive form of the ordained ministry and is entrusted with the threefold task of teaching, sanctifying and governing. (Priests and laity also are entrusted with the ministry of teaching, sanctifying and governing, in proportion to their calling, since this ministry is given them through baptism by means of their participation in the threefold messianic office of Jesus Christ as prophet, priest and king: for the laity see Ombres in Timms and Wilson 2000: ch. 6.) The bishops, like the pope, are 'vicars of Christ'; they are not 'vicars of the Roman Pontiff' (LG 27: Abbott 1966: 51–52). The sacramental understanding of the episcopate in Vatican II is immensely significant for collegiality. As Quinn points out, 'the College of Bishops is constituted not by a juridical act but by a sacrament ... Collegiality is a property of the sacramental nature of the episcopal office ... Collegiality is embedded in ... *communion* and *sacrament*' (Quinn 1999: 98–101, italics original).

Roman Catholic collegiality is focused on the universality of the college of bishops, whereas mediaeval (and Anglican) ideas give more weight to national expressions of collegiality (White 1987). The Roman Catholic Church holds that Jesus Christ constituted the Twelve Apostles as a college in fellowship with Peter and that bishops in fellowship with the pope are their successors. The episcopal 'college' (including the pope) is not a metaphor but a 'juridical person' which always exists concretely. Full authority in teaching, sanctifying and governing the Church is committed to the episcopal college in communion with the pope who is the head of the college. The college is not a body of equals with the head as *primus inter pares*. A bishop 'is constituted a member of the episcopal body by virtue of sacramental consecration and by hierarchical communion with the head and members of the body' (LG 22: Abbott 1966: 43). However, a bishop cannot be constituted a member of the college by communion with other members alone without the head, but only with the other members through the head.

It follows that a bishop who is not in communion with the pope, even though his orders might be recognized by Rome (e.g. an Orthodox bishop) is not a member of the episcopal college. Obviously the Anglican episcopate is not regarded by Rome as part of the episcopal college, since in the view of the Roman Catholic Church Anglican bishops are not sacramentally ordained to the episcopate (or to the priesthood or to the diaconate, for that matter) and are not in hierarchical communion with the pope. Sacramental consecration (*ordo*) makes a bishop a bishop, but the authority (*potestas*) to exercise episcopal functions comes from the pope.

In Roman Catholic ecclesiology, the supreme exercise of episcopal authority is an Ecumenical Council which consists entirely of bishops and is called, presided over and ratified by the pope. A council so constituted teaches infallibly. The college of bishops has no authority without the authority of the pope who has full, supreme and universal power over the Church and can always exercise this power freely. The college of bishops is nothing without the pope. It is made clear that the authority of the pope is not delegated by the college of bishops. The bishops as a college under the leadership of the pope are entrusted with leadership of the universal Church in mission (see LG 22–24 and *Nota praevia*; *Catechism of the Catholic Church*, nos. 877–887, 1560; Kasper 1989: 158). Thus, whatever is said by Vatican II about the authority of bishops corporately, as a college, and individually in their own dioceses, is subject to the massive proviso that their authority is non-existent apart from the pope. We are, I think, justified in deducing from these statements that, while the Second Vatican Council's view of authority certainly cannot be reduced to the monarchical model, that model in fact remains a powerful one. Its relation to the conciliar, collegial model is unclear and unresolved in post-conciliar discussion.

One reason for this disjunction between primacy and conciliarity is that the relation between the local church (the diocese, the sphere of the bishop's oversight and ministry of word and sacrament), on the one hand, and the universal Church, on the other, remains unresolved. Collegiality is an expression and outworking of communion (*communio*; *koinonia*) – the Church of England's bishops' discussion of this is entitled *Bishops in Communion* – but communion is established primarily between churches and only secondarily between their pastors. As Legrand points out, there was almost a total absence of thinking in the Roman Catholic Church about local churches before the Council; the collegiality of bishops was often discussed without regard to the collegiality of churches. But if the local church is a true manifestation of the Church of Christ, and is just as much the Church as the universal Church is the Church, collegiality can only be considered adequately in an ecclesiological framework and with the pneumatological perspective that the nature of the Church as the Spirit-bearing body of Christ requires (Legrand 1972; see also McPartlan 2004).

Henn points out that the explicit attribution by Vatican II of full and supreme power to the college of bishops, alongside similar attribution to the Bishop of Rome as the successor of St Peter and the Vicar of Christ, sharpens the question of how many subjects of such full and supreme power there are in the Roman Catholic Church. He suggests that there are three possible answers: (1) there is one subject, the pope, from whom all other expressions of authority flow; (2) there are two subjects, 'inadequately distinct', the pope alone and the pope in union with the episcopal college; (3) there is (again) one subject, the college of bishops, but the pope, as its head, may exercise the authority of the college freely. Henn finds difficulties with each of these: (1) the first seems to be excluded by the divine institution of the episcopal college and of its authority on behalf of Christ; (2) the second in practice marginalizes the episcopate over against the papacy; (3) the last is difficult to reconcile with the doctrine of the papacy as set out by Vatican I, which cannot be assimilated to episcopal collegiality. Henn concludes rather drily: 'Wide-ranging agreement by theologians about how the subject or subjects of full and supreme authority are to be understood and related obviously has not yet been achieved' (Henn 1998: 268; cf. Buckley 1998: 16).

Alongside this major ecclesiological *aporia*, there is another, crucial factor: the link between mission and unity. Vatican II injected a new note into Roman Catholic ecclesiology – the note of mission and evangelization. The Council proclaimed (*Ad Gentes*, 2: Abbott 1966: 585) that the Church was missionary by its very nature and was called to be the instrument of the mission of God to the world (*missio dei*: for this concept see Avis 2005: 4–9). What are the consequences for the structures of the Church, which in the Roman Catholic tradition are held to be God-given, of letting mission and evangelization shape ecclesiology? One answer is that there are consequences for our approach to issues of unity, for mission and unity are inextricable. As John Paul II put it in the encyclical *Ut Unum Sint*: 'Believers in Christ ... cannot remain divided ... How could they refuse to do everything possible ... to overcome obstacles and prejudices which thwart the proclamation of the Gospel of salvation in the cross of Jesus, the one Redeemer of Man?' (John Paul II 1995). However, the great question mark at the heart of the quest for unity is the question of authority. Precisely in this encyclical, John Paul II was testing the waters with regard to the ecumenical appropriation of papal authority.

The glaringly unresolved issues of authority mean that there is a sharp irony in the approach of *Ut Unum Sint* for, as Pope Paul VI explicitly confessed in 1967, it is the papacy itself that is the greatest obstacle to unity. In *Ut Unum Sint*, Pope John Paul II acknowledged this unpalatable truth and joined his predecessor in asking forgiveness for where his office had become a stumbling block to Christians. The purpose of the encyclical was to re-affirm the Roman Catholic Church's commitment to the quest for visible unity ('full and visible communion') and to invite other churches to help the pope to understand his unique ministry. The place of 'legitimate diversity' is recognized as essential to the mission of the Church. Although there is no suggestion that the classical claims of the Roman Catholic Church that the pope is the successor of Peter, the vicar of Christ, the supreme pastor of all Christians are negotiable, John Paul II was asking what that might mean today in an ecumenical context.

Roman Catholic theologians have not been slow to draw out the ecumenical significance of how Rome conducts its internal affairs. Archbishop Quinn points out that the manner in which the pope is seen to relate to the episcopal college reveals how the papacy would behave vis-à-vis the Orthodox or Anglican episcopates if re-union were achieved (Quinn 1999: 76). And Nichols alleges that, while 'the present trend towards a more authoritarian and centralized mode of hierarchy is disastrous for the Roman Catholic Church', it is also 'disastrous for ecumenism' and will effectively take the Roman Catholic Church out of the ecumenical movement: 'No-one is going to be interested in re-uniting with the Roman Church if it is perceived to be governed by a papal autocracy' (T. Nichols 1997: 4). But by the same token, Nichols emphasizes, *'The greatest gift that the Roman Church can give the ecumenical movement is to reform itself'*, so that it might become a model of salutary, participatory hierarchy and 'a sacramental sign of unity' (316, italics original). The clamour for reform of its authority structures – for decentralization, subsidiarity, the rights of the laity – continues unabated in the Roman Catholic Church (see, e.g., Timms and Wilson 2000; Hoose 2002). We will pick up the theme of reform again at the end of the book, but meanwhile, as we return to the historical background, we note without comment that when Joseph Ratzinger, Pope Benedict XVI, took possession of his cathedral church of St John Lateran in May 2005, he roundly stated: 'The pope is not an absolute monarch, whose thought and will are law' (Walsh 2005: 16).

Anglicanism as an Expression of Conciliar Catholicism

For well over a century, a somewhat muted, but nevertheless coherent – and I would say attractive – ecclesiology, both Catholic and reformed, has been affirmed by the Lambeth Conferences. Henry Lowther Clarke provided an early survey of *Constitutional Church Government* in the Anglican Communion (Lowther Clarke 1924), relating it to mediaeval precedents and stressing the principle of freedom from state interference. Philip E. Thomas brought the story of the constitutional articulation of Anglican ecclesiology up to 1978 in his unpublished thesis (Thomas 1982). In *The Transformation of Anglicanism*, W. Sachs has charted the evolution of Anglicanism into a world-wide communion led by bishops and governed by synods (Sachs 1993). W.M. Jacob has brought out the issues of governance and structure in his account of the making of the Anglican Communion and its institutions (Jacob 1997). Bruce Kaye describes the origins of synods in Australian Anglicanism (Kaye 2003). The formal resolutions of the Lambeth Conferences up to 1988 are gathered in Coleman 1992, while useful material from the committee and section reports that fed into the debates are gathered in Norgren 1994. The Windsor Report is now a resource that carries a degree of authority (Anglican Communion Office 2004); important reservations about its ecumenical stance are found in J.R. Wright 2005.

The Lambeth Quadrilateral (which originated in the then Protestant Episcopal Church of the USA in Chicago 1886, was adopted by the Lambeth Conference 1888 and revised in 1920) lists the minimum requirements to be sought in any steps towards unity: the Scriptures, the two creeds (Apostles' and Niceno-Constantinopolitan), the two dominical sacraments of baptism and the Eucharist, and a universally acknowledged ministry with its focus in the historic episcopate 'locally adapted in the methods of its administration'. The Lambeth Conference of 1920, in its *Appeal to All Christian People*, spoken to a fragmented Christendom from a church that knew itself to be incomplete. The appeal, addressed to all baptized Christians, whatever their tradition, conveyed a vision of catholicity – of unity and universality in the triune God's purpose for the Church – but acknowledged that it was a hitherto unrealized vision:

> We believe that God wills fellowship. By God's own act this fellowship was made, in and through Jesus Christ, and its life is in his Spirit. We believe that it is God's purpose to manifest this fellowship, so far as this world is concerned, in an outward, visible and united society, holding one faith, having its own recognized officers, using God-given means of grace, and inspiring all its members to the world-wide service of the Kingdom of God. This is what we mean by the Catholic Church.

The Lambeth Conference pointedly added: 'This united fellowship is not visible in the world today.' Archbishop Longley invited those bishops who were 'in visible communion with the United Church of England and Ireland' to the first Lambeth Conference in 1867 (Norgren 1994: 80).

The Church as a visible society, conceived, in such a way as this, as *in via*, on pilgrimage, requires structures for consultation and taking decisions. As we have seen, these structures have tended historically to fall into one of two models, or a combination of both: the monarchical and the conciliar. The monarchical model tends to be hierarchical and authoritarian: during the period of its development it rested on a supposed donation of imperial authority to the putative successors of Peter in the Roman see. The conciliar model aims to be representative and constitutional: it is founded on the concept of the whole body of the Church as the source of authority. Needless to say, monarchical Catholicism does not set out to be repressive: it is often a form of benevolent autocracy, comparable to the rule of the so-called 'enlightened despots' in eighteenth-century Europe. By the same token, conciliar Catholicism does not have a monopoly of virtues: the Council of Basel degenerated into a shambles – conciliar authority seems to have gone to its head – and the role of laypeople was only slowly accepted into the conciliar tradition.

We have glanced in the previous chapter at some examples of conciliar thought in the Church of England from the Reformation to modern times. This sets the scene for some reflections on the opportunities and challenges entailed in the practice of conciliarity in the Anglican Communion today. To begin with, we may ask, to what extent may Anglicanism today be regarded as an expression of conciliar Catholicism? Lambeth 1948 defined Anglicanism as 'Catholic in the sense of the English Reformation ... Catholic but reformed ... reformed but Catholic'. Lambeth 1968, while making it clear that the post-1870 papal claims were unacceptable, affirmed the principle of episcopal collegiality but insisted that this must be seen in the context of the conciliar character of the Church, which involves the *consensus fidelium*. The next Lambeth Conference picked this up, stressing the need for the 'study, prayer and witness of every member' in discerning Christian truth to shape the *consensus fidelium*. Anglican episcopacy was 'constitutional', that is to say, 'limited and supported' by synods, canons and other ways in which the whole Church participates in its governance and mission. Lambeth 1988 invoked the notion of reception to describe the 'gradual and dynamic process ... by which the people of God as a whole actively respond to decisions made by synods and councils ... a process which takes time and is always open to the guidance of the Holy Spirit within the community' (Norgren, ed. 1994: 114, 148, 155, 177). What does this mean in terms of Anglican polity?

The first thing to say is that, although the Anglican Communion, through the instrumentality of the Lambeth Conferences, has continued to maintain its inveterate hostility to papal centralism and hierarchicalism, it has always wished to leave the door open to re-union with a reformed Roman Catholic Church. A statement of Lambeth 1908 was repeated in 1920, 1930 and 1968 and still stands: there could be no fulfilment of God's purpose for his Church through any method of reunion that did not 'ultimately include the Great Latin Church of the West, with which our history has been so closely associated in the past, and to which we are still bound by many ties of common faith and tradition' (Norgren 1994: 148). What is slightly surprising in this declaration is that the Lambeth bishops did not say that the Church of England (and consequently the provinces of the Communion) had been and continued to be part of that 'Great Latin Church of the West'. Earlier Anglican apologists would have rejected any unqualified identification of the Western Church with the Church of Rome.

Anglicanism recognizes the authority of General Councils in principle and accepts the teaching of the early councils, especially as it is contained in the ecumenical creeds: the creeds are enshrined in the Book of Common Prayer, 1662, and affirmed in Article VIII of the Thirty-nine Articles. Anglicans would certainly expect to participate in a truly ecumenical General Council, if one were possible. Anglicans such as William Temple, George Bell and Oliver Tomkins took a leading role in the Ecumenical Movement, especially Faith and Order, which became part of the World Council of Churches in 1948 (though of course the World Council of Churches is not and does not claim to be a General Council in permanent session, but rather an 'interconfessional assembly' and an expression of the fellowship of the member churches).

However, a truly ecumenical General Council is not a realistic possibility in the present situation of a divided Church and it is unlikely to become more feasible in the immediate future. The Encyclical Letter of Lambeth 1878 said of General Councils that they originated 'with the inspired Apostles' and 'long served to hold all the Churches of Christ in one undivided and visible communion'. However, it went on, the holding of a General Council, 'such as the Church of England [*sic*] has always declared her readiness to resort to, is in the present condition of Christendom, unhappily but obviously impossible' (Norgren 1994: 88).

A General Council is an expression of a Church already united in eucharistic communion and on that foundation taking steps to deal with a common threat. Tragically, such eucharistic communion is not a feature of the fragmented Church that we know. The pluralism of faith and practice in the Christian Church seems to be increasing, not reducing. Churches and denominations have proliferated, especially in the twentieth century, and the total now stands at over 30,000. The prospect of an ecumenical council can be entertained only at the cost of a highly arbitrary limitation of what constitutes a Christian Church. For example, would a council be restricted to bishops (and thereby to episcopally ordered churches), or would it include other representative church leaders and senior pastors? What would be the role of the pope (according to Roman Catholic teaching, only the pope can convene a General Council, preside at it and ratify its decisions)? If it is true that Anglican ecclesiology is characterized by its realism, in this case realism inhibits romantic fantasizing about the chances of a General Council that would adjudicate on controversial issues (such as the ordination of women or issues in human sexuality perhaps). There is no hope of a General Council in the foreseeable future and there may very well never be another. But does that mean that conciliarism is a distant dream and that to dwell on it is an exercise in nostalgia? Far from it.

Anglicanism (like other reformed traditions) appears to work on the assumption that, in the absence of even a remote prospect of a General Council, branches or parts of the Christian Church must govern themselves responsibly and practise conciliarity as best they can. Anglicanism is not paralysed by the impossibility of a truly ecumenical council. It believes that conciliarity belongs to the nature of the Church and that particular churches (in this case, provinces gathered into communions) should act in a conciliar fashion within the limits imposed by the divisions in the Church. It is not perfectionist: it does not say: 'A General Council or nothing!' It sets out to practise conciliarity as far and wide as it can until it runs up against the barriers erected by broken communion, a brokenness caused by differences in doctrine or order and the rival claims to jurisdiction that these differences lead to.

The Anglican affinity to the conciliar tradition is seen in the way that Anglicanism acknowledges national identities and aspirations. Lambeth Conferences (e.g. that of 1930) have portrayed the Anglican Communion as a fellowship of national and regional churches. Lambeth 1878 wished to 'assert the just liberties of particular or national churches', but Lambeth 1930 warned against allowing a politically driven nationalism to undermine loyalty to the Catholic Church (Norgren 1994: 93, 109). Anglicanism recognizes the importance of cultural identity in its commitment to inculturation. While the autonomy of Anglican provinces as self-governing churches vis-à-vis the authority of the whole Anglican Communion is a matter that calls for continued hard thinking and some heart-searching, there is certainly a degree of continuity to be perceived here with the national aspirations and rivalries that helped to fuel the Conciliar Movement. These may not be the highest spiritual motives, but they are real ones and need to be taken into account. Anglicanism does not disdain or disparage national identities, traditions and aspirations. Its theologians have often seen the hand of God in the destiny of nations, just as the Old Testament prophets did.

Another feature of Anglicanism that links it with the Conciliar Movement is that it allows sound learning, freely pursued, to inform the mind of the Church – though of course Anglicanism is not unique in this. Following the definition of papal infallibility by Vatican I, the Lambeth Conference of 1878 offered support 'to all who are drawn to us in the endeavour to free themselves from the yoke of error and superstition' and welcomed 'every effort for reform upon the model of the Primitive Church'. Lambeth 1948 claimed that Anglicanism was continuous in essentials with the early Church and asserted that it stood for 'the unfettered study of Holy Scripture', appealed to reason, respected liberty and valued diversity. Anglicanism 'repudiates any idea of a central authority for the whole Church other than General Councils of Bishops' (Norgren 1994: 93, 111). Although the privileges that an openness to the findings of research tends to award to scholars are open to abuse, it certainly forms a point of contact with the conciliar tradition which, as we have seen, represented the highest point of influence of scholars and universities in the Western Church before the Reformation.

The Anglican Communion is a fellowship of forty-four self-governing national or regional churches, with a common faith and order, that are in communion with the See of Canterbury and with each other. In a world emerging from colonialism, the Anglican Communion embraced the principles of national self-determination and inculturation. It emphasized the constitutional constraints on authority. Its polity speaks the language of checks and balances: checks on central authority and a balance of power in favour of the autonomy of the provinces. These 'provinces' are fully constituted 'particular churches' with their own general synods (though the provincial structures vary), authorized liturgies and codes of canon law. The office of Archbishop of Canterbury, though one of considerable moral and pastoral authority, does not possess jurisdiction over these provinces. The Anglican Communion now has structures of synodical government at all appropriate levels: the diocese, the province and the particular (or national) church. In New Zealand synods were instituted by Bishop G.A. Selwyn in the mid-nineteenth century. In an episcopal charge to the Diocese of New Zealand in 1847 Selwyn said: 'I believe the monarchical idea of the Episcopate to be as foreign to the true mind of the Church as it is adverse to the Gospel doctrine of humility ... The bishop is the organ of the general sense of the Church' (Beeson 2002: 174). Lambeth 1867 strongly advocated diocesan and provincial synods for those provinces where the Church was not established and gave guidelines for their constitution (Norgren 1994: 82–86). The interesting attempt in Anglican polity to combine conciliar (synodical) governance with episcopal oversight (which Anglicans hold to be complementary) modifies both components of the polity, setting up tensions but also creating interactions and opportunities for collaboration and collegiality at several levels. While the episcopate has certain special responsibilities for faith and order matters (certainly in the Church of England), it is required to consult with the laity and other clergy in their synodical houses and to gain their consent. Conciliar thought was never simply concerned with General Councils, but picked up the early mediaeval precedent of regional and national councils which, as Archbishop Lanfranc for example had deplored, had fallen into disuse.

Anglicanism gives a voice in its conciliar institutions not only to bishops, but also to presbyters and deacons and laymen and laywomen. As we have seen, the pre-Reformation reforming councils were not restricted to bishops: presbyters were also involved, but the laity were represented mainly by civil rulers. Among influences on conciliar thought, Marsilius of Padua and William of Ockham were notable for giving a place to lay-people. Anglican thinkers were not, on the whole, keen to give the laity a voice, the Tractarians being particularly adamant about this (though Gladstone, as a lay theologian, did not agree with his colleagues). As early as 1867 the Lambeth Conference recommended that in diocesan and provincial synods there should be houses of laity alongside those of bishops and clergy (Norgren 1994: 93). The steps by which the laity were eventually incorporated into the synodical structure of the Church of England are recounted by Eric Kemp in *Counsel and Consent* (Kemp 1961: ch. 8). It is arguable that Anglican ecclesiology is orientated to the foundational sacrament of baptism: through their baptism all Christians are incorporated into Jesus Christ's threefold messianic mission as prophet, priest and king. By virtue of this royal priesthood all the baptized are mandated to play their part in the governance of Christ's kingdom.

Anglicanism also has universal structures of consultation – though not of jurisdiction or binding decision-making – in place in the Lambeth Conference, the Anglican Consultative Council and the Primates' Meeting (for recent discussion of these 'instruments of communion' see Anglican Communion Office, 2004). The Lambeth Conference is an interesting example of the conciliar principle. As Sachs has observed, it embodies the synodical principle without itself being a synod (Sachs 1993: 207). It has substantial moral – though not juridical – authority in the Communion. Its resolutions only become binding if they are adopted by provincial synods. The Lambeth Conference has on occasion pointedly repudiated a Roman model of centralized authority and has shied away from any form of universal jurisdiction. In the nineteenth century the Conference considered ideas for a pan-Anglican synod or central council only to reject them. It has seemed to bend over backwards to repudiate any suggestion that it might lay claim to an authority that would be binding on the member churches. Lambeth 1948 celebrated a 'dispersed' or 'distributed' pattern of authority as 'God's loving provision against the temptations to tyranny and the dangers of unchecked power' (Norgren 1994: 116). While many Anglicans now recognize that there is an authority deficit in Anglicanism, the muted character of authority within the Communion has been regarded as a virtue compared to papal and curial interventionism. Increasingly, however, Anglicans are looking for a way through this polarization. Are there structures of authority that escape both the fragmentation that untrammelled provincial authority can generate and the over-control of universal jurisdiction? The dilemma that Anglicans face is that any measures of this kind would have to be accepted by each of the provinces separately, through their synodical structures. Any attempt to foist on to the Communion a central authority, with the power to intervene, would be doomed to total failure.

It is within this conciliar context that the ministry of the Archbishop of Canterbury functions. While media pressure would like to give the Archbishop a more 'papal' role – as though only the Archbishop of Canterbury could speak for the Church of England and the Anglican Communion, and when he does so that settles the matter – this is inimical to the office as Anglicans understand it. There is also a certain reluctance to accept the enhanced role for the Archbishop, within the Primates' Meeting, that some conservative elements within the Communion would like to see. The Archbishop of Canterbury remains basically the incumbent of the most ancient metropolitan see of the English Church and the successor in that see of St Augustine of Canterbury. It is the see that for various historical reasons serves as a focus of communion and unity for those churches which have historical links with the Church of England. The Archbishop has modest powers of jurisdiction outside his own diocese of Canterbury, though what he does have is often overlooked (Podmore 1998; Thomas 2002). However, the office of Archbishop of Canterbury demonstrates in practice that – within the not inconsiderable constraints of a communion that is pluralistic in belief and practice – Anglicans respond positively to a central, symbolic representative ministry that can speak for Anglican Christians. Following the 1988 Lambeth Conference, the Primates and the Anglican Consultative Council meeting jointly resolved that the Archbishop of Canterbury 'serves as the principle focus of unity in the Communion. Initiatives are often taken by him with the concurrence, encouragement and understanding of other bodies. This involvement, and initiatives undertaken in his own right and later reported to the various appropriate bodies, are of vital importance' (cited by O. Chadwick in Coleman 1992: xiv).

Anglicanism: A Deficit of Authority?

Having now looked at some aspects of conciliarity in their Anglican expression, we must now ask: How effective is Anglican conciliarity, does it work? In 1988, as Anglican bishops from around the world gathered for the Lambeth Conference, the leader in *The Tablet* pronounced: 'There is a vacuum at the centre of the Anglican Communion where hard decisions affecting the whole body are required to be taken.' The editorial pointed out that the Lambeth Conference was not a legislative assembly, a Church Council or a tribunal and had no power of jurisdiction. 'Neither history nor the present mind of the churches that supply it give it authority beyond the considerable moral authority inherent in a large congregation of bishops.' This was fair comment at the time, and subsequent events have, if anything, reinforced it (see the discussion in Wright 1989, who brings out the fact that stronger options than mere consultation were considered in the late nineteenth century).

A series of developments over two decades has raised questions about the theological coherence and political cohesion of the Anglican Communion. The untidy emergence of women priests and (a few) women bishops was followed by some infringements of the territorial integrity of dioceses by irregularly consecrated bishops. The unilateral decision of the Diocese of New Westminster, in the Anglican Church of Canada, to make provision for public liturgical rites of blessing for same-sex unions was trumped by the consecration of a priest who was living openly in a same-sex relationship as a coadjutor bishop of the Diocese of New Hampshire (with the endorsement of the General Convention of the Episcopal Church of the USA, but against the warnings of the Archbishop of Canterbury and the Primates' Meeting). These last two actions prompted the Archbishop of Canterbury to set up the Lambeth Commission to look at the ecclesiological and legal issues raised by these developments. The resulting document *The Windsor Report* (Anglican Communion Office 2004), though bearing the marks of haste, has helpfully focused Anglican thinking on the tension inherent in a polity that seeks to do justice, in terms of the Church, to the integrity of the local and the demands of the universal. *Windsor* explores what is meant by 'autonomy in communion'. Though this is not perhaps the most felicitous phrasing of the issue, it does home in on a crucial dilemma for many churches and one that needs to be further addressed for the sake of unity. As Anglicans grapple with this problem, there are several building blocks that are available to them in their tradition.

First, alongside the emphasis on provincial autonomy, the Lambeth Conferences have consistently affirmed the duty of mutual obligation and of loyalty to the fellowship. They have spoken of bonds of communion and have never advocated a free-for-all when it comes to decision-making. The urgent question for Anglicans is how this principle of mutuality can be given constitutional expression.

Second, it is significant that Anglican polity embodies a principle of primacy, as well as of synodality. Being in communion with the See of Canterbury is the *sine qua non* of membership of the Communion. As well as the Lambeth Conferences, there are regular meetings of the Primates. As we have noted, recent Lambeth Conferences and other bodies have called for an enhanced role for the Primates' Meeting and for the Archbishop of Canterbury himself in situations of internal conflict. The Archbishop possesses a power of invitation to the Lambeth Conference and to the Primates' Meeting, the potential of which has not yet been fully explored. (See further below on Anglican views of a universal primacy.)

Third, Anglicanism has stood for the view that juridically binding authority is not the only valid form of conciliarity. It has played up other aspects: the value of consultation, bearing one another's burdens, a fellowship of prayer and study, a leadership that is offered rather than imposed. Conciliarity may be authentic, even when its conclusions cannot be enforced.

That need not mean that the Communion and its instruments can never have more than moral authority for the member churches. There is the potential to develop forms of mutual obligation that are intended to promote the common good of the Communion. Such protocols would concern forms of consultation leading to common action (or restraint), together with sanctions that would apply in circumstances where the agreed protocols had not been observed. These protocols would have to be freely accepted by the member churches through their own canonical processes. A majority of the provinces might wish to insist that continued full membership of the Communion and participation in its instruments required acceptance and observance of the protocols.

One possible way of entry would be a programme of concerted reflection, by appropriate bodies, across the Communion on what the common good of the Communion might entail. Anglican theological roots in the conciliar tradition, and beyond that in Thomistic philosophy and theology, suggest that an over-arching concept of the common good would be congenial to many Anglican theologians. It seems clear that the common good of the Communion could not be explored without taking into account the common good of the whole Church of Christ: it would need to have ecclesiological, missiological and ecumenical dimensions. This process of reflection would involve asking: what patterns of authority are needed to enable the Christian Church, and within it the Anglican Communion, to grow in unity, holiness, catholicity and apostolicity and thus to carry forward the mission of the gospel in the world?

A method for arriving at a set of protocols that would enable the Communion to act as one body has been proposed by Norman Doe. In a paper first presented to the Primates' Meeting in 2001 (Doe 2002), Doe distinguishes between the moral order and the juridical order in Anglican polity. The moral order is primarily located in the Communion as a whole, in the relations between the provinces, while the juridical order is primarily situated within the individual provinces. We might say that there is a voluntaristic, persuasive ecclesiology that pertains to the Communion and a binding, canonical ecclesiology that belongs to the provinces severally. Nevertheless, since Anglicanism calls itself a 'communion', the persuasive and the binding aspects cannot be ultimately held apart. Closer integration of the moral and the juridical orders is called for in the interests of cohesion and the resolution of conflict.

In this seminal article Doe then examines the various bodies of canon law of the provinces (he has written a book on this: Doe 1998) for signs of convergence. Some provincial legal systems have a centripetal thrust, in that they explicitly recognize the wider Communion and acknowledge obligations towards it. While most canon law is neutral in its effect, there are aspects that are centrifugal, stressing autonomy and pulling back from wider ties. The strong similarities within the legal systems of the provinces leads Doe to claim that a fundamental Anglican canon law already exists, albeit in a latent form. The shared principles that can be inferred from the complete corpus of Anglican canon law comprise an Anglican *ius commune* (common law). This fundamental canon law is currently dispersed, but if it were brought together in a synthesis it could provide a core canon law for the Communion. There is a commonality in what the various codes lay down about faith and order: the problem is that they have never been brought together into an overall set of principles. Doe believes that this could be done and that a core canon law for the Communion could certainly include obligations to the Communion as a whole (centripetal principles). These could well follow the pattern of the ecumenical agreements or concordats that have already become incorporated into the laws of many Anglican provinces.

A long-term project of induction and synthesis could result in a common or core canon law, consisting of ecclesiological truths and mutual agreements or agreed protocols, which every province would have to incorporate into its own legal system if it were willing to do so. (*The Windsor Report* suggested a covenant and offered a worked-out example in an appendix.) This intriguing combination of the persuasive and the mandatory offers Anglicans an attractive middle way between the unacceptable alternatives of rampant provincial independence, on the one hand, and unworkable central control, on the other. Even to attempt the exercise could well help Anglicans to become more conscious of the wider Anglican fellowship and of the imperatives of consultation and restraint in deference to the common good. In the process Anglicans might also become more aware of the pre-Reformation sources of aspects of their polity and have their sense of continuity with the undivided Western Church enhanced. It has long been clear that Anglicanism aspires to be an expression of conciliar catholicism. The conciliar ideal has been evoked more or less continuously in Anglican ecclesiology. Something like the Doe proposal (on which he has done further work: Doe 2003) seems essential to secure the conciliar integrity of the Anglican Communion for the future.

Anglican Views of Collegiality and Universal Primacy

Anglican views on a ministry of universal primacy have to be set within the context and tradition of conciliarity and collegiality. Roman Catholic scholars naturally think in terms of the relation between *monarchical* and conciliar principles. Thus Rahner writes: 'the fundamental-theological structure of the Church ... demands a bipolar unity of a monarchical and a conciliar element, inseparably related to each other' (Rahner 1969: 340). Anglicans, on the other hand, with their principle of dispersed sovereignty, are resistant to ideas of monarchy (i.e. of a sole or single centre of authority) that are not expressions of 'constitutional monarchy' – and strictly speaking constitutional monarchy is not pure monarchy at all. For Anglicans, the authority structure of the Church is a complex of conciliar, collegial and primatial elements. In this constellation of authority, which reflects the ecumenical paradigm of *Baptism, Eucharist and Ministry* (BEM 1982), conciliarity stands for the responsibility and appropriate involvement of the whole people of God; collegiality is the corporate exercise of oversight by bishops with each other and with their college of presbyters; and primacy is the personal leadership and oversight of the bishop in the diocese, the metropolitan in the province and the Archbishop of Canterbury in the world-wide Communion.

The way that Anglican principles and structures of conciliarity have developed has been influenced by reaction to papal claims and to the way that authority has been exercised concretely in the Roman Catholic Church. The Lambeth Conferences, which began in 1867, close to Vatican I, tended to pointedly distance themselves from Roman models of authority. Lambeth 1878 applauded the outburst of protest around the world that greeted the definition of papal infallibility and universal jurisdiction. But Anglicanism is not without experience of primacy *tout court*. While Anglican controversialists from Jewel to Gore have excoriated the papacy for abuses of power and distortions of authority, they have nevertheless tended to leave the door open to a reformed, constitutional papacy. The Anglican–Roman Catholic International Commission (ARCIC) has devoted three reports to this issue and while it has undoubtedly made progress and achieved some convergence, it can fairly be said that Anglicans retain considerable suspicion of the papacy as an institution and look for greater reassurance, both theological and practical, with regard to constitutional constraints on a ministry of universal primacy, than ARCIC has so far been able to provide. Moreover, there has been no positive indication from the Vatican over the thirty-five years of ARCIC's work that its modest proposals in this area (as distinct from its marked convergence in the areas of ministry and ordination, on the one hand, and eucharistic theology, on the other) would be acceptable to Rome (Anglican–Roman Catholic International Commission, 1982, 1999; critique of the methodology of earlier reports in Avis 1986a).

In essence, it can confidently be said that Anglicanism as a whole has never excluded the possibility of accepting a universal ministry of the Bishop of Rome. This may seem surprising, or at least paradoxical, in view of the implacable and vehement denunciations of the papacy that have studded Anglican polemical theology from the mid-sixteenth century to the end of the nineteenth. The fact is, however, that Anglican views on the papacy have been twin-track: on the one hand, forceful critique of papal claims and of the manner in which authority is exercised by the papacy; on the other, irenic and constructive dialogue about future reform and reunion (though, not seldom the olive branch has been fired from a catapult!). Historical documentation in Avis 2002; modern discussion in Allen and Allchin 1965; Wright 1972, 1988, 2004; *May They All Be One* 1997; Nazir-Ali 1997; Williams 1997; Hind 1999, 2003; Sykes 2001.

The Anglican tradition has been drawn to what is sometimes called the Cyprianic conception of the Church and of the episcopate (Nazir-Ali 1997; cf. Cyprian 1957). The universal or Catholic Church consists of local churches (dioceses) and particular churches (national churches or provinces, made up of those dioceses, though properly constituted churches that are not episcopally ordered have not generally been excluded). The ecclesial reality of the universal Church does not depend on the papacy for validation and Rome does not provide a necessary centre of unity (so Palmer). The world-wide episcopate constitutes a corporate body, a college, and all bishops have an equal share in their responsibility for the oversight of the Church. Lambeth 1968 affirmed that the principle underlying episcopal collegiality was that the apostolic calling to exercise authority in the Church was given to the whole body of bishops. Each bishop has a dual oversight: in his diocese as its chief pastor; and 'with his brother bishops throughout the world a concern for the wellbeing of the whole Church' (Norgren 1994: 147). Bishops are the successors of the Apostles and the power of the keys is given to each. There is an important sense in which the Petrine ministry is inherited by every bishop. A.M. Allchin spoke for the Anglican tradition in a symposium on the Petrine office in 1971 when he said: 'An apostolic and Petrine ministry exists in the Church. It is shared by the whole college of bishops. It is not the exclusive prerogative of any one See.' Allchin went on to point out that, on this point, there is striking agreement between what Anglican divines have said since the seventeenth century and what Orthodox theologians have been saying since the later Middle Ages (Allchin 1971: 128–29).

As far as Anglicans are concerned, papal universal jurisdiction, which is claimed by Vatican I to be fully episcopal, makes the pope bishop of the whole Church and therefore of every diocese (Williams 1997); it puts two bishops into each diocese (cf. Wright 1988). Although this interpretation of what was defined by Vatican I and re-affirmed by Vatican II is unpalatable to many Roman Catholics and notwithstanding the fact that considerable energy has been expended by Roman Catholic scholars in arguing that it is not the correct interpretation (Pottmeyer 1998), Anglicans do tend to read it this way and can point to the canonical texts, as well as to current practice in the Roman Catholic Church, in their support. Anglicans could say that the Church's centre is everywhere, because each local church is fully the Church of Christ; but the truth is that the unity of the Church demands a visible, physical symbol and Anglicans increasingly recognize this.

Anglican polity, shaped as we have seen by the conciliar tradition, developed parallel to representative political institutions and in interaction with them. Anglicans have regarded it as perfectly normal that political principles, principles of governance, should be common to Church and State. They have not insisted that the Church, as an institution, is exempt from the ethical and political considerations that have to be taken into account in the civil sphere. The Church is itself a 'politic society' as well as 'a society supernatural' (thus Hooker). That does not mean that the Church should slavishly emulate whatever populist trends prevail in society, or that it should behave as though it were a pure democracy where everything is ostensibly decided by majority vote, but rather it means that abiding principles of constitutionality, representation and consent, constraints on unchecked authority and on human love of power are applicable to the Church as well as to the State (cf. Sykes 2001; Wright 1988; Avis 1992).

Anglicans share the Conciliar Movement's sense of the wholeness and fullness of the Church. Unlike some mediaeval theologians Anglicans have never located the Church in the hierarchy or made it practically synonymous with the clergy. The involvement of laypeople in its structures of governance, in the parish, in Parliament, in the person of the sovereign, in the houses of laity or their equivalents in the General Synods or Conventions of the modern Anglican Communion, encourage an awareness of the Church as the people of God. The way that the Second Vatican Council evokes the people of God as a whole body strikes a chord with Anglicans.

Primacy is a reality in Anglican churches and in the life of the Communion. Clergy in parishes, deans in cathedrals and bishops in dioceses exercise a sort of primacy in their respective contexts. But primacy extends beyond the diocese: the Anglican episcopacy is not a level structure, but provides for metropolitical jurisdiction, though the arrangements vary from province to province of the Communion. Primacy extends beyond the province too: the Archbishop of Canterbury is Primate of All England and has some responsibilities beyond his own diocese in the Church of England as a whole. In the Communion he has a presidential role as the one who calls together the Lambeth Conference and the Primates' Meeting and who presides at the Anglican Consultative Council. The Communion is wrestling with the question whether the Archbishop of Canterbury should have an enhanced role with some powers of intervention in situations of conflict that cannot be resolved locally. What is perfectly clear is that Anglicanism is not averse in principle to a ministry of primacy at the global level; in fact it seems to feel the need of it more and more (see Podmore 1998, 2005; and for historical background Thomas 2002). What Nazir-Ali (1997) calls 'the logic of primacy' is securely embedded in Anglican ecclesiology, but the logic of conciliarity, which is probably even stronger, ensures that primacy is constructed in a constitutional way.

Anglicans have always recognized a certain primacy of the Roman See and of its bishop and have been open to according to them their ancient or 'primitive' prerogatives. When Field advocates this, he points out that he is is proposing no more than Luther himself was willing to accord to the pope. The pope cannot be universal bishop (we see this issue in play here at the turn of the sixteenth century, long before Vatican I defined it) because 'every bishop hath his place'. The Bishop of Rome should by all means preside at a General Council, but should not control the proceedings or have a veto over the decisions (Field 1847: IV, 382; III, 264; IV, 33). Wake, similarly, grants what the early councils and Fathers allowed and the same position is set out by Palmer (Avis 2002: 123, 191).

This primacy, of a certain, as yet undefined sort, but which is more than one of honour, is derived for Anglicans from the unfolding history of the Church. It has been seen as resting on ecclesiastical and imperial constitutions (so Cosin), not on divine right (*iure divino*). If there is in some sense a universal ministry of the Bishop of Rome, it is a human institution (so Bramhall), but may be said to be founded 'on reason and Christian charity' (Palmer). Although in modern ecumenical dialogue with the Roman Catholic Church the distinction between *iure divino* and *iure humano* has tended to break down (e.g. with Lutherans as well as Anglicans: Empic and Murphy 1974: 31), it signals an important truth: if the primacy is the will of God for the Church, why is it not more securely grounded in Scripture (ARCIC admits that the institution of a continuing Petrine office cannot be explicitly found in the Gospels) and where does its status in divine law leave Christians and churches, both now and through the centuries, who do not or did not accept it? Woe betide those who disobey God's will.

So Anglicans are wary of an institutionalized Petrine office, with built-in powers, but are willing to recognize a Petrine charisma (Williams 1997) and, like other non-Roman Catholic Christians, Anglicans certainly saw this in some, but by no means all, aspects of John Paul II's papacy.

It is not too much to say that Anglicans are appalled by the progressive accretion of power to the papacy during the last millennium and a half of Christian history and by the concrete consolidation of papal authority during the past 150 years. Rowan Williams speaks for many Anglicans when he says: 'from an Anglican, as from an Orthodox point of view – almost everything said theologically about the papacy between 1000 and 1500 is at best outrageous and at worst materially blasphemous' (Williams 1997: 6). Anglicans instinctively view this process as the self-aggrandizement of the papacy: they do not always make allowances for the struggle for pre-eminence between pope and emperor and are just as guilty as many Roman Catholics of not taking the contingencies of history into account. Many Anglicans probably find it mildly disturbing that Anglican historians – a Mandell Creighton or an Owen Chadwick – can relate the power-play of the popes with urbane equanimity and without implying any judgement (they find Acton more congenial, if a little over-heated).

The fact that Anglicans, like Orthodox, do not accept an immediate and ordinary jurisdiction for the universal primate, does not mean that they exclude the possibility of any jurisdiction pertaining to that role. Anglicans could probably live with an appellate jurisdiction (Nazir-Ali 1997) in which the Bishop of Rome acted as arbiter in disputes and might accept the possibility of visitation on behalf of a universal primate, which implies occasional and limited ordinary jurisdiction in extreme circumstances, since they have those already (Podmore 1998, 2005). But what they almost certainly would insist on is that the scope and limits of a universal primacy should be clearly set out (the principle of constitutionality) and that the subsidiary principles of consent and of reception should be honoured. This implies that the laity should be encouraged to exercise the kingly or royal office (as well as the priestly and prophetic office) that belongs to them by baptism and so fulfil their appropriate role in the governance of the Church, that the integrity of the local church should be respected, that no one should be above church law or be free to make it unilaterally, that sub-sidiarity should be axiomatic and that the collegiality of the bishops should flourish and should not be curtailed or suppressed.

   While Anglicans are better at knowing what they do not want than at knowing what they do want, and are past masters at finding fault with other churches' structures when their own are patently creaking at the seams, the above desiderata are not a mere Anglican wish list, but are in tune with the conciliar tradition as it has evolved in the Western Church over the past 700 years. The best Anglican discussions of universal primacy ask hard questions about what teeth that primacy needs to have as well as about what constraints there will be on how it chooses to use them (cf. Wright 2004; Hind 2003). However, some Anglicans do tend to become rather dewy-eyed at the vision of a Pope John XXIII figure, a caring pastor who will preside in love and gather the universal Church into one fold. That raises questions about the iconographic status of the modern papacy and about projection and about whether any human person or institution can mediate without friction and distortion the one true 'Shepherd and Bishop of your souls' (1 Peter 2.25, AV).

The Eastern Orthodox Churches

Although the Eastern churches often complain that they are marginalized within the Ecumenical Movement, the truth is that they have profoundly influenced ecumenical ecclesiology, even to the extent of shaping certain models of unity that have been proposed. Conciliar fellowship between churches that already enjoy a sufficient degree of ecclesial communion is a model of unity that was much discussed at a certain point in the Ecumenical Movement. The Fifth Assembly of the World Council of Churches, meeting at Nairobi in 1975, proposed 'conciliar fellowship' between truly united local churches as a model of the 'unity we seek'. The Assembly stated:

The one Church is to be envisioned as a conciliar fellowship of local churches which are themselves truly united. In this conciliar fellowship, each local church possesses, in communion with the others, the fullness of catholicity, witnesses to the same apostolic faith and therefore recognizes the others as belonging to the same church of Christ and guided by the same Spirit ... They are bound together because they have received the same baptism and share in the same eucharist: they recognize each other's members and ministries. They are one in their common commitment to confess the gospel of Christ by proclamation and service to the world. To this end, each church aims at maintaining sustained and sustaining relationships with her sister churches, expressed in conciliar gatherings whenever required for the fulfilment of their common calling (Keshishian 1992: xv; Keshishian provides an extended exposition of ecumenical conciliarity from an Oriental Orthodox point of view).

For the Eastern churches, matters of authority, unity and primacy revolve around the key ecclesiological idea of *sobornost*: the answers that Orthodox theology gives to the questions that the Western tradition, with its characteristic juridical mentality, has thrown up are determined by that concept (Schmemann 1962). *Sobornost* points to communal solidarity, to mutual mystical indwelling in love. It evokes conciliarity in the broadest sense of the community of the Church, guided and governed by the Holy Spirit, consulting its deepest mind. It elevates the Church as mystery above the Church as institution. *Sobornost* has affinities with the Western conciliar tradition's sense of the whole Church as the bearer of truth.

Modern Orthodox theology is an expression of 'eucharistic ecclesiology', even where it does not follow Nikolai Afanasief, the pioneer of this mode of theology, into a sort of eucharistic totality. Eucharistic theology brings every affirmation about the Church to the touchstone of the Divine Liturgy, where the bishop gathers the local Church (the capital C is important here) as one body, united with the universal Church and with the saints in heaven. The Eucharist is seen as the supreme manifestation of the reality of the Church. Eucharistic ecclesiology, though it privileges the mystical above the institutional, on the whole affirms the visibility of the Church (though this is tenuous in Khomiakov) and its hierarchical aspect through the role of the bishop or priest in eucharistic presidency. In contrast to the western, Roman tendency to exalt the universal over the local, in eucharistic ecclesiology the particular, local expressions of unity and catholicity are affirmed (though in Afanasief the universal is rather downplayed) (Zizioulas 2001: 13; Nichols 1995: 128). It is the Eucharist that unites the Church in space and time and the Eucharist cannot happen without the bishop.

To pick up the guiding thread of this study, the models and structures of authority that have developed in the Church from early mediaeval times: the Orthodox theologian Stylianos Harkianakis put the question with an absence of diplomatic nuance: 'Is the structure of the Christian Church in the light of the gospel, monarchical or collegial?' (Harkianakis 1971: 116–17). Orthodox theologians trace the divergence of paradigms of authority back to the interpretation of Matthew 16.18 ('You are Peter and on this rock I will build my Church'). Meyendorff (1975: 98) asserts equally bluntly: 'The whole ecclesiological debate between East and West is thus reducible to the issue of whether the faith depends on Peter or Peter on the faith.' Appealing to the tradition of Eastern exegesis, Meyendorff quotes Origen to the effect that the words of Jesus here have a soteriological, not an institutional, significance. In confessing Jesus to be the Christ, Peter is the pioneer of faith and the representative of believing Christians. So every believer receives the same keys to the Kingdom of Heaven as Peter did and in that sense becomes Peter. Thus in Eastern exegesis Peter's successors are found wherever the true faith is confessed and as such 'cannot be localized geographically or monopolized by a single church or individual'. However, a particular responsibility belongs to the bishop of each local church. There is only one see, the chair of Peter, and all the bishops sit on it (Meyendorff in Meyendorff 1992: 89).

If, as in Orthodox theology, ecclesiology is explicitly trinitarian, if the Holy and Undivided Trinity, both Three and One, is our model of unity, a collegial, not a monarchical paradigm of authority is implied. The structure of the Church must reflect (does necessarily reflect) the economy of salvation, in which Father, Son and Spirit act in harmony and so reveal the eternal intra-trinitarian relations of the Godhead. This is what enables one Orthodox theologian to claim that episcopal synodality is a soteriological matter (Harkianakis 1971).

For Orthodoxy there is no visible head of the Church on earth (Fouyas 1972: 127) and there is no universal jurisdiction by divine right (Meyendorff 1966: 149). Orthodox ecclesiology presupposes the integrity and solidarity of local churches without an external superior authority that can intervene, because that would imply an incursion into their celebration of the eucharistic mystery, at which the bishop, as their chief pastor, presides. Each local church is the Church in its integrity and wholeness, the *una sancta*, the Catholic Church (Clément 2003: 12), and is identical with the Church founded by Christ on Peter's confession of faith. It is not that Christ built his universal Church on Peter as an individual and thereby gave him authority over that universal Church; but rather that there is one Church, simultaneously local and universal, and each bishop is both Peter and the college of the Apostles (Clément 2003: 27). In fact, modern Orthodox theology opposes eucharistic ecclesiology to universal ecclesiology (Meyendorff in Meyendorff 1992). The event of Caesarea Philippi is replicated in every episcopally gathered eucharistic community. The East does not accept the mystical identity of the Bishop of Rome and Peter that emerged in the West and attained its zenith in Gregory VII, who believed that he was not only Peter's successor, but that Peter acted and spoke through him.

For Orthodoxy, the equality of bishops is not an economy and is not a political matter: it is ontological. No bishop can be more of a bishop than another. The concept of a 'universal bishop' is scandalous (so Afanasief in

McManus 2000: 235). There may be 'administrative' differences in bishops' responsibilities, says Evdokimov, but 'from the charismatic point of view, all bishops are perfectly equal; there is no super-bishop, no *episcopus episcoporum*. That there is no power higher than that of the bishop in his diocese is a basic principle in the East' (Evdokimov 1971: 124). Zizioulas robustly states the fundamental principle that he believes was abandoned by the Roman Catholic Church at Vatican I: 'Each bishop is absolutely equal to all the other bishops in every way as presiding over a complete Church' (2001: 33, n. 32). Any ecclesiastical power that was intrinsically superior to the local bishop within the local church would 'disavow the plenitude of the eucharistic mystery and imply a source of grace and charism heterogeneous to the [local] Church itself' (McManus 2000: 237). 'Supreme power' over the local church would mean power over Christ himself, because his fullness is present in every local church (Schmemann in Meyendorff 1992: 153–54). The fact that Orthodoxy recognizes a eucharistic (priestly/episcopal) hierarchy does not imply the subordination of one bishop to another or of one see to another; the solidarity and equality of bishops in collegiality is inviolate. The 'Cyprianic ecclesiology' that affirms the indivisible unity of the episcopate within which each bishop takes his place (*Episcopatus unus est cuius a singulis in solidum pars tenetur*) unites Orthodox and Anglicans (cf. Cyprian 1957). Zizioulas (2001) gives a sustained exposition of Cyprian's *On the Unity of the Catholic Church* and other writings.

For Orthodoxy, the papacy is the greatest obstacle to the reconciliation of East and West and the papal claim to universal ordinary jurisdiction is a bigger problem than the claim to infallibility (Clément 2003: 9). However, Orthodox theologians insist that the idea of primacy as such is not in dispute; primacy is pervasive in Orthodoxy (Harkianakis 1971: 115–16). For Afanasief, a universal primacy of the Bishop of Rome would be acceptable, provided that it were a primacy centred on witness to the faith and on the reception (or non-reception, that is to say, the discernment) of what was happening in other local churches (Nichols 1995: ch. 7).

Because of the debacle of the Council of Florence (the continuation of Basel), when Eastern bishops accepted an agreement with the West that they could not sell when they got back home, Orthodox theologians tend to be unenthusiastic about Ecumenical Councils as such, sometimes seeing them as an imposition of Roman imperialism (Khomiakov; for an exposition of Afanasief's view of councils see Nichols 1989: 62–75). Naturally, the Orthodox do not accept the authority of Councils summoned by the pope since the Great Schism that came to a head in 1054. On the other hand, they believe that they have the authority, as the true Church without remainder, to convene an Ecumenical Council (which would be purely Orthodox), though they have not done so since the breach with the West.

Orthodox theologians feel little affinity with fifteenth-century conciliarism in the West because (as they see it, perhaps through official Roman

Catholic eyes) it polarized conciliarity and primacy. N. Lossky (1999: 134) asserts that the question of the Conciliar Movement, whether a Council was above the pope, or the pope above the Council, 'has no place in true conciliarity', because conciliarity and primacy 'necessarily imply one another'. Orthodox theology seeks an integration of conciliarity and primacy that avoids both ecclesiastical democracy and the autocracy of a super-bishop (McManus 2000: 248). In Orthodoxy synodality is not a function of the Church, but an essential dimension of its life (see Duprey 1971). On the other hand, the Orthodox tradition has not condemned the Reformation, in the sense of the breach with Roman jurisdiction (Fouyas 1972: 85), though it tends to see Protestantism as a particularly aggravated form of the disease of Western Christendom (Khomyakov 1977).

Zizioulas on Conciliarity and Primacy

The most impressive exposition (at least to Anglican eyes) of the issues of authority, unity and primacy, within the tradition of Orthodox eucharistic ecclesiology, is found in the combination of the two seminal works by John Zizioulas, Metropolitan of Pergamon: *Eucharist, Bishop, Church* (new edition 2001) and *Being as Communion* (1985). The highly personalist and relational theology of *koinonia* in *Being as Communion*, though published after the ecclesiological spade work of *Eucharist, Bishop, Church*, provides the ontological structure for Zizioulas's synthesis. His is a confessedly holistic theology, attempting to hold together unity and multiplicity, the one and the many. The co-inherence of the one and the many is found in the local and universal Church, the bishop and the people, primacy and conciliarity. These are not in conflict!

This is in the tradition of a eucharistic ecclesiology – in the New Testament, Zizioulas argues, it is the coming together, the gathering for the Eucharist that constitutes the Church – but Zizioulas demurs at what he sees as Afanasief's absorption of the Church into the Eucharist. Over against eucharistic totalism Zizioulas stresses the collateral conditions for the Church: faith, love, baptism, holiness (Zizioulas 2001: 17). The institutional aspect of the Church is of little concern to Zizioulas: what excites him is its mystical nature: the 'mystical identity' between the Church on earth, gathered in the celebration of the Eucharist, and the Church in heaven, joining with angels and archangels in worship. Correspondingly, the ministries of the Church are 'mystical radiations' of Christ's authority, because there is a mystical relationship between the Sender and the sent, the Apostle: Luke 10.16 (2001: 60, 78, n. 108). Nevertheless, Zizioulas explicitly rejects the Harnackian disjunction between spirit and order, charism and structure: the hierarchy is itself charismatic (2001: 62).

Zizioulas sees the modern Roman Catholic idea of episcopal collegiality as an analytical or arithmetical concept: the addition of separate parts, rather than as the mystical identity of each bishop with the apostolic college. Collegiality is not the sum of its parts, but an organic unity, a whole that does not need the pope to complete it (Zizioulas 2001: 262). Catholicity for Zizioulas is a qualitative concept, having to do with wholeness and integrity, not geographical extension or universality, as Cyril of Jerusalem had adumbrated and Augustine was the first to propose systematically (2001: 171–73, n. 106). The local Church is catholic because of the presence of Christ in the Eucharist at which the bishop presides as his representative (Zizioulas prefers 'presentation' to 'representation': 2001: 186, n. 275). Therefore, it is true to say that each bishop sits on the throne of Peter. In an extended discussion of Cyprian, Zizioulas assimilates the third-century martyred bishop into his framework of mystical identity. There is a unity of identity between the individual bishop and the college, 'not as a part of the whole, but as an expression of the whole' (Zizioulas 2001: 155). The Eucharist celebrates the 'simultaneous instantiation of the local and universal Church' (McManus 2000: 243; cf. McPartlan 2004).

Zizioulas lays down what universal primacy can and cannot be for Orthodoxy (Zizioulas 1978, 1999). Orthodox are not interested in an institutionalized primacy; they might warm to one that was not juridical, not a primacy of jurisdiction, nor of an individual, but one that was pneumatological, that is to say, one that evoked the life-giving work of the Holy Spirit in the deepest life of the Church. Such a primacy would be the primacy of a local church (that of Rome), but one that was exercised in a synodical context: locally in the college of presbyters with their bishop (it is conciliarity that gives the local church its structure), regionally in provincial councils, and globally in collegial consultation, ultimately and potentially in an Ecumenical Council. Zizioulas (2001: 261) sees the emergence of councils in the fourth century as an expression of the unity of the churches in one body, but thinks (wrongly) that the Conciliar Movement defined itself by its opposition to papal primacy (McManus 2000: 243). Understood in the way outlined above, a universal primacy would be 'an ecclesial necessity' in a united Church (Zizioulas 1999: 125).

Chapter 13

SEMPER REFORMANDA: THE IMPERATIVE OF REFORM IN THE CONCILIAR MOVEMENT, THE REFORMATION AND THE MODERN CHURCH

The Legacy of the Conciliar Tradition

The central conviction of conciliarism – its pivotal ecclesiological axiom – is the belief that responsibility for the well-being (the doctrine, worship and mission) of the Church rests with the whole Church. Hardly less fundamental is the conciliar principle that this responsibility is exercised in a constitutional and representative way through councils, supremely through a General Council. Conciliarism was essentially a theological movement: it brought the ecclesiological work of theologians to bear on intractable problems of ecclesiastical power struggles; it critiqued obstructive legal and administrative systems in the name of higher truths. Nevertheless, conciliarism was politically realistic: it recognized national aspirations and brought civil rulers and non-episcopal scholars into its deliberations. Through all this it appealed to the common good of the Church, elevating the well-being of the whole over that of the constituent parts, and infused the practice of authority with ideas drawn from the tradition of natural law, particularly equity (*aequitas*) and flexibility in the administration of positive, human law (*epieikeia*). On the other hand, none of that made it a movement towards democratic church government, though the seeds of democracy were present in Marsilius of Padua's *Defensor Pacis*. Conciliarism remained hierarchical and hierocratic – especially in Jean Gerson and Nicholas of Cusa, two of its most impressive exponents – an assertion of the principle of aristocracy over against that of monarchy. General Councils not only had supreme authority, emulating the *plenitudo potestatis* claimed by the late mediaeval papacy, but could not err in matters of faith. This was one area where the Protestant Reformers parted company with the 'classical' conciliarists. While the rump of the Council of Basel would not have stopped short of a completely depotentiated papacy, the consensus of conciliar thought aimed at what today we might call an integration of primacy and conciliarity. The right combination of conciliarity, collegiality and primacy is the Holy Grail of modern ecumenical dialogue.

The debate over the relative strengths of various centres of authority in the Church remains unresolved. It remains unresolved not only in Roman

Catholicism (witness the spate of books and journalism contesting the current administration of authority in that church), but in Anglicanism and in the historic Protestant churches. The existence of the Eastern churches calls into question the very notion of an Ecumenical or General Council on which the whole problematic pivots. There has not been a truly Ecumenical Council since before the decisive break between East and West in the mid-eleventh century. To concede, as Pope Paul VI did, that Councils of the Catholic Church are General rather than Ecumenical simply sharpens the issue. The Council of Constance drew up a profession of faith for the new pope to make. It distinguished between 'the eight holy ecumenical (*universalia*) councils' and 'the general (*generalia*) councils at the Lateran, Lyons and Vienne' (Tanner 2004: 18). Paul VI's speech in 1974 on the seventh centenary of the Council of Lyons (1274) referred to that council and the other mediaeval councils as 'general councils of the western world' (*generales synodos in occidentali orbe*) (20, citing AAS, 66 [1974], 620).

In the present state of the Christian Church conciliarity is fragmented and inchoate; it is not a panacea for the divisions of Christendom but an expression of them. Conciliarity is imperative and belongs to the essential life of the Church, but it is compromised, flawed, imperfect and ambiguous. All Christian churches are in the same boat with regard to conciliarity: Roman Catholics, Orthodox, Anglicans and Protestant churches, all attempting to practise conciliarity according to their lights but crucially without each other – when conciliarity is predicated precisely on invoking or mobilizing the whole Church.

Issues of authority in the churches today look different from the perspective of the conciliar tradition – and all the more so if we address the deep ethical principles that are embedded in its ecclesiology, the concepts of the common good of the Church and of the relation of church law to natural law.

The Common Good of the Church

The familiar prayer, inscribed in the intercessory texts of various churches, that 'we may seek the common good', reflects the concern of the apostolic and post-apostolic writers that Christians should be loyal, law-abiding citizens of the Roman Empire. The Christians of the New Testament should have the good of the community at heart and should pray for God's blessing on those who are in authority (Romans 13.1–7; 1 Timothy 2.1–4; 1 Peter 2.13–17). The New Testament comes close to speaking about the common good in one place: the NRSV and the NIV use 'for the common good' to translate *pros to sympheron* in the context of charismata in 1 Corinthians 12.7, whereas the AV (King James Bible) is closer to the Greek with 'to profit withal'. Thiselton follows Margaret Mitchell in rendering it 'for common advantage' (Thiselton 2000: 936). The inter-testamental background should not be overlooked (Ullmann 1975: 211–12): 2 Maccabees refers to the national welfare (13.3) and distinguishes between the private and the public good (4.5).

The idea of the common good also continues a substantial tradition, going back at least to Augustine of Hippo, of Christian thinking about the nature of community and society. That tradition drew in turn, critically and reflectively, on the pre-Christian classical tradition, particularly as that was shaped by Aristotle and Cicero, read in the light of the Bible (for the connections between the classical and theological understandings of *koinonia* see Sagovsky 2000).

In *The City of God* Augustine spoke of the peace, harmony and tranquillity that was possible in this world, as a reflection and anticipation of the life of heaven, and of the political good order and discipline that was needed to preserve it (Augustine 1972: 599–600, 870 [CD XV.4; XIX.13]. Augustine's exposition of this theme was hardly expansive or effusive – for him the supreme good that is found in God completely dominates and partly eclipses the earthly expression of the good, but it gave authority for mediaeval writers to carry the argument further in the direction of a common good of this world.

Mediaeval theologians reflected on the relation between the good of individuals and the good of the Christian commonwealth. The common good, they generally said, was greater than the individual good but included it. Thomas Aquinas insisted that all law must be promulgated for the common good (Aquinas, n.d. 28: 16–17 [ST, I–II, q. 90, a. 4]; cf. Lisska 1996). Thomas Aquinas followed Augustine in affirming that the supreme common good was to be found in God. As Aquinas put it: 'the supreme good, namely God, is the common good, since the good of all things depends on him' (Hollenbach 2002: 4, citing *Summa Contra Gentiles*, III, 17; cf. Finnis 1998: 111–17; Kempshall 1999). This synthesis of classical and Christian ideas, forming a coherent body of thought, affirmed that happiness and virtue belong together and that the aim of civil government is to provide not merely for the material needs of citizens and for their physical security, but to promote the common good by fostering the life of virtue that brings happiness. For the aim of human life was, as Aristotle had put it in the *Politics*, not just to live, but to live well, to lead 'the good life' in community (*koinonia*) (Aristotle 1995: 7–12 [I, 1–2]).

What mediaeval scholars built on this tradition was the application of the criterion of the common good to the Church itself. Exponents of Roman law and canon law, kings and popes alike appealed to the notion of the public welfare. The parallel concepts of 'the state of the realm' (*status regni*) and 'the state of the Church' (*status ecclesiae*) were developed to uphold the welfare of the Christian commonwealth against the assertion of individual or private rights (Post 1964: 12). Those who longed to see the reform of abuses in the mediaeval Latin Church appealed to the common good or well-being of the Church, insisting that no one (especially the pope) should act against the *status ecclesiae*. In calling for a General Council to heal the internal divisions of the church, the conciliar thinkers of the late fourteenth and early fifteenth centuries – notably Henry of Langenstein, Jean Gerson and Dietrich of Niem – invoked the biblical, Pauline language of the whole body of the Church and its proper functioning. The positive laws of the Church must not be allowed to impede reform; they were subject to correction by divine (biblical) law and natural law which always had in view the common good, not the advantage, in wealth or power, of the few.

The sixteenth-century Reformers (particularly Luther, Melanchthon, Bucer, Calvin and Bullinger) and their immediate successors laid out the conditions, not only for a faithful Church, but for a flourishing Christian society with the Church at the heart of it, though not trespassing on what were properly the responsibilities of the civil magistrate. Laws that promoted the common good would safeguard public order, decency and mutual care. The second generation of Lutheran Reformers paid greater attention than Luther himself had done to the institutions that would promote the common good, especially in law and education (Witte 2002; Hendrix 2004), though Luther's agenda for social reform in his *Appeal to the Nobility of the German Nation* of 1520 certainly set the pace.

The idea of the common good is integrally related to the concept of justice, and so also to natural law (connections fruitfully made by Finnis 1980: on the common good see especially ch. 6 and pp. 54–56). At the beginning of the eighteenth century, at a time when the discourse of the common good was giving way to the rhetoric of the rights of the individual, the Neapolitan philosopher of history Giambattista Vico gave a suggestive definition of the common good in his academic oration *On the Study Methods of Our Time* (1708) by linking justice, law and the common good:

> What is justice? It is constant care for the common good. In what does the science of law consist? In the knowledge of the best government. What is law? It is the art of watching over the public interest ... What is natural law? The private interest of each one of us. What is the law of nations? The common good of all nations. What is civil law? The good of the commonwealth (cited in Miller 1994: epigraph).

The rhetoric of the common good seems to have faded from Protestant consciousness today and has become the preserve of the Roman Catholic Church (but see now Miller and McCann 2005). The Anglican Communion, faced with the possibility of schism over the consecration of an American bishop in a same-sex relationship, appealed repeatedly to the common good of the Church and invoked the conciliar tradition in the Windsor Report 2004 (Anglican Communion Office 2004: 38, 49, 69, 83, 86). But, with that exception, when do we hear either Protestant or Roman Catholic voices today invoking the notion of *the common good of the Church*? We look briefly now at some contemporary applications of the common good of society before asking: How does all this relate to the Church? But let us keep one eye on the Church as we proceed; the implications are not far to seek.

The modern Roman Catholic Church has made extensive use of the idea of the common good, especially in the Second Vatican Council's 'Constitution on the Church in the Modern World' (*Gaudium et Spes*). The political life of humankind, the Council stated, exists to serve the common good, which it is the responsibility of government to promote. The common good embraces the fulfilment of individuals, families and communities: it is the sum of those conditions of social life which enable them all to achieve that fulfilment more completely and readily. Citizens should actively participate in political life and should use their vote, not for selfish ends, but to advance the common good. The Council was already aware of the global context of human relations and taught that particular communities should take into account the common good of other groups and indeed of the whole human family (Abbott 1966: esp. 225, 285 [GS 26, 74]).

Before the 1997 General Election in the United Kingdom the Roman Catholic Bishops Conference of England and Wales issued 'The Common Good and the Catholic Church's Social Teaching': in his Preface the late Cardinal Hume emphasized that the foundation of that teaching was the inalienable dignity of every human person, created in the image of God, and offered freedom through the gospel by God. Society should, therefore, encourage men and women to take responsibility for their own lives and encourage them to co-operate with others to promote the common good. The document went on to affirm that the common good must be the criterion and judge of political means as well as ends and that the well-being of persons in community was the primary consideration. It argued that the common good is achieved in two planes: 'horizontally', through human solidarity one with another, and 'vertically' through the subsidiarity of 'higher' levels of authority to the needs and responsibilities of 'lower' levels. While the common good varies according to circumstances and context, the report conceded, it always involves the informed tolerance of other views that are held in good conscience and respect for differences between one group of human beings and another.

The message of the late John Paul II for the World Day of Peace, 1 January 2005, extensively invoked the idea of the common good, stressing its global dimension, its universal scope – one might say, its catholicity – and its transcendent dimension, its source and destination in God.

The Roman Catholic Bishops' initiative in relaunching the vision of the common good and the late pope's application of it to the aspiration for a world community were timely. Today the language of the common good is almost forgotten. The voice of the common good is mute. There is widespread scepticism, encouraged by some political philosophers (e.g. Rawls and Dworkin), as to whether diverse western societies could ever agree on a good that they held in common. This philosophical scepticism is compounded by a widely held ideological suspicion (not without good reason, given the totalitarian history of the twentieth century) that appeals on behalf of the collective are a mask for an agenda of authoritarianism and the suppression of individual freedom. To the extent that any common good is recognized by society and culture in the West today, at the level of explicit agenda, it is the radically subjectivized desideratum of total untrammelled self-determination and self-expression (cf. O'Donovan and O'Donovan 2004: 244). The shibboleth of non-judgementalism (doing one's own thing provided it does not directly inflict harm on bystanders) and of indiscriminate toleration have replaced the ideal of the common good. A lazy tolerance actually militates against the common good, for as Hollenbach argues, in a maximally tolerant society there would be a minimum of meaningful human interaction (Hollenbach 2002: 69). When the value system has been radically privatized, it is unfashionable to argue that the good is by definition something held in common, because human beings are by nature social beings, created for relationship, fellowship, communion and mutual indwelling. 'We can know a good in common that we cannot know alone' (Michael Sandel, cited by Hollenbach 2002: 18). There is a challenge to the churches and to Christian theologians, to try to work out a viable meaning of the common good for a plural society. But it is actually the diverse texture, the tugs and tensions within the fabric of community, its inherent plurality, that makes sense of the concept of the common good. It is an idea that would be meaningless in a monolithic and monochrome society.

The idea of the common good weaves together concepts of society, community, moral virtue and of freedom combined with responsibility.

For the ideal of the common good to be viable, there must be a free, diverse but coherent society, held together by shared values and respect for both individual liberty and public authority. Freedom to work together for the common good depends on a healthy fabric of institutions, traditions, conventions and social practices, protected by a law that is not oppressive but sets the boundaries within which individuals and groups can exercise their initiative and take responsibility. It is the moral communities within civil society (among whom the Church or churches stand out) that uphold the common good by sustaining traditions and narratives that embody salutary social and personal values (cf. MacIntyre 1985; Gill 1992; Fergusson 1998; Avis 2003: ch. 7).

'Civil society' may be concisely defined as that diverse and complex collection of organizations and institutions that carry out their purposes in the extensive space for human activity that lies between the household on the one hand and the State on the other (cf. Avis 2003: 14–17). In that respect, the institutional churches and para-church organizations are components of civil society. They relate to other institutions and organizations and interact with them, as well as with the State itself through engagement with the legislature (Parliament and local government) and the executive (the national and local civil service). Does that mean that the Church is not a *societas perfecta*, as mediaeval papalists and conciliarists alike maintained? In one sense, no, the Church is not a society that is complete within itself, because it is intertwined with the wider civil society and is shaped by culture and economic and political forces in a way that was difficult to see when Church and State comprised one Christian commonwealth. But in another sense the Church is certainly a visible society, a society that is both divine and human, and it is a theological truth that the Church is inde-fectible (it will not finally fail as the agent of the gospel of Christ), guided by the Holy Spirit, and endowed with all the gifts and graces that are required for the fulfilment of its mission.

An essential characteristic of a healthy society – whether it is civil society or the society that is the Church – is confidence in justice: distributive justice (giving to all their due and treating everyone equally and fairly); commutative justice (that negotiates day-to-day transactions); and retribu-tive and restorative justice (through the administration of discipline and sanctions). When it is clear to all that laws (the laws of the state or of the Church) are being made purely for the common good, rather than for party advantage or for merely ideological reasons, and that the law is being upheld and administered with efficiency and impartiality, there the law is held in good repute and a crucial condition for social harmony is fulfilled. The conciliarists and the Reformers alike held that law should be adminis-tered with *epieikeia* (moderation, flexibility) and *aequitas* (equity, fairness), that it should be responsive to people's needs, and that all legislation should be brought to the touchstone of Scripture and natural law.

All societies are, however, sustained 'from below' by the energy generated by less formal and less structured bodies which we may call communities. The good life of which Aristotle spoke cannot be lived in splendid isolation, but is a life lived in fellowship with others. The message of the Bible and of Christian theology is the same: 'It is not good for man to be alone' (Genesis 2.18). There is a good life that can only be discovered through commitment and self-giving to others. The married couple or family is the base community, the paradigm of all communities and the building block for other expressions of community. The Christian married couple, united sacramentally in matrimony, as well as in baptism and the Eucharist (at least in principle), form the domestic church and comprise the smallest unit above the individual believer within the body of Christ. Communities are found also in the form of neighbourhoods, networks and other associations of like-minded people who come together to pursue common interests, hobbies or sport. Local churches, congregations and parishes are also forms of community. Communities create the social capital that enables societies to flourish. Institutions may be seen as aggregates of their stake-holding communities: they need to nurture them, for without them they are hollow structures. Local churches sustain the wider Church.

In their turn, civil societies and the institutions that form them provide the stability, underpinned by justice and the rule of law, that enables more local communities to flourish. While societies are concerned with justice, rather than with compassion, because they are impersonal collectivities of bodies with diverse and even conflicting ideas and goals, communities, held together as they are by bonds of affection and personal loyalty, are concerned with compassionate action for the sake of their members and – ideally – those outside their boundaries. Communities but not societies may love (cf. Kirkpatrick 2001). Churches, as societies formed of institutions, often present an impersonal face to those who look to them, so it is vital that the right balance is struck between the centre and the diaspora, or in ecclesiological language between the universal Church and the local and particular churches. The face of Christ will be glimpsed through the very local expression of the Church, or not at all.

The common good of the Church and the common good of society are bound together and mutually dependent. The one will not flourish without the other. Church leaders should not imagine that the Church will flourish if civilization goes to pot. When Christians work for the common good the Church receives a fresh access of energy. Grounded in their local Christian communities and working together through the institutional churches at regional and national level, Christians can co-operate and collaborate – with discretion – with those of other religious beliefs, or none, in pursuit of specific shared goals. The Bible and the Christian tradition teach that all human beings can know the basic moral requirements of the good life that make for the common good, such as the knowledge of good and evil and the 'Golden Rule' that we should treat others as we would wish them to treat us (the essential core of the natural law). Christians hold, of course, that the ultimate good is uniquely revealed in Scripture: it is to be found in God as he is known in Jesus Christ through the power of the Holy Spirit; it is experienced in the body of the Church through all the means of grace, especially word and sacrament. Christians therefore work with zeal and devotion to make that truth known through mission and evangelization. But Christians also typically work with inspired energy for lesser goods, precisely because they know that they are derived from the ultimate source of all good and that they approximate to it to various degrees.

The theological good, as understood by Christians and other theistic believers, is to know, love and serve God, 'to glorify God and to enjoy him for ever', as the Westminster Shorter Catechism put it. The social good, as embraced by Christians and non-Christians alike, is to live in harmonious fellowship, in love and charity, first with our neighbours, then with our nation and ultimately with global humankind. Christians are committed to pursue the social good because their faith teaches them that their neighbours, their fellow citizens and all their fellow human beings are created in the image of God (*imago dei*), are loved by God and are the subjects of the working of the Holy Spirit in every human heart and life that calls them to conversion, to live henceforth in tune with God's will for human well-being. Human fellowship and communion (*koinonia*), in friendship, marriage, the family, the neighbourhood and beyond – for all its short-comings, fragility and imperfections – reflects, anticipates and points to that communion (*koinonia*) with God that is the fruit of redemption.

The deep connection in theology between the common good and the vision of God surely tells us that the ideal of the common good of the Church – that is, of the whole Church, not merely of one part of it – should guide the policy and decisions of all the churches, for at the heart of the common good of the Church is its unity; and, in turn, the salutary exercise of authority is a crucial condition of unity. The common good of the Church is not a confessional matter, one that can be appropriated by par-ticular Christian world communions and applied to their domestic diffi-culties (which is as far as the Windsor Report takes it; and does the Roman Catholic Church take it any further?). We are not talking about the common good of 'our church'. It is an intrinsically ecumenical concept: just as we need to think globally about the common good of humankind (as Vatican II and John Paul II reminded us), so too we need to think ecu-menically about the common good of the Church, of the *whole* Church, and need to bring the rules, policies and decisions of particular churches, especially as they affect other churches, to that touchstone.

Natural Law and Church Law

One of the striking features of conciliar thought in the late mediaeval period and through the Reformation and beyond is its insistence that the life of the Church should be ordered in accordance with natural law. During the crisis periods of the Great Schism of the West and the Reformation both conciliarists and Reformers asserted that the reform, not only of particular abuses but of structures of authority in the Church, was required by natural law, as well as by divine, biblical law. In gathering up the harvest of the conciliar tradition in this final chapter, we need to explore the significance of the natural law tradition for ecclesiology.

The history of various approaches to natural law, from classical sources in Aristotle and the Stoics to its definitive theological florescence in St Thomas, is usefully traced by Crowe 1977. Looking somewhat beyond our period, the later 'rationalistic' development of natural law in secular jurisprudence and political thought, which cut loose from the Church and Christian doctrine, is charted in Gierke 1958b which has a helpful introduction by Ernest Barker. Natural law was defended by Anglican theologians in a hostile, positivistic intellectual climate: Ramsey 1966; Macquarrie 1970.

Natural law is a somewhat elusive and certainly a far from monolithic idea. It is variously interpreted, not to say highly contested. Aristotle set the lines of conceptual definition. He distinguished in the *Rhetoric* between specific or particular law, on the one hand, and law that was 'common' or 'according to nature', on the other. The first, what we would call positive law, was written, the latter unwritten. He observed that written law may not always fulfil the true function of law: positive laws may actually be unjust (Aristotle 1991: 102, 110 [1373b, 1374b, 1375b]). In the *Nichomachean Ethics*, Aristotle distinguished two elements within civic justice: a natural element, which is valid everywhere and is not dependent on legislation, and a conventional element, which is the product of legislation (Aristotle 1953: 157–58 [1134b]). The Stoics identified nature and reason and saw these reflected in a common or universal law (*koinos nomos*). Cicero spoke of *ius naturale*, a law that belonged to humankind by virtue of our common human nature and which corresponded to universal human needs and instincts.

In early mediaeval times natural law began to diverge between descriptive and prescriptive concepts of the law of nature and this twin track follows through to the major scholastic thinkers and to the Reformers. (We have seen that Luther repudiated the descriptive view of natural law and saw it as an imperative.) The descriptive approach is classically expressed in Ulpian's definition, incorporated into Justinian's *Digest*: 'Natural law is what nature has taught all animals' (seen in the urge to procreate and the instinct to nurture offspring). The prescriptive law of nature tended to identify natural law with divine law. It is classically expressed in Gratian's definition: 'Natural law is what is contained in the law and the gospel, in virtue of which each is commanded to do to others as he would wish to be done to himself and is forbidden to do to another what he would not have done to himself.' Bonaventure accepts Ulpian's 'naturalistic' definition, while Albert the Great rejects it.

Aquinas reconciles these contraries and creates a synthesis (though this is not complete or unambiguous) by setting humanity's animal and moral natures in a hierarchy, so providing continuity with the humbler creation while at the same time according natural law its full force as law. The Creator impresses a law of action or behaviour upon all creatures as the supreme legislator, but orders human life towards a transcendent goal which has to be voluntarily pursued. Aquinas should not be credited with the view that natural law is always and everywhere the same. Although the eternal law is of course unchanging, the way that we participate in it (which is precisely his understanding of what natural law is) varies. Natural law is adapted to the complexity of circumstances, the uneven and unequal development of reason in peoples, and the corruption of human nature through sin. Human nature itself is not static and unvarying, but dynamic and responsive to changing circumstances (*natura humana mutabilis est*: Aquinas ST, II-IIae, q. 57, a. 2; Crowe 1977: 45, 75, 120, and for Aquinas chs 6 and 7).

Aquinas has been (and is) interpreted in either 'rationalist' or 'theological' modes. Finnis (1980 and 1998) follows Grisez in attempting to detach natural law in the Thomistic tradition from Christian theology, specifically from its doctrines of creation and providence, and from the metaphysics presupposed by Thomas, and to ground it instead in self-evident truths. These deliverances of the practical reason refer to certain basic goods for human life that are incontestable: knowledge is the first of these; relationships and social life also figure prominently; freedom and pleasure are not included (cf. Finnis 1998: 79–86; Biggar and Black 2000; these 'basic goods' are reminiscent of Hart's 'natural necessities': Hart 1961). Lisska (1996) gives a detailed exposition of Aquinas on natural law that bypasses the theological and metaphysical foundation as far as possible, while George (1999) further distances the Grisez-Finnis approach from Aquinas, expounding it largely in terms of self-evident rational insights.

However, Jean Porter (1999 and 2005) has placed Aquinas firmly back in his proper context: in Scripture, in the patristic and scholastic tradition, and in the Christian doctrines of creation, the *imago dei*, and the providential ordering of the world to a supreme good that lies beyond this life. Similarly, Biggar has claimed that the idea of the moral good, that Grisez and Finnis present as attainable 'naturally', is actually formed by specifically Christian presuppositions: 'It is in fact a Christian theory, formally abstracted from the theological context in which alone it makes sense' (Biggar in Biggar and Black 2000: 179). Porter significantly criticizes Finnis *et al.* for supposing that the natural law can be appropriated and that the common good can be realized apart from particular moral communities: for her (though this is implied rather than stated), the moral community that forms their proper home is the Christian Church, made up of the local churches.

Kerr suggests that natural law is 'currently perhaps the most contested topic in Thomas' work' (Kerr 2002: 111: modern interpretations of Aquinas on natural law are discussed in ch. 6). In spite of this variety of interpretation, certain clear common threads can be discerned in the natural law tradition. First, it stands for the belief that certain norms of the good life and of right conduct are known to all people: the imperative to seek the good and to shun evil (the irreducible bedrock of natural law) is universal. The Golden Rule that we should do to others as we would that they should do to us is found in many religions and philosophies, including the Christian Scriptures.

Second, the natural law tradition holds that the way that we should behave is related to the sort of beings that we are and to the way the world is, to the nature of things. There is a connection between fact and value, though not one that can be read off in a crude or simplistic fashion that would incur the gross *faux pas* of the naturalistic fallacy. There is a basic fit or congruity between the way we are made and the way we are meant to live.

Third, natural law doctrine affirms that there is an intrinsic connection between law and ethics. As H.L.A. Hart (1961) rather grudgingly acknowledged, some kind of natural law concept is needed to save us from the dictatorship of legal positivism. Laws may not be detached from moral truths. Legislators are not free to enact whatever laws they choose. Laws are not free standing, but are subject to a higher authority, that of ethical principles concerning right and wrong. Laws gain their ultimate legitimation, not from the power and authority of those who promulgate them, but from the ethical truths that they embody and apply. Who makes this judgement? The natural law tradition has been hospitable to emerging ideas of constitutionality, representation and consent. According to these political principles, it is not merely for those who legislate and those who enforce the law to decide whether their laws conform to ethical truths (though they should satisfy themselves on that score): it is for those on the receiving end to discern whether that is so, and if and when they do, to signal that this is the case by giving their consent.

Finally, natural law teaching qualifies the force of positive law in practice when it points out, as we have just noted, that laws do not have their legitimation in themselves. The fact that the law (the law of the land, or of any institution that legislates for its members) requires something of us is not a sufficient ultimate claim on our obedience; an unjust law is not a true law, is not *law*, but an abuse of law-making powers. At this point, natural law privileges conscience as the ultimate forum in which the decision whether or not to obey a law that appears to us unjust and unjustified or not must be made. At this point the study of natural law flows into the necessary casuistry of moral theology or moral philosophy.

To return to history: the conciliarists and the Reformers alike maintained that the positive laws of the Church must not be allowed to prevent the sort of reforms that, they believed, were required by natural and divine (biblical) law. Church law must give way to the eternal principles of the law that is grounded in the mind of God, inscribed in the order of nature and society, and overseen by God's providence. The principles of constitutionality (the scope and limits of power), representation of the whole body, and the consent of the governed were inscribed in ancient legal adages such as *Quod omnes tangit* ... The concentration of sovereignty in the papacy that had led to all pressure for reform of abuses being resisted was called into question by these principles of authority that stemmed from natural law. Laws should be conducive to fairness and equity (*aequitas*). Positive laws should be interpreted and applied with flexibility and in the light of circumstances (*epieikeia*). Aristotle had said in the *Rhetoric* that 'fairness' (*epieikes*) is justice that goes beyond the written law; and in the *Ethics* he had pointed out that laws inevitably generalize, but the wise dispenser of justice takes account of particular circumstances (Aristotle 1991: 105 [1373b]; 1953: 166–68). Conciliarists varied in the extent to which they explicitly invoked natural law, but they were of one mind in upholding these rational principles of governance.

The sixteenth-century Reformers maintained the mediaeval natural law tradition. Although it has been widely assumed that either a vicious nominalism in philosophy or an extreme transcendentalism in theology would have made it *a priori* impossible for them to work within the natural law framework, the evidence that they did so is overwhelming. Not only Melanchthon, but Luther himself; not only Bucer but Calvin invoked natural law principles. They applied them both to the ordering of society in the world (the temporal sphere) and to the right ordering of the Church (the spiritual sphere – though of course they saw Church and society as forming one integrated Christian commonwealth). Luther often quoted the adage *Quod omnes tangit* ... and enthused about *epieikeia*. The Reformers brought not only the findings of Renaissance biblical research but also considerations derived from natural law to bear in their critique of the Roman Church. The pope multiplied human rules and regulations that were hard to bear. Devout Christian souls should not be bowed down by them. On the other hand, *epieikeia* required reasonableness and compromise in dealing with one's opponents and demanded that one should not quibble about secondary issues. This is the spirit that informs a good deal of the Reformers' dealings with the Roman Catholic authorities: it is seen in the Augsburg Confession, the *Augustana*, and in much of the conciliar activity of the Protestants, including the preparations for a council that would seek to reconcile the opposing sides.

Modern Roman Catholic teaching insists that the content of natural law is for the Church's magisterium to define. *Humanae Vitae* (1968) made this claim explicit (Kerr 2002: 99). This claim is in tension with the fundamental insight of the natural law tradition that the basic principles of natural law are discernible by all people of goodwill, even though the tradition recognizes, following Aquinas particularly, that there is an element of discursive thinking involved in the concrete application (*determinatio*) of natural law to specific circumstances and therefore the possibility of error. The fact that the possibility of error or misjudgement in the determination of natural law is not entertained, at least in practice, by the Roman magisterium, is an obstacle to moving beyond the Reformation.

Continuity and Discontinuity

At the beginning of this book we took von Hügel's schema of the three elements in the Church (the mystical, the intellectual and the institutional) as an heuristic framework. An issue that links the three elements together is that of continuity and discontinuity in the life of the Church. We would expect to see aspects of continuity and of discontinuity in the institutional, the intellectual and the mystical dimensions of the Church's history.

All churches like to think (and probably need to believe) that they stand in visible continuity with the Church of the Apostles. The Lima statement of the World Council of Churches *Baptism, Eucharist and Ministry* (BEM 1982) described apostolic continuity in terms of the permanent character-istics of the apostolic community. Eastern Orthodox Christians affirm an unchanging continuity: the identity of the Church is unvarying. For the Orthodox the Church is synonymous with changelessness; its identity is unvarying (though its existence is far from static). Roman Catholic Christians assert the unbroken continuity of the Catholic Church from the time of the Apostles and trace the succession of occupants of the See of Rome back to Peter the fisherman, though Roman Catholic theology, if not official teaching, has since Newman in 1845 (Newman 1974) recognized a degree of real development, not mere fresh expression of the same ideas, within this continuous tradition (Chadwick 1957; Avis 2002: ch. 12; Nichols 1990). Anglicans, for their part, tend to point with typical pragmatic instincts to the unbroken continuity of parishes, dioceses and cathedrals, as well as of episcopal consecrations, through the political upheavals of the English Reformation. Anglicans claim that the Church of England is the continuation of the Catholic Church in England, not a sub-stitute or replacement for the pre-Reformation Church. Some Lutherans strongly affirm the continuity of their churches with the patristic Church (and that means that the line of continuity passes through the mediaeval Church), though others are rather ambivalent (even though on the Continent of Europe, Lutherans often worship in mediaeval church buildings). Methodists certainly see themselves as a branch of the one, holy, catholic and apostolic Church – which seems to imply that the Church of England, from which Methodism came forth, is the historical link. Even churches with a congregational, independent polity, rather than structures of oversight that extend beyond the local, point to ancient (seventeenth-century) chapels and delight to recall the worthies of earlier times.

As far as the Western Church is concerned, the Great Schism of 1378–1417 was without question a major caesura, a catastrophic event importing radical discontinuity and disruption, that split the Western Church into two jurisdictions. As we have noted, continuity was resumed and the split was healed only by the unprecedented exercise of conciliar authority. Not for the first time, the visible continuity of the Catholic Church was secured not by a pope, nor even by the episcopate as a whole, but by a General Council acting at the instigation of an emperor. The events of that era challenge the claim that the monarchical papacy has guaranteed the continuity and unity of the Church through the ages.

The conciliar tradition has seen continuity (including development and diversity) in its ideas and core principles, but the institutional continuity of conciliarism is fragile. Conciliarism exists in the mystical and intellectual modes, as well as in its institutional forms. More as a mystical apprehen-sion of the essential life of the whole Church and as an intellectual tradition of reflection on salutary forms of ecclesiastical polity than as a persisting institution, the Conciliar Movement bridges the divide caused by the

Reformation. It is one of the neglected threads of continuity between Roman Catholic, Anglican and Protestant churches. While fully fledged conciliar ideas have been suppressed in the Roman Catholic Church, they have suffered from benign neglect in the other branches of western Christendom. It would encourage a fresh perception of a continuity that is at once mystical, intellectual and institutional if all the traditions concerned were to re-appropriate the conciliar tradition that flourished in the late mediaeval period and allow it to become a common focus between them.

Alongside conciliar ideas, there are other major threads of continuity linking the pre- and post-Reformation churches.

First, the trinitarian and christological dogmas of the early councils and the creeds that they produced were not in dispute between the Protestant Reformers and the Roman authorities. That constitutes fairly massive common ground that should not be overlooked.

Second, Roman Catholics and Protestants shared the same heritage of political philosophy and repertoire of concepts, though obviously they appropriated it in different ways: they were using exactly the same bricks, though the resulting architecture was rather different. Sabine pointed out in his history of political theory that there was no such thing as a distinctively Roman Catholic or Protestant political doctrine.

> Catholics and Protestants alike, and every subdivision of Protestants, drew upon the same Christian heritage and the same body of European political experience. The scholars of all churches had the same stock of ideas, a rich and varied body of thought extending continuously back to the eleventh century and embodying a tradition which carried it back to antiquity (Sabine 1963: 354).

Third, the religious orders provide continuity as well as the obvious discontinuity of dissolution. It is a striking fact that the religious orders produced a large number of Reformers. The Reformers were not thrown up by radical sectarian movements of the late Middle Ages: they were not Lollards, Hussites or Waldensians, let alone descendants of the Cathars. Perhaps the majority of significant reforming figures emerged from the religious orders. They did so, not because these communities were generally corrupt, but because they were undergoing renewal and generating fresh energies. As J.T. McNeill pointed out half a century ago, 'None of the Reformers had a background of medieval sectarianism. They were men trained in monasteries and universities and nursed on the bosom of the medieval Church' (McNeill in Rouse and Neill 1954: 27). The Observants among the mendicant orders produced not only Luther and a long list of other German Reformers, but also reforming figures who did not break with Rome: notably Savonarola (d. 1498) and Francisco Ximinez de Cisneros (d. 1517). In Reformation England, of the twenty-four Tudor bishops on the bench at a certain juncture, sixteen had once been members of a religious order (not to mention the many lower-ranking active reformist figures). Protestant ideas appealed to them in a way that Wycliffite notions did not (Rex 2002: 134).

Though Luther renounced his vows as a religious, he did not reject the rigorous demands of the monastic ideal, but applied and adapted them, including the evangelical counsels of the Sermon on the Mount, to all Christians (Hendrix 2004: 24–26). Luther was not interested in structures, but in the evangelical vitality of Christian Europe, especially Germany; his aim as a Reformer was 'to help the German nation to be free and Christian again, after the wretched, heathenish, and unchristian rule of the pope' (LW 44: 161). Hendrix comments:

> Luther was not speaking about continuity between institutions as if the essentials of Christianity had been transferred across the Reformation divide from the Roman Church to Protestant churches ... [I]n spite of the papal tyranny that almost destroyed Christendom, the essentials of the faith had survived in order to serve the cause of a newly Christianized Europe. In his eyes there was both continuity and discontinuity, not between churches in their modern confessional forms, but between a captive Christendom, in which authentic Christianity had barely survived, and a liberated Christendom, in which the centrality of faith and love was being restored (Hendrix 2004: 45).

Fourth, the vision of reform is a further link connecting the pre- and post-Reformation churches, the Roman Catholics and the Protestants. Like MacCulloch (2003), Hendrix sees the whole period of the sixteenth century as comprising a reformation that embraced Protestant, Radical and Roman Catholic developments. This designation not only gives Roman Catholic reforming intentions their due, but also 'avoids casting Protestants and dissenters in the role of schismatics from the one true church' (Hendrix 2004: 123). The Roman Church had its complement of great reformers and the Council of Trent enacted nearly one hundred canons on issues that required reform (*super reformatione*). Just as the Protestant Reformers protested, with Calvin, that they wished simply to renew the face of the Catholic Church, so Giles of Viterbo deplored innovation (*res novae*) stating: 'We are not innovators. We are simply trying, in accordance with the will of God, to bring back to life those ancient laws whose observance has lapsed' (O'Malley 1968: 142). It is good to remember that before 1521 no reformer of any stripe could have envisaged that some of the reshaping of Christian institutions that seemed necessary would leave them outside the Roman Church.

Finally, if catholicity is concerned with the wholeness of the Church (*kata holon*), we can affirm that the conciliarists and the Reformers are linked by a catholic concern. The conciliarists invoked the authority of the whole body to redress the failure of its earthly head, while retaining a broadly hierarchical and centrally focused view of authority. The Protestant Reformers sought the renewal, the renovation of the *corpus christianorum* and in their diatribes against Rome they distinguished between the pastoral needs of the faithful and the obstructiveness of the hierarchy. For them the institutional fabric of the Latin Church could be sacrificed in order to save the essentials of word and sacrament. They saw catholicity as a qualitative rather than a quantitative concept (see Braaten and Jenson 1996; Aulén 1962).

These considerations – to look no further – enable us to say that the entire historical continuum, comprising the mediaeval struggles between popes and emperors and popes and popes, the Conciliar Movement, the Reformation, the Counter-Reformation, the Vatican Councils and the Ecumenical Movement, resides within the Western Church. The debate is an internal one, a family affair – that is why it has often been so impassioned, so inflamed. If Ockham belongs to the Western Church, so does Luther; if Gerson does, so does Calvin; if Cusanus does, so does Hooker. Cranz has demonstrated mystical and epistemological (intellectual) continuity between Cusanus and Luther (Cranz 2000: 151–203): this is to throw a bridge over the chasm of the Reformation. If, notwithstanding the wayward and perverse tendencies of human nature, the crooked timber of humanity, as Kant called it, the Catholic intention of the conciliarists cannot well be doubted, neither can the Catholic intention of the Reformers.

The Reformation Impetus in the Roman Catholic Church

Yves Congar was the prophet bearing the dangerous message of the imperative of reform to the Roman Catholic Church in the first half of the twentieth century. In Congar's vision reform and reunion were already inextricably linked. His *Chrétiens Désunis* (1937; ET *Divided Christendom* [1939]) ended with a call to reform for the sake of unity. But this was nothing strange, for the Church is always reforming herself (1937: 272). When Congar returned to the theme after the War in *Vrai et Fausse Réform dans l'Église* (Congar 1950) he faced the problem of sin in the Church and stressed that it is the nature of the Church to undergo 'ceaseless reform'. In both these works, Congar was labouring under a caricatured notion of Reformation theology, particularly of Lutheran doctrine; e.g. that the Church is invisible and that justification does not bring internal moral renewal, which supported his assertion that reform for Roman Catholics and reform for Protestants were very different things (Congar 1950: 461–62). One wonders how he would have expressed the imperative of reform if he had been working with an idea of the Reformation that was not a gross distortion. Congar shaped what Vatican II and Karl Rahner said about reform, but their statements are somewhat better informed about Protestant theology.

Vatican II, which belatedly came to terms with much that had turned out to seem valid in the legacy of the Reformation, echoed in its own tones the

Protestant mantra *ecclesia reformata semper reformanda*. The Council acknowledged that, because the Church was (among other things) a human institution, it was prone to decline from its divine calling. *Lumen Gentium* remarkably echoed Luther's *simul iustus, simul peccator* (at the same time holy and sinful), applying this notion to the Church rather than to the imperfect individual Christian. The Church, embracing sinners in her bosom, is at one and the same time holy and always in need of being purified, and therefore incessantly pursues the path of penance and renewal (*sancta simul et semper purificanda, poenitentiam et renovationem prosequitur*: LG 8: Tanner 1990: II, 855). And the decree on ecumenism says:

> Christ summons the Church, as she goes her pilgrim way, to that continual reformation (*ad hanc perennem reformatio*) of which she always has need, insofar as she is an institution of men here on earth. Therefore, if the influence of events or of the times has led to deficiencies in conduct, in Church discipline, or even in the formulation of doctrine (*in doctrinae enunciandae modo*) (which must be carefully distinguished from the deposit itself of faith), these should be appropriately rectified at the proper moment (UR 6: Abbott 1966: 350).

Unitatis Redintegratio set the cause of continual reformation in the context of ecumenism: reform was an aspect of the drawing together of the churches towards that full and complete unity which God in his goodness desires (*ad plenam perfectamque unitatem secundum Dei benevolentiam conducit*: UR 5: Tanner 1990: II, 912). Church renewal (*renovatio*) therefore has notable (*insigne*) ecumenical importance. The renewal that was taking place in, for example, the biblical and liturgical movements, preaching and catechetics, the apostolate of the laity, the spirituality of married life and the Church's social teaching and activity, the Council believed, should be considered as favourable pledges and signs of ecumenical progress in the future (UR 6: Tanner 1990: II, 913).

In a series of articles Karl Rahner has pushed the Council's teaching on the need for continual reform and renewal close to the limits that Roman Catholic theology needs to observe (collected in Rahner 1969: chs 17–19). The crucial issue (what Rahner calls 'one of the most agonising questions of ecclesiology which persistently recurs throughout the history of dogma': 253) is whether, because the Church contains sinners, the Church itself is sinful. Writing well before Vatican II (in fact as early as 1947), Rahner quotes Vatican I's affirmation of the Church's 'extraordinary holiness and inexhaustible fruitfulness in all that is good'. This is the ultimate truth about the Church, the 'default position', as we might say today: sin remains in the Church as a reality, yes, but one that contradicts her nature, for holiness belongs to her essential being (263–64). Nevertheless, the truth that sinners are members of the Church is an article of faith, taught by the Council of Constance against the views of Wyclif and Hus and (Rahner wrongly asserts) denied by the Reformers. The visible, institutional reality of the Church was, as we have seen, maintained by the magisterial

Reformers, though rejected, needless to say, by the radicals, the Anabaptists, etc. All who believe the Church to be a continuous visible society in the world will warm to Rahner's definition of Church in this context as 'the visible presence of God and his grace in this world in sacramental signs, it means the historical embodiment of Christ in the here and now of the world until he comes again'. So the fact that a real unregenerate sinner can belong to the real Church comprises 'a truth which in sheer incomprehensibility far outstrips anything' that hostile unbelievers can throw at the Church in exposing her failings (257). (Rahner is clear, just as the Reformers were, that there is a deeper, mystical sense of Church and to that these sinners do not and cannot belong.)

We cannot separate, Rahner insists, the visible society of the Church from its constituent members or the actions of its members from the actions of the body; the Church does not exist as an abstraction. Therefore we have to confess that the Church itself is sinful (Rahner 1969: 259). 'The Church is a sinful Church: this is a truth of faith, not [merely] an elementary fact of experience. And it is a shattering truth' (260). Expounding the Johannine passage about the woman taken in adultery (usually placed at John 8) as a parable of the Church, Rahner says (in words that would give even a pretty extreme Protestant a frisson of shock) that Christ looks upon 'this prostitute, his bride' (269).

When Rahner returned to the theme of the sinful Church after Vatican II, he was better informed about the Reformation: he noted that the teaching of the Church through the centuries, defined by the Council of Constance against Wyclif and Hus, that unregenerate sinners were members of the Church, was accepted 'in part even in the theology of the Reformers' (Rahner 1969: 270 n. 1). In this later article, Rahner pointed to the tendency in Roman Catholic 'official' theology to 'hypostatize' the Church as an independent entity, clerical and hierarchical, over against the people of God, and so to be blind to the extent to which the failings of its members actually corrupt the institution itself (277). Referring to Congar's question, 'How can the Church renew itself without ceasing?', Rahner adopts the Reformation watchword *ecclesia semper reformanda*, about which Congar had been ambivalent. Rahner speaks of a state of permanent repentance (*metanoia*), and acknowledges truth as well as falsity in Luther's theological principle *simul iustus et peccator* (at one and the same time righteous and sinful). Although, Rahner points out, this is a challenge directed at Roman Catholics by Protestant theology and has huge ecumenical significance, Vatican II evaded it. The pilgrim Church, of which the Council spoke so eloquently, is in constant need of cleansing, penitence and inner reform. Only the grace of God can sustain her in holiness (278–92).

In 'The Church and the Parousia of Christ' (Rahner 1969: ch. 19), written during the Council, Rahner speaks more strongly in the accents of the Reformation, echoing its eschatological ecclesiology. He highlights the tension, not only between the charismatic and the institutional dimensions of the Church, but also between the Church *in via* as pilgrim and the eschatological fulfilment of God's purposes for her, when she will be perfected by being 'eliminated' as an institution, a structured society, and be united with God, her destination and goal. Despite the promise that her mission will not fail (the doctrine of indefectibility which, though variously articulated within as well as between the Roman and reformed churches, is not controversial), both the Church and the individual Christian must 'laboriously make their pilgrimage through the obscurity of this aeon, and for both there ultimately remains only one thing: trust in the grace of God alone' (310).

Vision and Realism in Ecclesiology

As we noted at the beginning of this book, both monarchical and conciliar models of authority presuppose a Catholic ecclesiology. The catholicity of the Church implies certain given truths: that the Church is a visible ordered community, a society, and one that continues through history; that it is bound together by a common confession of the apostolic faith, by mutually recognized sacraments, by a ministry that is accepted as a ministry of the whole Church and by forms of oversight that express the authority that belongs to the whole Church.

Not only the papalists but the conciliarists too thought of the Church as a society that was complete in itself (*societas perfecta*), lacking nothing to remedy its temporary defects. It is a moot point whether the Reformers, or at least some of them, thought so too. Luther's mind did not run on these lines: the Church was a dynamic and elusive reality that lent itself to personal and relational rather than societal language. Luther was not interested in the institutional aspect of the Church's life, though he was passionately concerned for the renewal of the German nation. Calvin is the Reformer who comes closest to thinking in *societas perfecta* terms. Since for him the ordered existence of the Church, in its broad structure, comes from God and has the authority of revelation, the Church is more than a gathered community; it is nothing less than a society and one that is complete in itself. As far as the English Reformers, on the other hand, were concerned, the openness of the Church to civil government, particularly in the person of the monarch, and to culture, the integration of the Church into the Christian commonwealth, meant that the notion of the *societas perfecta* was inimical to them.

Were the papalists, the conciliarists and such Reformers as Calvin misguided in thinking of the Church in this way? Were they losing touch with Scripture and the apostolic vision? This is not the place to consider the numerous biblical images and concepts of the Church, but there is little doubt that during the later New Testament period a more societal, less dynamic or charismatic, ecclesiology did emerge – though this should not be exaggerated or seen as in contradiction to the original messianic vision. What is fairly unchallengeable is that an enhanced ecclesial self-awareness or self-consciousness is evident in the Pastoral Epistles where the Church is described as 'a people of his [God's] own' (Titus 2.14) and as the household (*oikos*) of God (1 Timothy 3.15). The Christian community is compared to a family and oversight is likened to the responsibility of a steward in a household (1 Timothy 3.5, 12; Titus 1.7). Solid architectural imagery ('the pillar and bulwark of the truth') reinforces the sense of the physical presence and permanent reality of the Church (1 Timothy 3.15). Schweizer comments that the Church is presented in the Pastorals as a body that attracts ideas of social order, especially of the house and family. 'It lives in a historical tradition' (Schweizer 1961: 81).

Even in Ephesians we have the beginning of a sense of the Church as a political society with the use of *politeia* language in 2.12 ('commonwealth of Israel') to describe the people of God, the Jewish-Christian Church. Although the Revised English Bible inadequately renders this 'community', other English translations (notably the New Revised Standard Version) follow the Authorized Version (King James Bible) with 'commonwealth'. The language is political and there is a suggestion of citizenship, of membership of a *polis* or polity. Lincoln points to overtones of constituted government and statehood and suggests that Israel/the Church is being viewed as a theocratically constituted nation (Lincoln 1990: 137). Similar solid physical imagery to that of the Pastorals is found here in Ephesians 2: the imagery of household, foundation, cornerstone and temple.

The idea of the Church as a visible, organic society, held together by the means of grace, principally the sacraments and extending through time and space, suggests that it is characterized by the conjunction of unity and mission; that is to say that it is united in its mission. Of course, to say that is to state an ideal, for the visible world-wide community of the baptized is in fact appallingly divided in certain crucial ways. Probably there is not a single code of beliefs or a single sacramental and ministerial structure that is universally recognized; and a divided Church is by definition divided in its exercise of oversight. We should say then of every part of the Christian Church that it aspires to catholicity and to some degree approximates to it. But because of the intrinsic connection between the four credal notes of the Church, and particularly in this case between catholicity and unity, we should not credit any ecclesial body with participating in catholicity unless it is not only open in relationship and dialogue to other churches, but is manifestly striving to heal the wounds of division in the body of Christ (cf. Volf 1998: ch. 7).

Ecclesiology, and not least ecumenical ecclesiology, is commonly stated in the ideal mode. It airily evokes what the Church is in the purposes of God, but disdains the messy human reality. So often ecclesiology offers a 'God's eye view', but turns a blind eye to the human aspect. To adapt something Luther said, it shows what the Church is in the eyes of God: a pure, holy, spotless dove. But it does not seem to acknowledge what the Church is in the eyes of the world: disfigured, wounded, dying. As we hear it we ask ourselves, What sort of language is this? The sentiments are admirable, but what is their status? The tense is the present indicative, but is the state of affairs it describes real? Are the statements empirical, descriptive statements or prophetic, eschatological statements? The Rolls Royce ecclesiology of the Ecumenical Movement, infused with a serene Platonism borrowed from the rather different theological assumptions of Orthodoxy, glides effortlessly on its way!

The mystery of the Church is that it reflects at one and the same time both the crucified Jesus and the glorified Christ. Our language can barely cope with the task of articulating it, but it ought to try harder to do so. Realism, as well as idealism, should characterize our ecclesiology and chasten its rhetoric (cf. Healy 2000). In the final analysis, it is when the mystical and the intellectual come together in theological vision, to counteract cynical political pragmatism of the ecclesiastical kind, that the institution can undergo change. That is what effects reform and creates unity. Institutions are deservedly under suspicion today, just as they were in the fifteenth and sixteenth centuries. A liberating, enabling and therapeutic expression of authority is like gold dust in our institutions. A liberating authority is one that reflects its root meaning of enabling, generating and strengthening (rather than dominating, controlling or inhibiting). It is an authority that is justified by pastoral skill and theological expertise. It invites a voluntary response and elicits free co-operation, rather than attempting to enforce compliance. A therapeutic leadership rejects the temptation to play on people's vulnerability or dependence and enables individuals and communities to take responsibility for themselves because it affirms, sustains and guides them in following their own proper calling (cf. Avis 1992). The Christian Church needs to rediscover this vision of true and salutary authority for its own well-being and for the sake of effective mission within the great *missio dei*. For 'where there is no vision the people perish' (Proverbs 29.18, Authorized Version [King James Bible]).

BIBLIOGRAPHY

Aarflot, A.
    1988   'The Collegiality of Bishops: A Lutheran Perspective', *The Jurist* 48: 359–75.
Abbott, W.M. (ed.)
    1966   *The Documents of Vatican II* (London and Dublin: Geoffrey Chapman).
Acton, Lord [J.E.E.D.]
    1952   'Nicholas of Cusa', in D. Woodruff (ed.), *Essays on Church and State* (London: Hollis and Carter), 246–50.
Aeneas Sylvius Piccolominus (Pius II)
    1992   *De Gestis Concilii Basiliensis Commentariorum Libri II* (ET; ed. D. Hay and W.K. Smith; Oxford: Clarendon Press [1967]).
Alberigo, J., P.-P. Joannou, C. Leonardi, and P. Prodi (H. Jedin) (eds.)
    1962   *Conciliorum Oecumenicorum Decreta* (Freiburg im Briegau: Herder).
Allchin, A.M.
    1971   'Can a Petrine Office be Meaningful in the Church? An Anglican Reply', in Küng 1971: 127–31.
Allen, D.W., and A.M. Allchin
    1965   'Primacy and Collegiality: An Anglican View', *Journal of Ecumenical Studies* 2: 63–80.
Allmand, C. (ed.)
    1998   *The New Cambridge Medieval History. VII. 1415–1500* (Cambridge: Cambridge University Press).
Althaus, P.
    1966   *The Theology of Martin Luther* (Philadelphia: Fortress Press).
    1972   *The Ethics of Martin Luther* (Philadelphia: Fortress Press).
Andrewes, L.
    1843   *Ninety-six Sermons* (Works, 5; Oxford: Parker).
    1920   *The Devotions of Bishop Andrewes* (2 vols. in one; trans. J.H. Newman and J.M. Neale; London: SPCK; New York: Macmillan).
Anglican Communion Office
    2004   *The Windsor Report: The Lambeth Commission on Communion* (London: Anglican Communion Office).
Anglican–Roman Catholic International Commission
    1982   *The Final Report* (London: SPCK and CTS).
    1999   *The Gift of Authority* (London: CTS; Toronto: Anglican Book Centre; New York: Church Publishing Inc.).
Aquinas, T.
    n.d.   *Summa Theologiae* (Blackfriars edn; 60 vols.; London: Eyre and Spottiswoode).
Aristotle
    1953   *Ethics* (trans. J.A.K. Thomson; Harmondsworth: Penguin).
    1991   *On Rhetoric* (trans. and ed. G.A. Kennedy; New York: Oxford University Press).
    1995   *Politics* (trans. E. Barker, intro. R.F. Stalley; Oxford: Oxford University Press [The World's Classics]).

Arnold, F.X.
    1937   *Zur Fräge des Naturrechts bei Martin Luther* (Münschen: M. Hueber).
Aston, M.
    1965   'John Wycliffe's Reformation Reputation', *Past and Present* 30: 23–51.
Auerbach, E.
    1961   *Dante: Poet of the Secular World* (trans. R. Manheim; Chicago: University of Chicago Press).
Augustine
    1972   *City of God* (ed. D. Knowles, trans. H. Bettenson; Harmondsworth: Penguin).
Aulén, G.
    1962   *Reformation and Catholicity* (trans. E.H. Wahlstrom; Edinburgh and London: Oliver and Boyd).
Avis, P.
    1975   'Moses and the Magistrate: A Study in the Rise of Protestant Legalism', *JEH* 26: 149–72.
    1986a *Ecumenical Theology and the Elusiveness of Doctrine* (London: SPCK).
    1986b *The Methods of Modern Theology* (Basingstoke: Marshall Pickering).
    1990   *Christians in Communion* (London: Geoffrey Chapman Mowbray).
    1992   *Authority, Leadership and Conflict in the Church* (London: Mowbray).
    1999   *God and the Creative Imagination: Metaphor, Symbol and Myth in Religion and Theology* (London: Routledge).
    2002   *Anglicanism and the Christian Church: Theological Resources in Historical Perspective* (London: T. & T. Clark/Continuum, rev. and exp. edn).
    2003   *A Church Drawing Near: Spirituality and Mission in a Post-Christian Culture* (London: T. & T. Clark).
    2005   *A Ministry Shaped by Mission* (London: T. & T. Clark).
Barth, K., and E. Brunner
    1946   *Natural Theology* (trans. P. Fraenkel; London: Bles).
Baumer, F. Le Van
    1940   *The Early Tudor Theory of Kingship* (New Haven: Yale University Press).
Baur, J.
    1965   *Gott, Recht und Weltliche Regiment im Werke Calvins* (Bonn: H. Bouvier).
Beeson, T.
    2002   *The Bishops* (London: SCM Press).
Bieckler, J.E.
    1975   'Nicholas of Cusa and the End of the Conciliar Movement: A Humanist Crisis of Identity', *CH* 44: 5–21.
Biel, G.
    1968   *Defensorium Obedientiae Apostolicae et alia documenta* (ed. and trans. H.A. Oberman *et al.*; Cambridge, MA: Bellknap Press of Harvard University Press).
Biggar, N., and R. Black (eds.)
    2000   *The Revival of Natural Law: Philosophical, Theological and Ethical Responses to the Finnis-Grisez School* (Aldershot: Ashgate).
Bishops in Communion
    2000   House of Bishops of the Church of England (London: Church House Publishing).
Black, A.J.
    1969   'The Political Ideas of Conciliarism and Papalism, 1430–1450', *JEH* 20: 45–65.
    1970   *Monarchy and Community: Political Ideas in the Late Conciliar Controversy 1430–1450* (Cambridge: Cambridge University Press).
    1971   'The Council of Basle and the Second Vatican Council,' in G.J. Cuming and D. Baker (eds.), *Councils and Assemblies* (Cambridge: Cambridge University Press [Ecclesiastical History Society]).

1979 *Council and Commune: The Conciliar Movement and the Fifteenth Century Heritage* (London: Burns and Oates; Shepherdstown: Patmos Press).

1980 'What was Conciliarism? Conciliar Theory in Historical Perspective', in B. Tierney and P. Lineham (eds.), *Authority and Power: Studies on Medieval Law and Government* (Cambridge: Cambridge University Press), 213–24.

1988 'The Conciliar Movement', in Burns 1988: 573–87.

1992 *Political Thought in Europe 1250–1450* (Cambridge: Cambridge University Press).

1998 'Popes and Councils', in Allmand 1998: 65–86.

Blockmans, W.
1998 'Representation', in Allmand 1998: 29–64.

Boase, T.S.R.
1933 *Boniface VIII* (London: Constable).

Bohatec, J.
1937 *Calvins Lehre von Staat und Kirche* (Breslau: M. and H. Marcus).

Boyde, P.
1981 *Dante, Philomythes and Philosopher* (Cambridge: Cambridge University Press).

Braaten, C.E., and R.W. Jenson (eds.)
1996 *The Catholicity of the Reformation* (Grand Rapids: Eerdmans).

1998 *Union with Christ: The New Finnish Interpretation of Luther* (Grand Rapids: Eerdmans).

2001 *Church Unity and the Papal Office: An Ecumenical Dialogue on John Paul II's Encyclical* Ut Unum Sint *(That All May Be One)* (Grand Rapids, MI: Eerdmans).

Bray, G. (ed.)
2000 *Tudor Church Reform: The Henricean Canons of 1535 and the* Reformatio Legum Ecclesiasticarum (Woodbridge, Suffolk: Boydell Press and the Church of England Record Society).

Brooke, Z.N.
1931 *The English Church and the Papacy* (Cambridge: Cambridge University Press).

Bucer, M.
1952 *Instruction in Christian Love* (trans. P.T. Fuhrmann; Richmond, VA: John Knox Press).

Buckley, M.
1998 *Papal Primacy and the Episcopate* (New York: Crossroad).

Burns, J.H.
1992 *Lordship, Kingship and Empire: The Idea of Monarchy 1400–1525* (Oxford: Clarendon Press).

Burns, J.H. (ed.)
1988 *The Cambridge History of Medieval Political Thought* (Cambridge: Cambridge University Press).

Burns, J.H., and T.M. Izbicki (eds.)
1997 *Conciliarism and Papalism* (Cambridge Texts in the History of Political Thought; Cambridge: Cambridge University Press).

Butler, Cuthbert
1962 *The Vatican Council 1869–1870* (ed. Christopher Butler; London: Collins and Harvill Press [1930]).

Butler, J.
1889 *The Analogy of Religion, Natural and Revealed* (London: George Bell and Sons).

Calvin, J.
1958 *Tracts and Treatises* (ed. T.F. Torrance; 3 vols.; Grand Rapids: Eerdmans).

1962 *Institutes of the Christian Religion* (trans. H. Beveridge; 2 vols.; London: James Clarke).

Cameron, E.
1991 *The European Reformation* (Oxford: Clarendon Press).

Carlson, E.M.
1946 'Luther's Conception of Government', *CH* 15: 257–70.

Casteel, T.W.
1970 'Calvin and Trent: Calvin's Reaction to the Council of Trent in the Context of his Conciliar Thought', *Harvard Theological Review* 63: 91–117.

Catechism of the Catholic Church
1994 London: Geoffrey Chapman.

Chadwick, H.
1994 'The Status of Ecumenical Councils in Anglican Thought', in *idem*, *Tradition and Exploration: Collected Papers on Theology and the Church* (Norwich: Canterbury Press), 258–69.
2003 *East and West: The Making of a Rift in the Church* (Oxford: Oxford University Press).

Chadwick, O.
1957 *From Bossuet to Newman: The Idea of Doctrinal Development* (Cambridge: Cambridge University Press).
1998 *A History of the Popes 1830–1914* (Oxford: Clarendon Press).
2001 *The Early Reformation on the Continent* (Oxford: Oxford University Press).

Clément, O.
2003 *You are Peter: An Orthodox Theologian's Reflection on the Exercise of Papal Primacy* (London: New City Press).

Cochrane, A.C.
1966 'Natural Law in Calvin', in E.A. Smith (ed.), *Church-State Relations in Ecumenical Perspective* (Louvain: Duquesne University Press).

Coleman, R. (ed.)
1992 *Resolutions of the Twelve Lambeth Conferences 1867–1988* (Toronto: Anglican Book Centre).

Congar, Y.
1939 *Divided Christendom* (London: Geoffrey Bles, The Centenary Press).
1950 *Vrai et Fausse Réform dans l'Église* (Unam Sanctam, 20; Paris: Les Éditions du Cerf).
1958 '*Quod Omnes Tangit ab Omnibus Tractari et Approbari Debet*', *Revue Historique de Droit Francais et Etranger*, Series 4, 35: 210–59.
1965 *La collégialité épiscopale, histoire et théologie* (Unam Sanctam, 52; Paris: Les Éditions du Cerf).

Cowdrey, H.E.J.
1998 *Pope Gregory VII, 1073–1085* (Oxford: Clarendon Press).
2003 *Lanfranc: Scholar, Monk and Archbishop* (Oxford: Oxford University Press).

Cranz, F.E.
1959 *An Essay on the Development of Luther's Thought on Justice, Law and Society* (Cambridge, MA: Harvard University Press).
2000 *Nicholas of Cusa and the Renaissance* (ed. T.M. Izbicki and G. Christianson; Aldershot: Ashgate).

Creighton, L.
1904 *Life and Letters of Mandell Creighton* (2 vols.; London: Longmans, Green and Co.).

Creighton, M.
   1892   *A History of the Papacy during the Period of the Reformation*. I: *The Great Schism – The Council of Constance*; II: *The Council of Basel – The Papal Restoration 1418–1464* (London: Longmans, Green and Co., new edn).
Cromartie, A.
   2000   'Theology and Politics in Richard Hooker's Thought', *History of Political Thought* 21: 41–66.
Cross, C.
   1999   *Church and People: England 1450–1660* (Oxford: Blackwell, 2nd edn).
Crowder, C.M.D. (ed.)
   1977   *Unity, Heresy and Reform, 1378–1460: The Conciliar Response to the Great Schism* (London: Arnold).
Crowe, M.B.
   1977   *The Changing Profile of the Natural Law* (The Hague: Martinus Nijhoff).
Cuming, G., and D. Baker (eds.)
   1971   *Councils and Assemblies* (Cambridge: Cambridge University Press [Ecclesiastical History Society]).
Cyprian
   1957   *The Lapsed. The Unity of the Catholic Church* (intro. M. Bevenot; London: The Newman Press and Longmans, Green and Co.).
d'Entrèves, A.P.
   1951   *Natural Law* (London: Hutchinson).
   1952   *Dante as a Political Thinker* (Oxford: Oxford University Press).
   1959   *The Medieval Contribution to Political Thought* (Oxford: Oxford University Press).
Dante
   1903   *Convivio* (trans. P. Wicksteed; London: Temple Classics).
   1954   *Monarchy and Three Political Letters* (ed. D. Nicholl; London: Weidenfeld and Nicholson).
   1981   *The Divine Comedy* (trans. C.H. Sisson; London: Pan).
Davis, C.T.
   1957   *Dante and the Idea of Rome* (Oxford: Clarendon Press).
Denzinger, H., and A. Schönmetzer (eds.)
   1963   *Enchiridion Symbolorum* (Freiburg im Breisgau: Herder).
Dixon, R.W.
   1878   *History of the Church of England from the Abolition of the Roman Jurisdiction* (6 vols.; London: Routledge).
Doe, N.
   1998   *Canon Law in the Anglican Communion* (Oxford: Clarendon Press).
   2002   'Canon Law and Communion', *ELJ* 6: 241–63.
   2003   'The Common Law of the Anglican Communion', *ELJ* 7: 4–16.
Doumergue, E.
   1917   *Jean Calvin: Les Hommes et les Choses de son Temps* (7 vols.; Lausanne: G. Bridel).
Du Boulay, F.R.H.
   1965   'The Fifteenth Century', in D. Knowles (ed.), *The English Church and the Papacy* (New York: Fordham University Press).
Duffy, E.
   1997   *Saints and Sinners: A History of the Popes* (New Haven and London: Yale University Press [in association with S4C]).
Duprey, P.
   1971   'The Synodical Structure of the Church in Eastern Theology', *OIC* 7: 152–82.

Dyson, R.W. (ed. and trans.)
> 1986 *Giles of Rome on Ecclesiastical Power: The* De Ecclesiastica Potestate *of Aegidius Romanus* (Woodbridge, Suffolk: Boydell Press).

Elton, G.R.
> 1972 *The Tudor Constitution* (Cambridge: Cambridge University Press).

Empie, P.C., and T.A. Murphy (eds.)
> 1974 *Papal Primacy and the Universal Church* (Lutherans and Catholics in Dialogue, 5; Minneapolis: Augsburg Press).

Eschmann, T.
> 1943 'A Thomistic Glossary on the Principle of the Pre-eminence of the Common Good', *Medieval Studies* 5: 123–65.

Evans, G.R. (ed.)
> 2001 *The Medieval Theologians* (Oxford: Blackwell).

Evdokimov, P.
> 1971 'Can a Petrine Office be Meaningful in the Church? A Russian Orthodox Reply', in Küng 1971: 122–26.

Farr, W.
> 1974 *John Wyclif as Legal Reformer* (Studies in the History of Christian Thought, 10; Leiden: E. J. Brill).

Fenner, C.J.
> 1974 'The Concept and Theological Significance of Ecumenical Councils in the Anglican Tradition' (PhD diss., Washington, DC: Catholic University of America).

Fergusson, D.
> 1998 *Community, Liberalism and Christian Ethics* (Cambridge: Cambridge University Press).

Ferrante, J.M.
> 1984 *The Political Vision of the* Divine Comedy (Princeton, NJ: Princeton University Press).

Fiddes, P.S.
> 2003 *Tracks and Traces: Baptist Identity in Church and Theology* (Carlisle: Paternoster Press).

Field, R.
> 1847 *Of the Church* (4 vols.; Cambridge: Cambridge University Press [EHS]).

Figgis, J.N.
> 1916 *Studies of Political Thought from Gerson to Grotius, 1414–1625* (Cambridge: Cambridge University Press, 2nd edn).

Finnis, J.
> 1980 *Natural Law and Natural Rights* (Oxford: Clarendon Press).
> 1998 *Aquinas: Moral, Political and Legal Theory* (Oxford: Oxford University Press).

Fouyas, M.
> 1972 *Orthodoxy, Roman Catholicism and Anglicanism* (Oxford: Oxford University Press).

Fransen, P.
> 1962 'The Authority of the Councils', in J.M. Todd (ed.), *Problems of Authority* (London: Darton, Longman & Todd; Baltimore: Helicon Press).

George, R.P.
> 1999 *In Defense of Natural Law* (Oxford: Oxford University Press).

Gerrish, B.A.
> 1962 *Grace and Reason: A Study in the Theology of Luther* (Oxford: Clarendon Press).

Gerson, J.
    1985   'Jean Gerson, "Propositio Facta coram Anglicis": a Translation' (trans. G.R Dunstan), in C.M. Barron and C. Harper-Bill, *The Church in Pre-Reformation Society: Essays in Honour of F. R. H. Du Boulay* (Woodbridge, Suffolk: Boydell Press), 68–81.

Gewirth, A.
    1951   *Marsilius of Padua: The Defender of the Peace. I: Marsilius of Padua and Medieval Political Philosophy* (New York and London: Columbia University Press).

Gibson, E.C.S.
    1910   *The Thirty-nine Articles of the Church of England* (London: Methuen).

Gierke, O. von
    1958a   *Political Theories of the Middle Age* (trans. F.W. Maitland; Cambridge: Cambridge University Press [1900]).
    1958b   *Natural Law and the Theory of Society 1500-1800* (trans. E. Barker; Cambridge: Cambridge University Press).

Gill, J.
    1961   *Eugenius IV: Pope of Christian Union* (London: Burns and Oates).
    1971   'The Representation of the *Universitas Fidelium* in the Councils of the Conciliar Period', in Cuming and Baker 1971.

Gill, R.
    1992   *Moral Communities* (Exeter: Exeter University Press).

Gilson, E.
    1963   *Dante and Philosophy* (New York: Harper Torchbooks [1949]).

Grace, D.
    1997   'Natural Law in Hooker's *Of the Laws of Ecclesiastical Polity*', *JRH* 21: 10–22.

Gray, J.S., and J.C. Tucker
    1999   *Presbyterian Polity for Church Officers* (Louisville, KY: Geneva Press, 3rd edn).

Greenslade, S.L.
    1967   'The English Reformers and the Councils of the Church', *Oecumenica: An Annual Symposium of Ecumenical Research* (1967), 95–115.

Haikola, L.
    1967   'Luther und das Naturrecht', in *Vierhundertfünfzig Jahre lutherische Reformation 1517–1967, Festschrift für Franz Lau* (Gottingen: Vandenhoeck & Ruprecht), 126–33.

Haile, H.G.
    1980   *Luther: A Biography* (New York: Doubleday; London: Sheldon Press, 1981).

Hardwick, C.
    1851   *A History of the Articles of Religion* (Cambridge: John Deighton; London: F. & J. Rivington).

Harkianakis, S.
    1971   'Can a Petrine Office be Meaningful in the Church? A Greek Orthodox Reply', in Küng 1971: 115–21.

Hart, H.L.A.
    1961   *The Concept of Law* (Oxford: Oxford University Press).

Harvey, M.
    1983   *Solutions to the Schism: A Study of Some English Attitudes 1378–1409* (Kirchengeschichtliche Quellen und Studien, 12; St Ottilien: EOS Verlag).
    1987   'Lollardy and the Great Schism: Some Contemporary Perceptions', in Hudson and Wilks 1987: 385–96.

Hastings, A. (ed.)
    1991   *Modern Catholicism: Vatican II and After* (London: SPCK).

Hawkins, P.S.
  1999   *Dante's Testaments: Essays in Scriptural Imagination* (Stanford, CA: Stanford University Press).
Hazlett, W.I.P.
  2003   *The Reformation in Britain and Ireland* (London: T. & T. Clark).
Healy, N.
  2000   *Church, World and the Christian Life* (Cambridge: Cambridge University Press).
Helmholz, R.
  2001   'Richard Hooker and the European *Ius Commune*', *ELJ* 6: 4–11.
Hendrix, S.
  2004   *Recultivating the Vineyard: The Reformation Agendas of Christianization* (Louisville, KY: Westminster John Knox Press).
Henn, W.
  1998   'Historical-Theological Synthesis of the Relation Between Primacy and Episcopacy during the Second Millennium', in *Il Primato del Successore di Pietro* (Vatican City: Liberia Editrice Vaticana), 222–73.
Hillerbrand, H.J., *et al.* (eds.)
  1996   *The Oxford Encyclopedia of the Reformation* (4 vols.; New York and Oxford: Oxford University Press).
Hind, J.
  1999   'Primacy and Unity: An Anglican Contribution to a Patient and Fraternal Dialogue', in Puglisi 1999: 35–57.
  2003   'Papal Primacy: An Anglican Perspective', *ELJ* 7: 112–26.
Holl, K.
  1948   'Luther und das Landesherrliche Kirchenregiment', *Gesammelte Aufsätze zur Kirchengeschichte*, I (Luther; Tübingen: Mohr), 326–80.
Hollenbach, D.
  2002   *The Common Good and Christian Ethics* (Cambridge: Cambridge University Press).
Hooker, R.
  1845   *Works* (ed. J. Keble; 3 vols.; Oxford: Oxford University Press).
  1977–98   *Works, Folger Library Edition* (ed. W. Speed Hill; 7 vols.; vols. I–V; Cambridge, MA and London: Belknap Press of Harvard University Press, 1977–90; vol. VI, Binghampton, NY: Medieval and Renaissance Texts and Studies, 1993; vol. VII, Tempe, AZ: Medieval and Renaissance Texts and Studies, 1998).
Hoose, B. (ed.)
  2002   *Authority in the Roman Catholic Church* (Aldershot: Ashgate).
Hopf, C.
  1946   *Martin Bucer and the English Reformation* (London: Oxford University Press).
Höpfl, H.
  1982   *The Christian Polity of John Calvin* (Cambridge: Cambridge University Press).
Hudson, A.
  1992   'John Wyclif', in G. Rowell (ed.), *The English Religious Tradition and the Genius of Anglicanism* (Wantage: Ikon).
Hudson, A., and M. Wilks (eds.)
  1987   *From Ockham to Wyclif* (Oxford: Blackwell).
Hughes, G.
  1996   *God of Surprises* (London: Darton, Longman & Todd, 2nd edn).
Hus, J.
  1974   *De Ecclesia* (trans. D.S. Schaff; Westport, CT: Greenwood Press [1915]).

Jacob, E.F.
  1963   *Essays in the Conciliar Epoch* (Manchester: Manchester University Press, 3rd edn).

Jacob, W.M.
  1997   *The Making of the Anglican Church Worldwide* (London: SPCK).

Jansen, J.F.
  1956   *Calvin's Doctrine of the Work of Christ* (London: James Clarke).

Jedin, H.
  1957   *A History of the Council of Trent*, I (trans. E. Graf; London: Nelson).

John of Paris
  1971   *On Royal and Papal Power* (trans. with an introduction J.A. Watt; Toronto: Pontifical Institute of Medieval Studies).

  1974   *John of Paris on Royal and Papal Power* (trans. with introduction A.P. Monahan; New York and London: Columbia University Press).

John Paul II
  1995   *Ut Unum Sint* (Vatican City: Libraria Editrice Vaticana).

Jordan, G.J.
  1930   *The Inner History of the Great Schism of the West* (London: Williams & Norgate).

Kantorowitz, E.H.
  1957   *The King's Two Bodies: A Study in Medieval Political Thought* (Princeton, NJ: Princeton University Press).

Kasper, W.
  1989   *Theology and Church* (trans. M. Kohl; London: SCM Press).

Kaye, B.
  2003   'The Strange Birth of Anglican Synods in Australia', *JRH* 27: 177–97.

Kelley, F.
  1987   'Ockham: Avignon, Before and After', in Hudson and Wilks 1987: 1–18.

Kelly, J.N.D.
  1986   *The Oxford Dictionary of Popes* (Oxford: Oxford University Press).

Kemp, E.
  1961   *Counsel and Consent: Aspects of the Government of the Church as Exemplified in the History of the English Provincial Synods* (London: SPCK).

Kempshall, M.S.
  1999   *The Common Good in Late Medieval Political Thought* (Oxford: Clarendon Press).

  2001   'Ecclesiology and Politics', in Evans 2001: 303–33.

Kenny, A.
  1985   *Wyclif* (Past Masters; Oxford: Oxford University Press).

Kenny, A. (ed.)
  1986   *Wyclif in his Times* (Oxford: Clarendon Press).

Kerr, F.
  2002   *After Aquinas: Versions of Thomism* (Oxford: Blackwell).

Keshishian, A.
  1992   *Conciliar Fellowship: A Common Goal* (Geneva: WCC Publications).

Khomyakov, A.S.
  1977   'On the Western Confessions of Faith', in A. Schmemann (ed.), *Ultimate Questions: An Anthology of Modern Russian Religious Thought* (London: Mowbray).

Kirby, W.J. Torrance
  1990   *Richard Hooker's Doctrine of the Royal Supremacy* (Leiden: E.J. Brill).

  1999   'Richard Hooker's Theory of Natural Law in the Context of Reformation Theology', *Sixteenth-Century Journal* 30: 681–703.

Kirkpatrick, F.G.
 2001 *The Ethics of Community* (Cambridge: Cambridge University Press).
Klibansky, R.
 1982 *The Continuity of the Platonic Tradition and Plato's Parmenides in the Middle Ages* (New York and London: Kraus International Publications [1939, 1942]).
Koch, K.
 1962 *Studium Pietatis: Martin Bucer als Ethiker* (Neukirchen: Neukirchener Verlag).
Küng, H.
 1965 *Structures of the Church* (London: Burns and Oates).
Küng, H. (ed.)
 1971 *The Petrine Ministry in the Church* (Concilium, 4.7; London: Burns and Oates).
Ladner, G.B.
 1959 *The Idea of Reform: Its Impact on Christian Thought and Action in the Age of the Fathers* (Cambridge, MA: Harvard University Press).
Lake, P.
 1988 *Anglicans and Puritans: Presbyterian and English Conformist Thought from Whitgift to Hooker* (London: Unwin Hyman).
Lang, A.
 1909 'The Reformation and Natural Law', *Princeton Theological Review* 7.
 1941 *Puritanismus und Pietismus* (Darmstadt: Neukirchen Kreis Moers).
Laud, W.
 1849 *Works* (Oxford: LACT, 6th edn).
Leff, G.
 1967a *Heresy in the Later Middle Ages* (2 vols.; Manchester: Manchester University Press; New York: Barnes and Noble).
 1967b 'The Apostolic Ideal in Later Medieval Ecclesiology', *JTS* NS 18: 52–82.
 1987 'The Place of Metaphysics in Wyclif's Theology', in Hudson and Wilks 1987: 217–32.
Legrand, H.-M.
 1972 'The Revaluation of Local Churches: Some Theological Implications', *Concilium* 1.8: 53–64.
Lenkeith, N.
 1952 *Dante and the Legend of Rome* (London: Warburg Institute).
Lieburg, H.
 1962 *Amt und Ordination bei Luther und Melanchthon* (Gottingen: Vandenhoeck & Ruprecht).
Lincoln, A.
 1990 *Ephesians* (Word Biblical Commentary; Dallas, TX: Word Books).
Lisska, A.
 1996 *Aquinas' Theory of Natural Law* (Oxford: Clarendon Press).
Little, D.
 1968 'Calvin and the Prospects for a Christian Theory of Natural Law', in G.H. Outka and P. Ramsey (eds.), *Norm and Context in Christian Ethics* (New York: Charles Scribner's Sons; London: SCM Press, 1969).
Lloyd, C. (ed.)
 1856 *Formularies of Faith put Forth by Authority during the Reign of Henry VIII* (Oxford: Oxford University Press).
Loades, D.
 1997 *Tudor Government: Structures of Authority in the Sixteenth Century* (Oxford: Blackwell).
Locher, G.W.
 1981 *Zwingli's Thought: New Perspectives* (Leiden: E.J. Brill).

Logan, F.D.
    1961   'The 1875 Statement of the German Bishops on Episcopal Powers', *The Jurist* 21.

Lohse, B.
    1999   *Martin Luther's Theology: Its Historical and Systematic Development* (Minneapolis, MN: Fortress Press).

Loomis, L.R., trans. (eds. J.H. Mundy and K.M. Woody)
    1961   *The Council of Constance: The Unification of the Church* (Records of Civilization, Sources and Studies, 63; New York and London: Columbia University Press).

Loserth, J.
    1884   *Wiclif and Hus* (London: Hodder & Stoughton).

Lossky, N.
    1991   *Lancelot Andrewes the Preacher* (Oxford: Clarendon Press).
    1999   'Conciliarity-Primacy in a Russian Orthodox Perspective', in Puglisi 1999: 127–35.

Lowther Clarke, H.
    1924   *Constitutional Church Government in the Dominions beyond the Seas and in other parts of the Anglican Communion* (London: SPCK).

Luscombe, D.
    1991   'John Gerson and Hierarchy', in I. Wood and G.A. Loud (eds.), *Church and Chronicle in the Middle Ages* (London: Hambledon), 194–200.

Luther, M.
    1883–   *D. Martin Luthers Werke (Weimarer Ausgabe)* [WA] (Weimar).
    1955–   *Luther's Works* [LW] (St Louis: Concordia; Philadelphia: Fortress Press).

Lytle, G.F. (ed.)
    1981a   *Reform and Authority in the Medieval and Reformation Church* (Washington, DC: Catholic University of America Press).
    1981b   'Universities as Religious Authorities in the Later Middle Ages and Reformation', in Lytle 1981: 69–97.

MacCulloch, D.
    1996   *Thomas Cranmer: A Life* (New Haven and London: Yale University Press).
    2003   *Reformation: Europe's House Divided, 1490–1700* (London: Allen Lane).

MacDonald, A.J.
    1932   *Hildebrand: A Life of Gregory VII* (London: Methuen).

MacIntyre, A.
    1985   *After Virtue* (London: Duckworth, 2nd edn).

Macquarrie, J.
    1970   *Three Issues in Ethics* (London: SCM Press).

Mannermaa, T.
    2005   *Christ Present in Faith: Luther's View of Justification* (trans. and ed. K. Stjerna; Minneapolis, MN: Fortress Press).

Mansi, J.D.
    1961   *Sacrorum Conciliorum Nova Amplissima Collectio*, vols. 26–31a (Graz: Akademische Druck – u. Verlagsanstalt).

Marsilius of Padua
    1956   *The Defensor pacis* (trans. A. Gewirth; New York and London: Columbia University Press).

Martinmort, A.G.
    1953   *Le Gallicanism de Bossuet* (Unam Sanctam, 24; Paris: Éditions du Cerf).
            May They All Be One: A Response of the House of Bishops of the Church of England to 'Ut Unum Sint' London: Church House Publishing, 1997.

Mayer, T.F.
    1989   *Thomas Starkey and the Commonweal: Humanist Politics and Religion in the Reign of Henry VIII* (Cambridge: Cambridge University Press).
Mazotta, G.
    1979   *Dante, Poet of the Desert* (Princeton, NJ: Princeton University Press).
McDermott, P.L.
    1998   'Nicholas of Cusa: Continuity and Conciliation at the Council of Basel', *CH* 67: 254–73.
McFarlane, K.B.
    1972   *Wycliffe and English Nonconformity* (Harmondsworth: Penguin [1952]).
McGrade, A.S.
    1974   *The Political Thought of William of Ockham* (Cambridge: Cambridge University Press).
McIlwain, C.H.
    1947   *Constitutionalism Ancient and Modern* (Ithaca, NY: Cornell University Press, rev. edn [1940]).
McManus, E.
    2000   'Aspects of Primacy According to Two Orthodox Theologians', *OIC* 36: 234–50.
McNeill, J.T.
    1930   *Unitive Protestantism* (New York: Abingdon Press).
    1941   'Natural Law in the Thought of Luther', *CH* 10: 211–27.
    1946   'Natural Law in the Teaching of the Reformers', *Journal of Religion* 26: 168–82.
McPartlan, P.
    2004   'The Local Church and the Universal Church: Zizioulas and the Ratzinger-Kasper Debate', *IJSCC* 4: 21–33.
McReady, W.D.
    1975   'Papalists and Antipapalists: Aspects of the Church-State Controversy in the Late Middle Ages', *Viator: Medieval and Renaissance Studies* 6: 241–73.
Melloni, A. and Scatena, S. (eds)
    2005   *Synod and Synodality: Theology, History, Canon Law and Ecumenism in New Contact* (Münster: Lit Verlag).
Meyendorff, J.
    1966   *Orthodoxy and Catholicity* (New York: Sheed and Ward).
    1975   *Byzantine Theology: Historical Trends and Doctrinal Themes* (Oxford: Mowbray; New York: Fordham University Press [1974]).
Meyendorff, J. (ed.)
    1992   *The Primacy of Peter* (Crestwood, NY: St Vladimir Seminary Press).
Meyjes, G.H.M. Posthumus
    1999   *Jean Gerson: Apostle of Unity: His Church Politics and Ecclesiology* (Studies in the History of Christian Thought, 94; trans. J.C. Grayson; Leiden: Brill).
Miethke, J., and L. Weinrich (eds.)
    1995, 2002   *Quellen zur Kirchenreform im Zeitalter der grossen Konzilien des 15. Jahrhunderts*, 2 vols: I. *Die Konzilien von Pisa (1409) und Konstanz (1414–1418)*; II. *Die Konzilien von Pavia/Siena (1423/24), Basel (1431–1449), und Ferrara/Florenz (1438–1445)* (Ausgewalte Quellen zur deutschen Geschichte des Mittelalters, 38a and b; Darmstadt: Wissenschaftliche Buchgesellschaft).
Miller, P.D. and McCann, D. (eds)
    2005   *In Search of the Common Good* (London and New York: T&T Clark).
Miller, P.N.
    1994   *Defining the Common Good: Empire, Religion and Philosophy in Eighteenth Century Britain* (Cambridge: Cambridge University Press).

Milton, A.
 1995 *Catholic and Reformed: The Roman and Protestant Churches in English Protestant Thought, 1600–1640* (Cambridge: Cambridge University Press).
More, P.E., and F.L. Cross (eds.)
 1935 *Anglicanism: The Thought and Practice of the Church of England Illustrated from the Religious Literature of the Seventeenth Century* (London: SPCK).
Morrall, J.B.
 1960 *Gerson and the Great Schism* (Manchester: Manchester University Press).
Morris, C.
 1989 *The Papal Monarchy: The Western Church from 1050 to 1250* (Oxford: Clarendon Press).
Morrisey, T.E.
 1973 'Franciscus de Zabarellis (1360–1417) and the Conciliarist Traditions' (PhD thesis, Cornell University).
 1978 'The Decree "Haec Sancta" and Cardinal Zabarella: His Role in its Formulation and Interpretation', *Annuarium Historiae Conciliorum* 10: 145–76.
 1981 'Franciscus Zabarella (1360–1417): Papacy, Community and Limitations upon Authority', in Lytle 1981: 37–54.
Morrison, K.F.
 1964 *The Two Kingdoms: Ecclesiology in Carolingian Political Thought* (Princeton, NJ: Princeton University Press).
 1969 *Tradition and Authority in the Western Church, 300–1140* (Princeton, NJ: Princeton University Press).
Müller, J.
 1965 *Martin Bucers Hermeneutic* (Gutersloh: Mohn).
Nazir-Ali, M.
 1997 'What Kind of Primacy Can Anglicans Accept?', *The Tablet*, 1 February 1997.
Nederman, C.J.
 1988 'Nature, Sin and the Origins of Society: The Ciceronian Tradition in Medieval Political Thought', *JHI* 49: 3–26.
 1991 'Aristotelianism and the Origins of "Political Science" in the Twelfth Century', *JHI* 52: 179–94.
Nederman, C.J., and K.L. Forhan (eds.)
 1993 *Medieval Political Theory: A Reader. The Quest for the Body Politic, 1100–1400* (London and New York: Routledge).
Neuner, J., and J. Dupuis (ed.)
 1983 *The Christian Faith in the Doctrinal Documents of the Catholic Church* (London: Collins).
Newman, J.H.
 1974 *An Essay on the Development of Christian Doctrine* (ed. J.M. Cameron; Harmondsworth: Penguin [1845]).
 1990 *The Via Media of the Anglican Church* (ed. with introduction and notes by H.D. Weidner; Oxford: Clarendon Press).
Nicholas of Cusa
 1991 *The Catholic Concordance* (ed. and trans. P.E. Sigmund; Cambridge: Cambridge University Press).
Nichols, A.
 1989 *Theology in the Russian Diapora: Church, Fathers, Eucharist in Nikolai Afanas'ev, 1893–1966* (Cambridge: Cambridge University Press).
 1990 *From Newman to Congar: The Idea of Doctrinal Development from the Victorians to the Second Vatican Council* (Edinburgh: T. & T. Clark).
 1995 *Light From the East: Authors and Themes in Orthodox Theology* (London: Sheed and Ward).

Nichols, T.
    1997   *That All May Be One: Hierarchy and Participation in the Church* (Collegeville:
            Liturgical Press).
Norgren, W.A.
    1994   *Ecumenism of the Possible* (Cincinnati: Forward Movement Publications).
O'Donovan, J. Lockwood
    1991   *Theology of Law and Authority in the English Reformation* (Emory University
            Studies in Law and Religion; Atlanta, GA: Scholars Press).
O'Donovan, O., and J.L. O'Donovan
    2004   *Bonds of Imperfection: Christian Politics, Past and Present* (Grand Rapids:
            Eerdmans).
O'Donovan, O., and J.L. O'Donovan (eds.)
    1999   *From Irenaeus to Grotius: A Sourcebook in Christian Political Thought* (Grand
            Rapids: Eerdmans).
O'Malley, J.W.
    1968   *Giles of Viterbo on Church and Reform* (Leiden: E.J. Brill).
Oakley, F.
    1960   'The *Propositiones utiles* of Pierre d'Ailly: An Epitome of Conciliar Theory',
            CH 29: 399–403.
    1962   'On the Road from Constance to 1688: The Political Thought of John Major
            and George Buchanan', *Journal of British Studies* 1: 1–31.
    1964   *The Political Thought of Pierre d'Ailly: The Voluntarist Tradition* (New Haven
            and London: Yale University Press).
    1965   'Almain and Major: Conciliar Theory on the Eve of the Reformation',
            American Historical Review 70: 673–90.
    1981   'Natural Law, the *Corpus Mysticum*, and Consent in Conciliar Thought from
            John of Paris to Matthias Ugonius', *Speculum: A Journal of Medieval Studies*
            56: 786–810.
    2003   *The Conciliarist Tradition: Constitutionalism in the Catholic Church,
            1300–1870* (Oxford: Oxford University Press).
Oakley, F., and B. Russell (eds.)
    2004   *Governance, Accountability and the Future of the Catholic Church* (London
            and New York: Continuum).
Ockham, W.
    1927   *The* De Imperatorum et Pontificum Potestate *of William of Ockham* (ed. C.K.
            Brampton; Oxford: Clarendon Press).
    1995   *A Letter to the Friars Minor* [etc.] (ed. A.S. McGrade and J. Kilcullen;
            Cambridge: Cambridge University Press).
            Dialogus, www.britac.ac.uk/pubs/dialogus
Palmer, W.
    1842   *A Treatise on the Church of Christ* (2 vols.; London: Rivingtons, 2nd edn).
Pannenberg, W.
    1964   *Jesus: God and Man* (London: SCM Press).
Parker, T.M.
    1965   'The Conciliar Movement', in Smalley 1965: 127–39.
Pascoe, L.B.
    1973   *Jean Gerson: Principles of Church Reform* (ed. H.O. Oberman; Studies in
            Medieval and Reformation Thought, 7; Leiden: Brill).
Patterson, P.D.M.
    2002   'Hooker's Apprentice: God, Entelechy, Beauty, and Desire in Book One of
            Richard Hooker's *Lawes of Ecclesiasticall Politie*', *Anglican Theological
            Review* 84: 961–88.

Patterson, W.B.
  1997a   'Hooker on Ecumenical Relations: Conciliarism in the English Reformation', in
          S. McGrade (ed.), *Richard Hooker and the Construction of Christian
          Community* (Medieval and Renaissance Texts and Studies, 165; Tempe, AZ:
          Medieval & Renaissance Texts & Studies).
  1997b   *King James VI and I and the Reunion of Christendom* (Cambridge: Cambridge
          University Press).
Pauck, W.
  1928   *Das Reich Gottes auf Erden: Utopie und Wirklichkeit* (Berlin: W. de Gruyter).
Pauck, W. (ed.)
  1969   *Melanchthon and Bucer* (Library of Christian Classics, 19; London: SCM
          Press; Philadelphia: Westminster Press).
Pearson, J.
  1864   *Exposition of the Creed* (Oxford: Clarendon Press).
Pelikan, J.
  1964   *Obedient Rebels: Catholic Substance and Protestant Principle in Luther's
          Reformation* (London: SCM Press).
  1968   *Spirit Versus Structure: Luther and the Institutions of the Church* (London:
          Collins).
  1983   *The Christian Tradition. IV. Reformation of Church and Dogma (1300–1700)*
          (Chicago and London: University of Chicago Press).
Petrie, R.C.
  1962   'Unitive Reform Principles of the Late Medieval Conciliarists', *CH* 31: 164–81.
Pocock, G.J.A.
  1975   *The Machiavellian Moment: Florentine Political Thought and the Atlantic
          Republican Tradition* (Princeton, NJ: Princeton University Press).
Podmore, C.
  1998   'Primacy in the Anglican Tradition', in C. Podmore (ed.), *Community, Unity,
          Communion* (London: Church House Publishing).
  2004   'The Anglican Communion: Idea, Name and Identity', *IJSCC* 4: 34–49.
  2005   *Aspects of Anglican Identity* (London: Church House Publishing).
Porter, J.
  1999   *Natural and Divine Law: Reclaiming the Tradition for Christian Ethics* (Grand
          Rapids, MI: Eerdmans).
  2005   *Nature as Reason: A Thomistic Theory of the Natural Law* (Grand Rapids, MI:
          Eerdmans).
Post, G.
  1964   *Studies in Medieval Legal Thought: Public Law and the State, 1100–1322*
          (Princeton, NJ: Princeton University Press).
Pottmeyer, H.J.
  1998   *Towards a Papacy in Transition* (New York: Crossroad).
  2004   'The Petrine Ministry: Vatican I in the Light of Vatican II', *Bulletin* of the
          Centro Pro Unione, Rome, 65: 20–24.
Puglisi, J.F. (ed.)
  1999   *Petrine Ministry and the Unity of the Church: 'Toward a Patient and Fraternal
          Dialogue'* (Collegeville: Liturgical Press).
Quillet, J.
  1988   'Community, Counsel and Representation', in Burns 1988: 520–72.
Quinn, J.R.
  1999   *The Reform of the Papacy* (New York: Crossroad).
Rahner, K.
  1969   *Theological Investigations*, VI (London: Darton, Longman & Todd; Baltimore:
          Helicon Press).

Ramsey, I.T.
    1966   'Towards a Rehabilitation of Natural Law', in I.T. Ramsey (ed.), *Christian Ethics and Contemporary Philosophy* (London: SCM Press).
Ratzinger, J.
    1965   'The Pastoral Implications of Episcopal Collegiality', *Concilium* 1.1: 20–34.
    1988   *Church, Ecumenism and Politics* (Slough: St Paul Publications; New York: Crossroad).
Raunio, A.
    1998   'Natural Law and Faith: The Forgotten Foundations of Ethics in Luther's Theology', in Braaten and Jenson 1998: 96–124.
Reeves, M.
    1965   'Marsiglio of Padua and Dante Alighieri', in Smalley 1965: 86–104.
Renouard, Y.
    1970   *The Avignon Papacy 1305–1403* (trans. D. Bethell; London: Faber & Faber [French original, 1954]).
Rex, R.
    2002   *The Lollards* (Basingstoke: Palgrave).
Robinson, I.S.
    1988   'Church and Papacy', in Burns 1988: 252–305.
Rouse, R., and S. Neill (eds.)
    1954   *A History of the Ecumenical Movement* (London: SPCK).
Rupp, E.G.
    1953   *The Righteousness of God: Luther Studies* (London: Hodder & Stoughton).
    1966   'The Victorian Churchman as Historian: A Reconsideration of R.W. Dixon's *History of the Church of England*', in G.V. Bennett and J.D. Walsh (eds.), *Essays in Modern English Church History in Memory of Norman Sykes* (London: Black), 206–16.
Ryan, J.J.
    1979   *The Nature, Structure and Function of the Church in William of Ockham* (AAR Studies in Religion, 16; Missoula, MO: Scholars Press).
    1998   *The Apostolic Conciliarism of Jean Gerson* (Atlanta: Scholars Press).
Sabine, G.H.
    1963   *A History of Political Theory* (London: Harrap, 3rd edn).
Sachs, W.
    1993   *The Transformation of Anglicanism: From State Church to Global Communion* (Cambridge: Cambridge University Press).
Sagovsky, N.
    2000   *Ecumenism: Christian Origins and the Practice of Communion* (Cambridge: Cambridge University Press).
Salmon, J.H.M.
    1987   *Renaissance and Revolt* (Cambridge: Cambridge University Press).
Scarisbrick, J.J.
    1971   *Henry VIII* (Harmondsworth: Penguin).
    1984   *The Reformation and the English People* (Oxford: Oxford University Press).
Schuessler, H.
    1981   'Sacred Doctrine and the Authority of Scripture in Canonistic Thought on the Eve of the Reformation', in Lytle 1981: 55–68.
Schmemann, A.
    1962   'Towards a Theology of Councils', *St Vladimir's Seminary Quarterly* 6: 170–84.
Schweizer, E.
    1961   *Church Order in the New Testament* (trans. F. Clarke; London: SCM Press).

Schwiebert, E.G.
    1943   'The Medieval Pattern in Luther's View of the State', *CH* 12: 98–117.

Shuger, D.
    1997   '"Society Supernatural": The Imagined Community of Hooker's *Laws*', in C. McEachern and D. Shuger (eds.), *Religion and Culture in Renaissance England* (Cambridge: Cambridge University Press).

Sigmund, P.E.
    1962   'The Influence of Marsilius of Padua on XVth Century Conciliarism', *JHI* 23: 392–402.
    1963   *Nicholas of Cusa and Medieval Political Thought* (Cambridge, MA: Harvard University Press).
    1993   'Law and Politics', in N. Kretzmann and E. Stump (eds.), *The Cambridge Companion to Aquinas* (Cambridge: Cambridge University Press), 217–31.

Skinner, Q.
    1978   *The Foundations of Modern Political Thought. II. The Age of Reformation* (Cambridge: Cambridge University Press).

Smalley, B. (ed.)
    1965   *Trends in Medieval Political Thought* (Oxford: Blackwell).

Spinka, M.
    1966   *John Hus' Concept of the Church* (Princeton, NJ: Princeton University Press).
    1968   *John Hus: A Biography* (Princeton, NJ: Princeton University Press).

Spinka, M. (ed.)
    1953   *Advocates of Reform* (Library of Christian Classics, 14; London: SCM Press; Philadelphia: Westminster Press).

Spinka, M. (trans. and ed.)
    1966   *John Hus at the Council of Constance* (New York: Columbia University Press).
    1972   *Letters of John Hus* (Manchester: Manchester University Press; Totowa, NJ: Rowman and Littlefield).

Spitz, L.
    1953   'Luther's Ecclesiology and his Concept of the Prince as *Notbischof*', *CH* 22: 113–41.

Stephens, W.P.
    1970   *The Holy Spirit in the Theology of Martin Bucer* (Cambridge: Cambridge University Press).
    1986   *The Theology of Huldrych Zwingi* (Oxford: Clarendon Press).

Stieber, J.W.
    1978   *Pope Eugenius IV, the Council of Basel, and the Secular and Ecclesiastical Authorities in the Empire: The Conflict over Supreme Authority and Power in the Church* (Leiden: Brill).

Stout, H.
    1974   'Marsilius of Padua and the Henrican Reformation', *CH* 43: 308–18.

Stump, P.H.
    1994   *The Reforms of the Council of Constance* (Leiden: E.J. Brill).

Swanson, R.N.
    1979   *Universities, Academics and the Great Schism* (Cambridge: Cambridge University Press).
    1980   'The Problem of the Cardinalate in the Great Schism', in Tierney and Linehan 1980: 225–35.

Sykes, S.W.
    2001   'The Papacy and Power: An Anglican Perspective', in Braaten and Jenson 2001.

Tanner, N.P.
    1990   *Decrees of the Ecumenical Councils* (2 vols.; London: Sheed and Ward; Georgetown, Washington DC: Georgetown University Press).

2004 'The Book of the Councils', in R.N. Swanson (ed.), *The Church and the Book* (Studies in Church History, 38; Woodbridge, Suffolk: Boydell Press), 11–21.

Tappert, T.G. (ed.)
1959 *The Book of Concord* (Philadelphia: Fortress Press).

Tatnall, E.
1969 'John Wyclif and *Ecclesia Anglicana*', *JEH* 20: 19–43.

Tavard, G.
1992 *The Church, Community of Salvation: An Ecumenical Ecclesiology* (Collegeville, MN: Michael Glazier).
2000 'The Catholic Church as Conciliar Church', *Priests and People* 14: 3–7.

Tellenbach, G.
1940 *Church, State and Christian Society at the Time of the Investiture Contest* (trans. R.F. Bennett; Oxford: Blackwell).

Thiselton, A.
2000 *The First Epistle to the Corinthians* (NIGTC; Grand Rapids: Eerdmans; Carlisle: Paternoster).

Thomas, P.H.E.
1982 'The Lambeth Conference and the Development of Anglican Ecclesiology 1867–1978' (Ph.D. diss., University of Durham).
2002 'The Evolution of the Primates: Anglicanism, Primacy and Conciliarity', *IJSCC* 2: 79–95.

Thompson, W.D.J. Cargill
1969 'The "Two Kingdoms" and the "Two Regiments": Some Problems of Luther's *Zwei-Reiche-Lehre*', *JTS*, NS, 20, Pt 1: 164–75.
1972 'The Philosopher of the "Politic Society": Richard Hooker as Political Thinker', in W. Speed Hill (ed.), *Studies in Richard Hooker: Essays Preliminary to an Edition of his Works* (Cleveland and London: The Press of Case Western Reserve University).
1974 'The Source of Hooker's Knowledge of Marsilius of Padua', *JEH* 25: 75–81.
1984 *The Political Thought of Martin Luther* (ed. P. Broadhead; Preface A.G. Dickens; Sussex: Harvester Press; New Jersey: Barnes and Noble Books).

Thorndike, H.
1844 *Works* (Oxford: LACT).

Tierney, B.
1954 'Ockham, the Conciliar Theory, and the Canonists', *JHI* 15: 40–70.
1955 *Foundations of the Conciliar Theory* (Cambridge: Cambridge University Press).
1964 *The Crisis of Church and State, 1050–1300* (Englewood Cliffs, NJ: Prentice-Hall).
1969 'Hermeneutics and History: The Problem of *Haec sancta*', in T.A. Sandquist and M.R. Powicke (eds.), *Essays in Medieval History Presented to Bertie Wilkinson* (Toronto: Toronto University Press), 354–70.
1982 *Religion, Law and the Growth of Constitutional Thought, 1150–1650* (Cambridge: Cambridge University Press).

Tierney, B., and P. Linehan (eds.)
1980 *Authority and Power: Studies on Medieval Law and Government Presented to Walter Ullmann on his 70th Birthday* (Cambridge: Cambridge University Press).

Tillard, J.-M.R.
1985 'Did we "Receive" Vatican II?', *OIC* 21: 276–83.

Tillich, P.
1948 *The Protestant Era* (Chicago: University of Chicago Press; London: Nisbet, 1951).
1962 *The Courage to Be* (London: Fontana).

Tillmann, H.
>   1980   *Pope Innocent III* (trans. W. Sax; Amsterdam: North Holland Publishing Co. [German edn, 1954]).

Timms, N., and K. Wilson (eds.)
>   2000   *Governance and Authority in the Roman Catholic Church* (London: SPCK).

Torrance, T.F.
>   1956   *Kingdom and Church* (Edinburgh: Oliver and Boyd).

Trinkaus, C., and H.O. Oberman (eds.)
>   1974   *The Pursuit of Holiness in Late Medieval and Renaissance Religion* (Studies in Medieval and Renaissance Thought, 10; Leiden: E.J. Brill).

Troeltsch, E.
>   *The Social Teaching of the Christian Churches* (trans. O. Wyon; 2 vols.; London: George Allen and Unwin; New York: Macmillan).

Turner, F.M.
>   2002   *John Henry Newman: The Challenge to Evangelical Religion* (New Haven, CT: Yale University Press).

Ullmann, W.
>   1949   *Medieval Papalism: The Political Theories of the Medieval Canonists* (London: Methuen).
>   1961   *Principles of Government and Politics in the Later Middle Ages* (London: Methuen).
>   1962   *The Growth of Papal Government in the Middle Ages* (London: Methuen, 2nd edn).
>   1972a   *A Short History of the Papacy in the Middle Ages* (London: Methuen).
>   1972b   *The Origins of the Great Schism* (Hamden, CT: Archon Books, 2nd edn [London: Burns, Oates and Washbourne, 1948]).
>   1975   *The Church and the Law in the Earlier Middle Ages: Selected Essays* (London: Variorum).
>   1978   *Scholarship and Politics in the Middle Ages: Collected Studies* (London: Variorum).

Verkamp, B.J.
>   1977   *The Indifferent Mean: Adiaphorism in the English Reformation to 1554* (Athens, OH: Ohio University Press; Detroit, MI: Wayne State University Press).

Volf, M.
>   1998   *After Our Likeness: The Church as the Image of the Trinity* (Grand Rapids, MI: Eerdmans).

von Hügel, F.
>   1923   *The Mystical Element of Religion* (London: J.M. Dent, 2nd edn).

Wainwright, G.
>   1978   'Conciliarity and Eucharist', *OIC* 14: 30–49 (reprinted in *Churches in Conciliar Fellowship?* [Geneva: Conference of European Churches, 1978], 74–96).
>   1997   *For Our Salvation: Two Approaches to the Work of Christ* (Grand Rapids, MI: Eerdmans; London: SPCK).
>   2003   'A Primatial Unity in a Synodical and Conciliar Context', *OIC* 38: 3–25.

Wallace-Hadrill, J.M.
>   1983   *The Frankish Church* (Oxford: Clarendon Press).

Walsh, M.
>   2005   'Cause for Concern,' *The Tablet* (21 May): 16.

Walton, R.
>   1967   *Zwingli's Theocracy* (Toronto: University of Toronto Press).

Watanabe, M.
    1963   *The Political Ideas of Nicholas of Cusa with Special Reference to his* De Concordantia Catholica (Geneva: Libraire Droz).
    1972   'Authority and Consent in Church Government: Panormitanus, Aeneas Sylvius, Cusanus', *JHI* 33: 217–36.

Watt, J.A.
    1971   'The Constitutional Law of the College of Cardinals', *Medieval Studies* 33: 127–57.
    1980   'Hostiensis on *Per Venerabilem*: The Role of the College of Cardinals', in Tierney and Linehan 1980: 99–113.
    1988   'Spiritual and Temporal Powers', in Burns 1988: 367–423.

Weidner, H.D.
    2001   'Newman's Application of the Offices of the Church in the Search for a Reformed Catholicism', *IJSCC* 1: 43–54.

Wendel, F.
    1963   *Calvin: The Origins and Development of his Religious Thought* (London: Collins).

Westburg, D.
    1994   *Right Practical Reason: Aristotle, Action and Prudence in Aquinas* (Oxford: Clarendon Press).

White, G.
    1987   'Collegiality and Conciliarity in the Anglican Communion', in S. Sykes (ed.), *Authority in the Anglican Communion* (Toronto: Anglican Book Centre), 203–20.

Whitford, D.M.
    2004   '*Cura Religionis* or Two Kingdoms: The Late Luther on Religion and the State in the Lectures on Genesis', *CH* 73: 41–62.

Wilks, M.
    1963   *The Problem of Sovereignty in the Later Middle Ages: The Papal Monarchy with Augustinus Triumphus* (Cambridge: Cambridge University Press).
    1987   'Royal Patronage and Anti-Papalism from Ockham to Wyclif', in Hudson and Wilks 1987: 135–63.
    2000   *Wyclif: Political Ideas and Practice* (ed. Anne Hudson; Oxford: Oxbow).

Williams, R.
    1997   *The Future of the Papacy: An Anglican View* (Michael Richards Memorial Lecture, 1997; The Pelican Trust).

Wingren, G.
    1957   *Luther on Vocation* (Philadelphia: Muhlenburg Press) (reprinted in *The Christian's Calling* [Edinburgh: Oliver and Boyd, 1958]).

Witte, J., Jr
    2002   *Law and Protestantism: The Legal Teachings of the Lutheran Reformation* (Cambridge: Cambridge University Press).

Wood, D. (ed.)
    1991   *The Church and Sovereignty c.590–1918: Essays in Honour of Michael Wilks* (Oxford: Blackwell [Ecclesiastical History Society]).

Workman, H.B.
    1926   *John Wycliff* (2 vols.; Oxford: Clarendon Press).

Wright, D.F. (ed.)
    1972   *Common Places of Martin Bucer* (Appleford: Sutton Courtenay Press).
    1994   *Martin Bucer: Reforming Church and Community* (Cambridge: Cambridge University Press).

Wright, J.R.
    1972   'An Anglican Perspective', in H.J. Ryan SJ and J.R. Wright (eds.), *Episcopalians and Roman Catholics: Can They Ever Get Together?* (Denville, NJ: Dimension Books).

    1988   'Communion and Episcopacy: An ECUSA Perspective', in J. Draper (ed.), *Communion and Episcopacy: Essays to Mark the Centenary of the Chicago-Lambeth Quadrilateral* (Oxford: Ripon College Cuddesdon).

    1989   'The Authority of the Lambeth Conferences 1867–1988', *Anglican and Episcopal History* 58: 278–89.

    2004   'The Possible Contribution of Papal Authority to Church Unity: An Anglican/Episcopal Perspective', in C.E. Braaten and R.W. Jenson (eds.), *The Ecumenical Future: Background Papers for* In One Body Through the Cross: The Princeton Proposal for Christian Unity (Grand Rapids: Eerdmans).

    2005   'The Windsor Report: Two Observations on its Ecumenical Content', *Anglican Theological Review* 87 [forthcoming].

Wyclif, J.
    1886   *Tractatus de Ecclesia* (trans. J. Loserth; London: Trübner & Co. for Wyclif Society).

Zizioulas, J.
    1978   'Conciliarity and the Way to Unity: An Orthodox Point of View', in *Churches in Conciliar Fellowship?* (Geneva: Conference of European Churches), 20–31.

    1985   *Being as Communion* (New York: St Vladimir's Seminary Press).

    1999   'Primacy in the Church: An Orthodox Approach', in Puglisi 1999: 115–25.

    2001   *Eucharist, Bishop, Church: The Unity of the Church in the Divine Eucharist and the Bishop during the First Three Centuries* (trans. E. Theokritoff; Brookline, MA: Holy Cross Orthodox Press, 2nd edn).

Zwingli, H.
    1929   *The Latin Works of Huldreich Zwingli*, III (trans. S.M. Jackson; Philadelphia: Heidelberg Press).

INDEX